Betty Crocker's Do-Ahead Cookbook

Photography Director: GEORGE ANCONA

 GOLDEN PRESS • NEW YORK
Western Publishing Company, Inc.
Racine, Wisconsin

Fourth Printing, 1974

Library of Congress Catalog Card Number: 72-80848

To Busy Women Everywhere—

Your life is crowded; you don't have the time to spend in the kitchen that your mother and grandmother did. Wouldn't you like to put together real home-cooked meals in the limited time you have? Betty Crocker's Do-Ahead Cookbook was designed to help you do just that, by planning and doing ahead.

These recipes were developed because of today's life-style—hectic, informal, flexible, ever-changing. The idea behind the recipes is ahead-of-time; you prepare food at less-busy times, then store it in your freezer or refrigerator until it's needed.

For long-range planning, there are recipes for the freezer; for short-term planning, the refrigerator stores the food.

These foods-in-reserve can be thought of as a savings bank—not only for a rush-hour dinnertime, but throughout the day, or for spur-of-the-moment situations.

Main dishes, salads, vegetables, breads, desserts—they're all here, along with snack-type foods. Directions for preparing are ultra-clear, and we've made it especially easy for you to find the instructions for what-to-do when you're ready to serve the food.

A real boon to your plan-ahead cooking life is exact storage time—we give it with every recipe. Also detailed information on freezing—how to cool, wrap, label and freeze.

All of these recipes were tested in the Betty Crocker Kitchens, and then tested again by homemakers throughout the country. We're sure the recipes will pass the most crucial test of all—the on-the-spot cooking test conducted in the midst of your busy kitchen. Here's happy cooking and happy eating for all your family—from now on!

Cordially,

Betty Crocker

Contents

Your Freezer: Long-Range Planning

Your Freezer: Long-Range Planning

Without a doubt, one of the most valuable appliances you can own is a home freezer. It is responsible for a whole new world of food preparation and meal planning, and it really takes the burden out of day-to-day cooking.

If you use your freezer wisely, you will always be prepared for the expected as well as the unexpected situation. Use this do-ahead freezer section as a step-by-step workbook. With a freezer and the freezer recipes in this book, you'll be able to take advantage of your supermarket's food "specials," and use your time to best advantage.

Here are some of the special features in our freezer recipes:

1 The first item mentioned under the title of each recipe is its recommended storage time. This recommendation is the result of extensive storage tests made in the Betty Crocker Kitchens. It tells you how long this particular food will stay at its best while stored under the proper conditions (see pages 84-87). After that time, the food will not be spoiled, but it may lose some of its moisture or flavor.

2 The number of servings is indicated right after the storage time. You can, therefore, plan according to your needs.

3 After the cooking directions, the recipe will tell you to cool, wrap, label and freeze. This must be done correctly if your food is to maintain its high quality (see pages 84-87).

4 When you want to serve the food you have frozen, turn to the recipe once more for the post-freezing directions. These are listed below the cooking instructions. You'll find them quickly by looking for this symbol: ■—which is followed by **boldface type.** Read over all of the directions following the symbol when you're planning your meal—and be sure to see if there are other ingredients to be added. Note that most foods do not require thawing, but are heated immediately after they have been removed from the freezer.

Pictured on the preceding page:
Crêpes Suzette (page 63)

Meats and Main Dishes

FREEZER MEAT LOAF

Store no longer than 1 month. Makes enough for 2 meals—6 servings each.

    3 pounds ground beef
    ½ cup dry bread crumbs
  3½ cups milk
    1 cup minced onion
    2 eggs
  2½ to 3 teaspoons salt
    2 tablespoons Worcestershire sauce
    ¼ teaspoon pepper

Mix all ingredients. Divide in half; spread each half evenly in ungreased loaf pan, 9×5×3 inches. (To serve immediately, see below.) Wrap, label and freeze.

■ **2 hours 35 minutes before serving, remove Freezer Meat Loaf from freezer and unwrap.** Bake uncovered in 350° oven until done, about 2½ hours. Drain off fat once during baking. (1 loaf —6 servings.)

To Serve Immediately: Bake uncovered in 350° oven until done, about 1½ hours. Drain off fat once during baking. (1 loaf—6 servings.)

MEAT AND POTATO PIE

Store no longer than 2 months. Makes enough for 2 meals—4 or 5 servings each.

    2 pounds ground beef
  2⅔ cups instant mashed potato puffs
    2 eggs
    2 teaspoons salt
    ¼ teaspoon pepper
    2 tablespoons instant minced onion
    ½ cup catsup
    2 cups milk

Mix all ingredients. Divide between 2 un-greased 9-inch pie pans; spread evenly. (To serve one immediately, see below.) Wrap, label and freeze.

■ **1 hour 15 minutes before serving, remove 1 pan Meat and Potato Pie from freezer and unwrap. Have ready:** instant mashed potato puffs (enough for 4 servings); ½ cup shredded sharp Cheddar cheese.

Bake pie uncovered in 375° oven 1 hour. After 50 minutes of baking, prepare potato puffs as directed on package. Mound potato around edge of meat; sprinkle cheese on potato. Bake until cheese is melted, 3 to 4 minutes. (4 or 5 servings.)

To Serve Immediately: Have ready: instant mashed potato puffs (enough for 4 servings); ½ cup shredded sharp Cheddar cheese.

Bake meat pie in 350° oven 40 to 45 minutes. After 30 minutes of baking, prepare potato puffs as directed on package. Mound potato around edge of meat; sprinkle cheese on potato. Bake until cheese is melted, 3 to 4 minutes. (4 or 5 servings.)

CHILI

Store no longer than 4 months. Makes enough for 4 meals—6 servings each.

  4 pounds ground beef
10 medium onions, chopped (about 5 cups)
  4 cans (28 ounces each) tomatoes
  1 can (15 ounces) tomato sauce
¼ cup chili powder
  2 tablespoons sugar
  1 tablespoon plus 1½ teaspoons salt

Cook and stir meat and onion in Dutch oven or large roasting pan until meat is brown and onion is tender. Spoon off fat. Stir in remaining ingredients. Heat tomato mixture until it boils. Reduce heat; simmer uncovered 1 hour 15 minutes. Spoon off fat if necessary.

Divide Chili among four 5- to 6-cup freezer containers. Cool quickly. Cover, label and freeze.

■ **45 minutes before serving, remove 1 container Chili from freezer; dip container into very hot water just to loosen. Have ready:** 1 can (15½ ounces) kidney beans, drained (reserve liquid).

Place reserved bean liquid and frozen block in saucepan. Cover tightly; cook over medium-high heat, turning occasionally, 25 minutes. Uncover; cook 20 minutes longer, stirring in kidney beans 5 minutes before Chili is done. Season with additional chili powder if desired. (6 servings.)

CHILI AND DUMPLINGS

Makes enough for 5 or 6 servings.

  Chili (above)
1 can (15 ounces) chili beans
1 package (14 ounces) corn muffin mix
½ cup shredded sharp Cheddar cheese

Six hours before serving, remove 1 container Chili from freezer; thaw at room temperature just until softened, not warm. Heat Chili and beans (with liquid) in large skillet until mixture boils. Reduce heat slightly.

Prepare muffin mix as directed on package except—decrease milk to ½ cup and stir in cheese. Drop dough by tablespoonfuls onto boiling chili. Cook uncovered over low heat 10 minutes. Cover tightly; cook 10 minutes.

CHUCKWAGON TURNOVERS

Store no longer than 3 months. Makes enough for 4 or 5 servings.

Meat Filling
  1 pound ground beef
½ cup chopped onion
⅔ cup shredded Swiss cheese
  1 egg, beaten
¼ teaspoon red pepper sauce
1½ teaspoons salt
  2 tablespoons snipped parsley

Pastry
  2 cups all-purpose flour*
  1 teaspoon salt
⅔ cup plus 2 tablespoons shortening
  4 to 5 tablespoons cold water

Cook and stir meat and onion until onion is tender. Remove from heat; cool slightly. Stir in remaining Meat Filling ingredients; set aside.

Prepare Pastry. Measure flour and salt into bowl; cut in shortening thoroughly. Sprinkle in water, 1 tablespoon at a time, mixing until all flour is moistened and dough almost cleans side of bowl (1 to 2 teaspoons water can be added if needed). Gather dough into a ball; divide in half.

Roll each half into 10-inch circle on lightly floured cloth-covered board. Place 1½ cups meat filling on half of each circle. Fold pastry over filling and press edges to seal securely. Prick tops of turnovers several times. Carefully place turnovers on ungreased baking sheet. (To serve immediately, see below.) Freeze uncovered until firm, about 2 hours. Remove turnovers from baking sheet. Wrap, label and return to freezer.

■ **35 minutes before serving, remove Chuckwagon Turnovers from freezer and unwrap; place on ungreased baking sheet.** Bake in 425° oven until brown, 25 to 30 minutes. Gravy or a tomato sauce is a nice addition.

To Serve Immediately: Bake in 425° oven until brown, 20 to 25 minutes. Gravy or a tomato sauce is a nice addition.

*If using self-rising flour, omit salt from Pastry. Pastry made with self-rising flour differs in flavor and texture.

ITALIAN SPAGHETTI SAUCE

Store no longer than 4 months. Makes enough for 24 servings—⅔ cup each.

Tomato-Meat Sauce
- **4 pounds ground beef**
- **¼ cup olive oil**
- **6 medium onions, finely chopped (about 3 cups)**
- **1 cup finely chopped green pepper**
- **8 cloves garlic, minced**
- **4 cans (16 ounces each) tomatoes**
- **4 cans (15 ounces each) tomato sauce**

Seasonings
- **3 tablespoons parsley flakes**
- **2 tablespoons sugar**
- **1½ to 2 tablespoons salt**
- **1 tablespoon oregano**
- **1 tablespoon basil**
- **1 teaspoon pepper**

Cook and stir meat in large skillet or Dutch oven until meat is brown. Spoon off fat; set meat aside.

Heat oil in 7- to 8-quart pan. Cook and stir onion, green pepper and garlic in oil until onion is tender. Stir in tomatoes, tomato sauce, Seasonings and the meat. Heat, stirring occasionally, until Tomato-Meat Sauce boils. Reduce heat; simmer uncovered 4 hours. (To serve immediately, see below.) Divide spaghetti sauce among four 1-quart freezer containers or three 6-cup freezer containers. Cool quickly. Cover, label and freeze.

■ **45 minutes before serving, remove 1 container Italian Spaghetti Sauce from freezer; dip container into very hot water just to loosen.** Place frozen block in 3-quart saucepan. Cover tightly; heat over medium heat, turning occasionally, 20 to 30 minutes. Reduce heat; uncover and simmer 10 minutes. While sauce heats, prepare hot cooked spaghetti for 6 or 9 servings. Serve sauce on hot cooked spaghetti; pass Parmesan cheese.

To Serve Immediately: Serve on hot cooked spaghetti; pass Parmesan cheese. [24 servings (⅔ cup meat sauce each).]

CHILI-MAC

Makes enough for 5 or 6 servings.

- **Italian Spaghetti Sauce (left)**
- **1 can (15½ ounces) kidney beans, drained (reserve liquid)**
- **1 tablespoon chili powder**
- **4 cups hot cooked macaroni**

Forty-five minutes before serving, remove one 1-quart container Italian Spaghetti Sauce from freezer; dip container into very hot water just to loosen. Place reserved bean liquid and frozen block in 3-quart saucepan. Cover tightly; heat over medium heat, turning occasionally, 20 to 30 minutes. Reduce heat; stir in beans and chili powder. Simmer uncovered 10 minutes. Serve on macaroni.

Storage Time for Beef at 0°

Most cuts	9 months
Ground	3 to 4 months
For stewing	4 months
Liver, heart, tongue	3 to 4 months
Cooked	2 months

To prepare for freezing: Place double layer of freezer wrap between steaks, chops, hamburger patties—to make them easy to separate. Using moisture-vapor-proof wrap, wrap closely to eliminate air. Do not season before freezing. You can freeze-store meat prepackaged, just as you bought it, for up to 2 weeks. Cook meat thawed or frozen.

To cook: Thaw wrapped meat in refrigerator or place frozen steaks and patties further than normal distance from broiler. In 300 to 325° oven, allow ⅓ to ½ more than the normal cooking time for frozen roasts.

MINI MEATBALLS

Store no longer than 2 months. Makes enough for 3 meals—4 or 5 servings each.

  3 pounds ground beef
⅓ cup minced onion
1½ cups dry bread crumbs
  1 tablespoon salt
¼ teaspoon pepper
1½ teaspoons Worcestershire sauce
  3 eggs
¾ cup milk

Mix all ingredients. Shape one-third of meat mixture by level tablespoonfuls into 1-inch balls. Place in ungreased jelly roll pan, 15½ × 10½ × 1 inch. Bake in 400° oven until done, about 10 minutes. (Can be served immediately. About 8 dozen meatballs.) Cool about 5 minutes. Freeze uncovered 15 minutes. Place partially frozen meatballs in 1-quart freezer container. Cover, label and return to freezer. Repeat 2 times. For variety and ease in preparation, use any of the recipes on this page for serving Mini Meatballs.

SWEET AND SOUR MEATBALLS

Makes enough for 4 or 5 servings.

  Mini Meatballs (above)
1 cup sweet and sour sauce

Fifteen minutes before serving, remove 1 container Mini Meatballs from freezer. Heat sweet and sour sauce in large skillet until it boils. Place frozen meatballs in sauce. Reduce heat; cover tightly and simmer until meatballs are hot, about 10 minutes. Nice served on rice.

SPAGHETTI AND MEATBALLS

Makes enough for 4 or 5 servings.

  Mini Meatballs (left)
1 jar (about 16 ounces) spaghetti sauce
6 or 7 ounces spaghetti
  Parmesan cheese

Fifteen minutes before serving, remove 1 container Mini Meatballs from freezer. Heat spaghetti sauce in large skillet until it boils. Place frozen meatballs in sauce. Reduce heat; cover tightly and simmer until meatballs are hot, about 10 minutes.

While meatballs simmer, cook spaghetti as directed on package. Serve meatballs and sauce on spaghetti; pass Parmesan cheese.

MEATBALLS ROMANOFF

Makes enough for 4 or 5 servings.

  Mini Meatballs (left)
2 tablespoons butter or margarine
1 tablespoon flour
1 package (5.5 ounces) noodles Romanoff
1½ cups milk
  2 teaspoons parsley flakes
  2 tablespoons butter or margarine

Fifteen minutes before serving, remove 1 container Mini Meatballs from freezer. Melt 2 tablespoons butter in large skillet. Remove from heat; stir in flour and sauce mix from noodles Romanoff. Stir in milk slowly. Heat, stirring constantly, until sauce boils. Place frozen meatballs in sauce; heat until sauce boils. Reduce heat; cover tightly and simmer until meatballs are hot, about 10 minutes.

While meatballs simmer, cook noodles as directed on package except—stir parsley flakes and 2 tablespoons butter into cooked noodles. Serve meatballs and sauce on noodles.

Pictured at right, top to bottom: Spaghetti and Meatballs, Sweet and Sour Meatballs and Meatballs Romanoff

Arrange meat patties on a 10-inch pastry square and cover them with a 12-inch square.

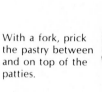

With a fork, prick the pastry between and on top of the patties.

Hamburger-Onion Hoedown

HAMBURGER-ONION HOEDOWN

Store no longer than 3 months. Makes enough for 2 meals—4 to 6 servings each.

Meat Patties
  2 pounds ground beef
  2 eggs, slightly beaten
  ⅔ cup dry bread crumbs
  ⅔ cup catsup
  ½ cup chopped parsley
  1 envelope (about 1½ ounces) onion soup mix
1⅓ cups warm water

Pastry
  4 cups all-purpose flour*
  2 teaspoons salt
1½ cups shortening
  ½ to ⅔ cup cold water

Mix Meat Patties ingredients; shape into 12 patties, ¾ inch thick.

Prepare Pastry. Measure flour and salt into bowl; cut in shortening thoroughly. Sprinkle in water, 2 tablespoons at a time, mixing until all flour is moistened and dough almost cleans side of bowl (1 to 2 teaspoons water can be added if needed). Gather dough into a ball; divide into 4 parts.

Roll 2 parts pastry into 10-inch squares for bottom crusts and 2 parts into 12-inch squares for top crusts. Place 10-inch squares on un-greased baking sheets; arrange 6 meat patties evenly on each square. Cover with 12-inch squares; seal edges. Press lightly between meat patties to mark servings. With fork, prick serving marks between patties and top of servings. Bake in 400° oven 40 to 45 minutes. (Can serve whole recipe immediately. 8 to 12 servings.) Cool quickly. Wrap, label and freeze.

■ **50 minutes before serving, remove 1 package Hamburger-Onion Hoedown from freezer and unwrap; place on ungreased baking sheet. Heat in 400° oven until hot, about 45 minutes. If desired, serve with tomato sauce or beef gravy. (4 to 6 servings.)**

*If using self-rising flour, omit salt. Pastry made with self-rising flour differs in taste and texture.

EASY POT-ROAST

Store no longer than 6 months. Makes enough for 6 to 8 servings.

3- pound beef chuck pot-roast (arm, blade, inside roll or shoulder clod)*
2 teaspoons salt
¼ teaspoon pepper
2 medium onions, sliced
1 can (8 ounces) tomato sauce
1 tablespoon brown sugar
1 tablespoon horseradish
1 teaspoon prepared mustard

Place meat on 30×18-inch piece of heavy-duty aluminum foil. Season with salt and pepper; sprinkle onion on meat. Mix remaining ingredients; pour on meat. Fold foil over meat and seal securely. (To serve immediately, see below.) Label and freeze.

■ **4 hours 15 minutes before serving, remove Easy Pot-Roast from freezer and place wrapped meat in baking pan, 13×9×2 inches.** (If foil has torn during storage, overwrap with foil.) Cook in 350° oven until tender, about 4 hours. Place meat on warm platter; keep warm while making Gravy (below).

GRAVY

Spoon off fat from broth. Add enough water to broth to measure 2 cups; pour into pan. Shake ½ cup water and ¼ cup all-purpose flour in covered jar; stir slowly into broth. Heat, stirring constantly, until gravy boils. Boil and stir 1 minute. If desired, add few drops bottled brown bouquet sauce.

To Serve Immediately: Place wrapped meat in baking pan, 13×9×2 inches. Cook in 300° oven until tender, about 4 hours. Place meat on warm platter; keep warm while making Gravy (above).

*Boneless rump, top or bottom round roast can be used in this recipe.

PEPPER STEAK

Store no longer than 4 months. Makes enough for 2 meals—4 or 5 servings each.

3 pounds beef round steak, 1 inch thick
½ cup soy sauce
1 cup water
¼ cup salad oil
¼ to ⅓ cup sugar
2 tablespoons cornstarch
½ teaspoon ginger
1 teaspoon garlic salt
2 medium onions, cut into ¼-inch slices

Trim fat carefully from meat; cut meat into strips, 2×1×¼ inch.* Place in baking dish, 11½×7½×1½ inches. Mix soy sauce and water; pour on meat. Refrigerate, turning meat occasionally, 2 hours. Remove meat from marinade; reserve marinade.

Heat oil in Dutch oven or large skillet. Cook meat in oil, turning frequently, until meat loses redness, about 15 minutes. Pour reserved marinade on meat. Mix sugar, cornstarch, ginger and garlic salt; stir into meat and marinade. Sprinkle onion on meat. Reduce heat; cover tightly and simmer 12 to 15 minutes. Divide meat and sauce between two 1-quart freezer containers. Cool quickly. Cover, label and freeze.

■ **30 minutes before serving, remove 1 container Pepper Steak from freezer. Have ready:** 2 medium green peppers, cut into strips (¾ inch wide); 2 medium tomatoes, peeled and cut into eighths; 3 to 4 cups hot cooked rice.

Dip container of meat and sauce into very hot water just to loosen. Place ½ cup water and frozen block in large skillet. Cover tightly; heat over medium-high heat, turning occasionally, until hot and bubbly, about 20 minutes. Stir in green pepper. Reduce heat; cover and simmer 5 minutes. Add tomato; cover and simmer 3 minutes. Serve on rice. (4 or 5 servings.)

*Meat is easier to cut when partially frozen.

HUNGARIAN GOULASH

Store no longer than 3 months. Makes enough for 6 to 8 servings.

- ¼ **cup shortening**
- 2 **pounds beef stew meat, cut into 1-inch cubes**
- 1 **cup sliced onion**
- ⅛ **teaspoon instant minced garlic**
- ¾ **cup catsup**
- 2 **tablespoons Worcestershire sauce**
- 1 **tablespoon brown sugar**
- 2 **teaspoons salt**
- 2 **teaspoons paprika**
- ½ **teaspoon dry mustard**
  Dash cayenne red pepper
- 1½ **cups water**

Melt shortening in large skillet. Cook and stir meat, onion and garlic in shortening until meat is brown and onion is tender. Drain off fat. Stir in remaining ingredients. Cover tightly; simmer 2 to 2½ hours. (To serve immediately, see below.) Pour into 1-quart freezer container. Cool quickly. Cover, label and freeze.

■ **45 minutes before serving, remove container Hungarian Goulash from freezer; dip container into very hot water just to loosen.** Place ½ cup water and frozen block in 3-quart saucepan. Cover tightly; heat over medium-low heat, turning occasionally, until hot and bubbly, about 30 minutes. While goulash heats, prepare hot cooked noodles for 6 to 8 servings. Serve goulash on noodles.

To Serve Immediately: Have ready: ¼ cup water; 2 tablespoons flour; hot cooked noodles for 6 to 8 servings.

Shake water and flour in tightly covered jar; stir slowly into meat mixture. Heat, stirring constantly, until gravy boils. Boil and stir 1 minute. Serve on noodles.

SWISS STEAK

Store no longer than 4 months. Makes enough for 2 meals—4 servings each.

Meat
- 2 **pounds beef round steak (top round, bottom round or sirloin), ½ inch thick**
- ¼ **cup all-purpose flour**
- ½ **teaspoon salt**
- ¼ **teaspoon pepper**
- 2 **tablespoons shortening**

Tomato Sauce
- ½ **cup minced green pepper**
- 1¼ **cups minced onion**
- 1 **can (16 ounces) tomatoes**
- 1 **teaspoon salt**
- ¼ **teaspoon pepper**

Lightly score surface of meat; cut meat into 8 serving pieces. Mix flour, ½ teaspoon salt and ¼ teaspoon pepper. Sprinkle half the flour mixture on one side of meat; pound in. Turn meat and pound in remaining flour mixture.

Melt shortening in large skillet. Brown meat in shortening over medium heat about 15 minutes. Reduce heat; cover tightly and simmer 1 hour. Add small amount of water if necessary.

Mix Tomato Sauce ingredients; pour on meat. (To serve whole recipe immediately, see below.) Cover; simmer 15 minutes. Divide meat between 2 ungreased baking pans, 8×8×2 inches. Spoon half the sauce on meat in each pan. Cool quickly. Wrap, label and freeze.

■ **45 minutes before serving, remove 1 pan Swiss Steak from freezer and unwrap.** Cook uncovered in 400° oven until tender, 30 to 40 minutes. (4 servings.)

To Serve Immediately: Cover tightly; simmer until tender, about 30 minutes. (8 servings.)

Pictured at right, top and bottom: Swiss Steak and Hungarian Goulash

Braised Beef on Rice. We show it here accompanied by Tomato Marinade (page 128).

Dividing meat and vegetables before freezing

BRAISED BEEF CUBES

Store no longer than 3 months. Makes enough for 2 meals—4 or 5 servings each.

Meat and Vegetables
- **¼ cup butter or margarine**
- **5 medium onions, sliced**
- **1 pound fresh mushrooms, sliced**
- **3 pounds beef stew meat, cut into 1-inch cubes**

Seasonings
- **1 clove garlic, minced**
- **2 teaspoons salt**
- **¼ teaspoon onion salt**
- **¼ teaspoon marjoram leaves**
- **¼ teaspoon thyme leaves**
- **⅛ teaspoon pepper**

Sauce
- **1 cup beef broth***
- **1 tablespoon plus 1½ teaspoons flour**
- **1½ cups red Burgundy**
- **2 or 3 drops red food color, if desired**

Melt butter in Dutch oven or large saucepan. Cook and stir onion and mushrooms in butter until onion is tender. Remove vegetables from pan; drain. Brown meat with garlic in same pan. Sprinkle remaining Seasonings on meat. Mix beef broth and flour; pour on meat. Heat, stirring constantly, until sauce boils. Boil and stir 1 minute. Stir in Burgundy. Cover tightly; simmer 1½ to 2 hours, stirring in onion and mushrooms 5 minutes before beef mixture is done.

Divide only the meat and vegetables between two 2-quart freezer containers. To 1 container, add ½ cup of the sauce in the pan. Cool quickly. Cover, label "Braised Beef" and freeze.

To other container, add remaining sauce and the red food color. Cool quickly. Cover, label "Beef Bourguignon" and freeze.

*Beef broth can be made by dissolving 1 beef bouillon cube or 1 teaspoon instant beef bouillon in 1 cup boiling water, or use canned beef broth (bouillon).

A hearty main dish *à la française*, Beef Bourguignon is perfectly complemented by crusty French bread.

BRAISED BEEF ON RICE

Makes enough for 4 or 5 servings.

1 container Braised Beef (page 16)
2 tablespoons cornstarch
2 tablespoons soy sauce
1 can (10½ ounces) condensed beef broth*
(bouillon)
3 cups hot cooked rice

Forty-five minutes before serving, remove container labeled "Braised Beef" from freezer. Dip container into very hot water just to loosen. Mix cornstarch, soy sauce and beef broth in medium saucepan. Place frozen block in broth. Heat uncovered over medium heat until hot, about 30 minutes. Serve on rice.

*Beef broth can be made by dissolving 2 beef bouillon cubes or 2 teaspoons instant beef bouillon in 1¼ cups boiling water.

BEEF BOURGUIGNON

Makes enough for 4 or 5 servings.

About 50 minutes before serving, remove container labeled "Beef Bourguignon" from freezer (see Braised Beef Cubes recipe on page 16).

Dip container into very hot water just to loosen. Place ½ cup water and frozen block in large saucepan. Heat uncovered over medium heat, turning occasionally, until hot, about 45 minutes. Traditionally served with French bread.

To Serve Immediately: Prepare Braised Beef Cubes (page 16) except—freeze only 1 container (for Braised Beef). Add remaining sauce and the red food color to remaining half of the meat mixture; serve.

Divide the ribs into serving pieces by cutting between bones with a sharp knife.

As they bake, brush the ribs 2 or 3 times with part of the sauce.

Pour the remaining sauce over the ribs.

BARBECUED RIBS

Store no longer than 4 months. Makes enough for 5 or 6 servings.

4½ pounds pork ribs (spareribs, back ribs or country-style ribs), cut into pieces

Sauce
¼ cup soy sauce
1 tablespoon cornstarch
1 bottle (18 ounces) barbecue sauce

Arrange meat meaty side up in open shallow roasting pan. Do not add water. Do not cover. Bake in 325° oven 1¾ hours.

Mix Sauce ingredients. (To serve immediately, see below.) Using ¾ cup of the sauce, baste ribs 2 or 3 times; bake 45 minutes longer.

Crisscross 2 pieces of heavy-duty aluminum foil, 28 × 18 inches; carefully mold to inside of Dutch oven. Arrange ribs in foil-lined Dutch oven. Pour the remaining sauce on ribs. Cool quickly. Wrap ribs securely in the foil, remove from Dutch oven, label and freeze.

■ **35 minutes before serving, remove Barbecued Ribs from freezer and unwrap.** Place ½ cup water and frozen block in Dutch oven. Cover tightly; heat over medium-high heat until it boils. Reduce heat; simmer covered until hot, about ½ hour.

To Serve Immediately: Using all of the sauce, baste meat 2 or 3 times while baking 45 minutes longer.

SWEET AND SOUR PORK

Store no longer than 1 week. Makes enough for 2 meals—5 or 6 servings each.

Meat
> **3 pounds lean pork butt, cut into 1½-inch cubes**
> **2 cups water**
> **3 eggs**
> **1½ cups all-purpose flour***
> **3¾ teaspoons salt**
> **Salad oil**

Sauce
> **1 can (about 30 ounces) pineapple chunks, drained (reserve syrup)**
> **¾ cup catsup**
> **¼ cup plus 2 tablespoons water**
> **3 tablespoons cornstarch**
> **¼ cup plus 2 tablespoons vinegar**
> **1 tablespoon sugar**
> **1 tablespoon Worcestershire sauce**

Heat meat and water in tightly covered Dutch oven until water boils. Reduce heat; simmer 15 minutes and drain. Cool quickly.

Beat eggs slightly in large bowl; add meat. Toss meat with egg until pieces are well coated. Mix flour and salt. Sprinkle flour mixture on meat; toss until well coated. Heat oil (½ inch) in large skillet or electric frypan over medium-high heat. Brown meat in oil, ⅓ at a time, about 5 minutes; drain. Do not overcook. (One meal can be served immediately. Reserve half of the meat; keep warm while making Sauce.) Cool quickly. Divide meat in half. Wrap, label and freeze.

Prepare Sauce. Add enough water to reserved pineapple syrup to measure 1½ cups. Mix pineapple syrup, catsup, water, cornstarch, vinegar, sugar and Worcestershire sauce in medium saucepan. Cook over medium-high heat, stirring constantly, until mixture thickens and boils. Remove from heat; stir in pineapple chunks. (To serve 1 meal immediately, reserve half of sauce in saucepan; see right.) Divide sauce between two 1-pint freezer containers. Cool quickly. Cover, label and freeze.

■ **20 minutes before serving, remove 1 package Sweet and Sour Pork cubes and 1 container Sweet and Sour Pork sauce from freezer. Have ready:** 2 medium green peppers, cut into 1-inch pieces; 1 medium onion, cut into 1-inch pieces; 4 cups hot cooked rice.

Dip container of sauce into very hot water just to loosen. Place ¼ cup water and frozen block in large saucepan. Cover tightly; heat over medium-high heat until thawed, about 15 minutes.

While the sauce is thawing, heat oven to 400°. Unwrap pork cubes; place frozen meat on ungreased baking sheet. Heat in oven until hot, 10 to 12 minutes.

Stir green pepper and onion into sauce (they will remain crisp). Reduce heat; cover tightly and simmer 5 minutes. Stir pork cubes into sauce just before serving. Serve on rice. (5 or 6 servings.)

To Serve Immediately: Have ready: 2 medium green peppers, cut into 1-inch pieces; 1 medium onion, cut into 1-inch pieces; 4 cups hot cooked rice.

Boil and stir sauce 1 minute. Reduce heat; stir in green pepper and onion. (They will remain crisp.) Cover tightly; simmer 5 minutes. Just before serving, stir in reserved pork cubes. Serve on rice. (5 to 6 servings.)

*If using self-rising flour, decrease salt to 2 teaspoons.

Storage Time for Pork at 0°	
Most cuts	4 to 5 months
Ground	2 months
Sausage	2 months
Cooked	2 months
Ham (unsliced)	2 months

Note: Ham slices, bacon and frankfurters lose quality when frozen.

PIZZA

Store no longer than 4 months. Makes 4 pizzas.

Sauce

¾ cup chopped onion
⅛ teaspoon instant minced garlic
2 cans (8 ounces each) tomato sauce or
   2 cups spaghetti sauce
½ teaspoon salt
¼ teaspoon pepper

Dough

2 packages active dry yeast
1⅓ cups warm water (105 to 115°)
5 cups buttermilk baking mix

Topping

2 cups sliced pepperoni (about 8 ounces)
2½ cups shredded mozzarella cheese
3 to 4 teaspoons oregano

Mix Sauce ingredients; set aside. To make Dough, dissolve yeast in warm water. Stir in baking mix; beat vigorously. Turn dough onto well-floured board. Knead until smooth, about 20 times. Allow dough to rest a few minutes. Divide dough into 4 parts; roll each part into 10-inch circle. Place on greased baking sheets.

Heat oven to 425°. Spread about ½ cup sauce on each circle. Arrange pepperoni on sauce; sprinkle cheese and oregano on top. (To serve immediately, see below.) Bake 10 minutes. Remove Pizzas from baking sheets; cool on wire racks. Place each Pizza on cardboard circle. Wrap, label and freeze.

■ **15 minutes before serving, heat oven to 425°.** Remove Pizzas from freezer; unwrap and remove from cardboard circles. Place Pizzas on oven rack. Bake until hot, about 10 minutes.

VARIATIONS

Omit pepperoni and substitute one of the following:

1 pound bulk Italian sausage, crumbled and browned
1 pound ground beef, browned and seasoned with 1 teaspoon salt and sprinkled with ½ cup chopped green pepper or 2 cups sliced pimiento-stuffed olives

To Serve Immediately: Bake in 425° oven until crust is brown and filling is hot and bubbly, 15 to 20 minutes.

LASAGNE

Store no longer than 3 weeks. Makes enough for 8 to 10 servings.

Meat Sauce

1 pound bulk Italian sausage or ground beef
¾ cup chopped onion
1 clove garlic, minced
1 can (16 ounces) tomatoes
1 can (15 ounces) tomato sauce
2 tablespoons parsley flakes
2 tablespoons sugar
1 teaspoon salt
1 teaspoon basil leaves

Cheese Filling

3 cups (two 12-ounce cartons) ricotta or creamed cottage cheese
½ cup grated Parmesan cheese
1 tablespoon parsley flakes
1½ teaspoons salt
1½ teaspoons oregano leaves

Base and Topping

1 package (8 ounces) lasagne noodles, cooked and drained
¾ pound mozzarella cheese, shredded
½ cup grated Parmesan cheese

Cook and stir meat, onion and garlic in large saucepan or Dutch oven until meat is brown and onion is tender. Spoon off fat.

Add tomatoes and break up with fork. Stir in remaining Meat Sauce ingredients. Heat, stirring occasionally, until mixture boils. Reduce heat; simmer uncovered until mixture is the consistency of spaghetti sauce, about 1 hour. Mix Cheese Filling ingredients.

Heat oven to 350°. Reserve ½ cup meat sauce for thin top layer. In ungreased baking pan, 13×9×2 inches, layer ¼ each of the noodles, remaining sauce, mozzarella cheese and ricotta cheese mixture. Repeat 3 times. Spread reserved meat sauce on top; sprinkle ½ cup Parmesan cheese on meat sauce. Bake uncovered 45 minutes. (Can be served immediately.) Cool quickly. Wrap, label and freeze.

■ **1 hour 10 minutes before serving, remove Lasagne from freezer and unwrap.** Bake uncovered in 375° oven until bubbly, about 1 hour.

EGG FOO YONG

Store no longer than 1 month. Makes enough for 4 or 5 servings.

2 tablespoons salad oil
3 eggs
1 cup bean sprouts, rinsed and drained
½ cup chopped cooked pork
2 tablespoons chopped onion
1 tablespoon soy sauce

Heat oil in large skillet. Beat eggs; stir in remaining ingredients.

Pour ¼ cup mixture at a time into oil. With a wide spatula, push cooked egg up over meat to form a patty. When patties are set, turn and brown other side. [Can be served immediately with Sauce (below).] Place in ungreased 13×9× 1½-inch foil pan. Cool quickly. Wrap, label and freeze.

■ **20 minutes before serving, heat oven to 375°. Have ready:** Sauce (below).

Remove Egg Foo Yong from freezer and unwrap. Heat uncovered until hot, about 15 minutes. Serve with Sauce.

Note: If you prefer, recipe can be doubled so that half can be served immediately and half can be frozen.

SAUCE

1 tablespoon cornstarch
1 teaspoon sugar
1 teaspoon vinegar
2½ tablespoons soy sauce
½ cup water

Mix all ingredients in small saucepan. Cook over medium heat, stirring constantly, until mixture thickens and boils. Boil and stir 1 minute.

VEAL WITH TOMATO SAUCE

Store no longer than 3 months. Makes enough for 6 servings.

Meat
6 boneless veal cutlets (about
    4 ounces each)
¼ cup salad oil
2 cloves garlic, crushed

Tomato Sauce
1 cup thinly sliced onion
1 jar (3 ounces) sliced mushrooms, drained
2 tablespoons flour
1 teaspoon salt
¼ teaspoon pepper
1 can (8 ounces) tomato sauce
⅔ cup water

Pound meat until ¼ inch thick. Heat oil and garlic in large skillet over medium-high heat. Brown meat quickly in oil, about 5 minutes. Remove meat from skillet; set aside. Reduce heat to medium. Cook and stir onion and mushroom in skillet until onion is tender. Stir in flour, salt and pepper; pour tomato sauce and water on onion mixture. Heat, stirring constantly, until mixture boils. Boil and stir 1 minute.

Return meat to skillet. Cover tightly; simmer until done, about 30 minutes. (Can be served immediately.) Arrange meat and sauce in ungreased baking dish, 11½×7½×1½ inches, or foil container. Cool quickly. Wrap, label and freeze.

■ **1 hour before serving, remove Veal with Tomato Sauce from freezer and unwrap.** Heat uncovered in 375° oven until hot and bubbly, 50 to 55 minutes. If desired, serve with hot cooked spaghetti.

VEAL PARMESAN

Store no longer than 3 months. Makes enough for 4 servings.

Meat
4 boneless veal cutlets (4 ounces each)
½ cup dry bread crumbs
¼ cup grated Parmesan cheese
½ teaspoon salt
⅛ teaspoon pepper
⅛ teaspoon paprika
1 egg
⅓ cup salad oil

Sauce and Topping
3 tablespoons water
1 can (8 ounces) tomato sauce
½ teaspoon oregano, if desired
3 slices mozzarella cheese

Pound meat until ¼ inch thick. Mix crumbs, Parmesan cheese, salt, pepper and paprika. Beat egg slightly. Dip meat in egg, then coat with crumb mixture.

Heat oil in large skillet. Brown meat quickly in oil, about 6 minutes. (To serve immediately, see below.) Remove meat to ungreased baking dish, 11½×7½×1½ inches. Heat water, tomato sauce and oregano in skillet, stirring constantly, until mixture boils. Pour sauce on meat; arrange mozzarella cheese on sauce. Cool quickly. Wrap, label and freeze.

■ **55 minutes before serving, remove Veal Parmesan from freezer and unwrap.** Bake uncovered in 375° oven until done, 45 to 50 minutes.

Note: A 1-pound veal round steak, ½ inch thick, can be substituted for the veal cutlets. Cut into 4 serving pieces.

To Serve Immediately: Reduce heat; add water. Cover tightly; simmer until done, about 30 minutes. (Add small amount of water if necessary.) Remove meat from skillet; keep warm. Pour tomato sauce into skillet; stir in oregano. Heat sauce until it boils; pour on meat and arrange mozzarella cheese on top.

VEAL BIRDS

Store no longer than 3 weeks. Makes enough for 2 meals—4 servings each.

Meat
8 boneless veal cutlets (4 ounces each)

Stuffing
2 cups packaged herb-seasoned stuffing
1 pound bulk pork sausage, browned and drained
½ cup finely chopped celery
⅓ cup shortening

Sauce
2 cans (10½ ounces each) condensed cream of mushroom soup
¾ cup milk

Pound meat until ¼ inch thick. Prepare stuffing as directed on package except—stir in sausage and celery. Press about ½ cup stuffing on each cutlet to within ½ inch of edge. Roll up, beginning at narrow end; secure with wooden picks.

Melt shortening in large skillet. Brown meat rolls in shortening. Remove meat from skillet; set aside. Pour off fat. Heat soup and milk in skillet, stirring constantly, until sauce is hot. Return meat to skillet. Cover tightly; simmer until done, about 45 minutes. (To serve whole recipe immediately, see below.) Divide rolls and sauce between 2 ungreased baking dishes, 8×8×2 inches. Cool quickly. Wrap, label and freeze.

■ **65 minutes before serving, remove 1 container Veal Birds from freezer and unwrap.** Cover tightly; heat in 400° oven 40 minutes. Uncover; heat 20 minutes. Place Veal Birds on warm platter and remove picks. Stir gravy; spoon on Veal Birds. (4 servings.)

To Serve Immediately: Place Veal Birds on warm platter and remove picks. Spoon gravy on Veal Birds. (8 servings.)

LAMB CURRY

Store no longer than 4 months. Makes enough for 4 to 6 servings.

¼ cup butter or margarine
1 medium onion, chopped (about ½ cup)
¼ cup chopped green pepper
¼ cup chopped celery
1 apple, pared and thinly sliced
1 to 2 teaspoons curry powder
¼ to ½ teaspoon salt
¼ cup all-purpose flour
2 cups chicken broth*
2 cups cubed cooked lamb

Melt butter in large saucepan. Cook and stir onion, green pepper, celery and apple in butter until onion is tender. Stir in curry powder, salt and flour. Cook over low heat, stirring constantly, until mixture is hot. Remove from heat; stir in broth. Heat, stirring constantly, until broth boils. Boil and stir 1 minute. Stir in meat. Cook, stirring occasionally, until hot, about 10 minutes. (To serve immediately, see below.) Pour into 1-quart freezer container. Cool quickly. Cover, label and freeze.

■ **35 minutes before serving, remove Lamb Curry from freezer. Have ready:** 3 cups hot cooked rice; chopped peanuts; hard-cooked eggs and chutney for accompaniments.

Dip container of curry into very hot water just to loosen. Place ½ cup water and frozen block in 3-quart saucepan. Cover tightly; heat over medium heat, turning occasionally, until hot and bubbly, about 30 minutes. Serve on rice. Pass peanuts, hard-cooked eggs and chutney.

To Serve Immediately: Serve on 3 cups hot cooked rice. Pass chopped peanuts, hard-cooked eggs and chutney.

*Chicken broth can be made by dissolving 2 chicken bouillon cubes or 2 teaspoons instant chicken bouillon in 2 cups boiling water, or use canned chicken broth.

SHEPHERDS' PIE

Store no longer than 2 months. Makes enough for 2 meals—4 servings each.

4 cups cubed cooked lamb, beef or veal
¼ cup chopped onion
3 cups cooked mixed vegetables (e.g., peas, carrots and/or corn)
2 cups gravy*

Mix all ingredients. Divide between 2 ungreased 1-quart casseroles. (To serve immediately, see below.) Wrap, label and freeze.

■ **65 minutes before serving, heat oven to 425°. Have ready:** instant mashed potato puffs (enough for 4 servings); 2 tablespoons snipped parsley.

Remove 1 casserole Shepherds' Pie from freezer and unwrap. Bake uncovered until hot and bubbly, about 1 hour. After casserole has baked 55 minutes, prepare potato puffs as directed on package. Mound potato on meat mixture; sprinkle parsley on potato. (4 servings.)

To Serve One Immediately: Have ready: instant mashed potato puffs (enough for 4 servings); 2 tablespoons snipped parsley.

Heat oven to 350°. Prepare potato puffs as directed on package. Mound potato on meat mixture; sprinkle parsley on potato. Bake uncovered until hot and bubbly, about 30 minutes. (4 servings.)

*Two cans (10¼ ounces each) gravy can be used.

Storage Time for Lamb and Veal at 0°	
Most cuts	6 to 9 months
Ground	3 to 4 months
Cooked	2 months

COOKED CHICKEN

Store no longer than 6 months. Makes enough for 2 meals—6 servings each.

3- to 3½-pound broiler-fryer chicken, cut up
1 sprig parsley
1 celery stalk with leaves, cut up
2 teaspoons salt
½ teaspoon pepper

Place all ingredients (with giblets) in large kettle. Add enough water to cover. Heat until water boils. Reduce heat; cover tightly and simmer until done, about 45 minutes.

Cool quickly. Remove skin and meat from pieces. Cut meat into large pieces. Divide meat between two 1-quart freezer containers (1½ to 2 cups in each). Strain broth (2 to 3½ cups). Divide broth between containers. Cover, label and freeze.

Use for Chicken Rice Casserole (right) and Chicken Tetrazzini (page 25).

Storage Time for Poultry at 0°

Chicken and Turkey	9 months
Ducks and Geese	6 months
Giblets	3 months
Cooked Poultry	1 month
in broth or gravy	6 months

Note: Do not freeze any stuffing.

To Thaw Frozen Poultry

In the Refrigerator: Leave in its wrapping. Allow about 2 hours per pound. Cook immediately.

At Room Temperature: Leave wrapped; put into brown paper bag on a tray. Allow about 1 hour per pound. Refrigerate or cook immediately.

Under Running Water: Leave wrapped. Allow about ½ hour per pound. Refrigerate or cook immediately.

CHICKEN RICE CASSEROLE

Makes enough for 6 servings.

Cooked Chicken (left)

Sauce
¼ cup butter or margarine
⅓ cup all-purpose flour
1½ teaspoons salt
⅛ teaspoon pepper
1½ cups milk

Base
1½ cups cooked white or wild rice
1 can (3 ounces) sliced mushrooms, drained
⅓ cup chopped green pepper
2 tablespoons chopped pimiento
¼ cup slivered almonds

One hour before serving, remove 1 container Cooked Chicken from freezer. Dip container into very hot water just to loosen. Place frozen block in large saucepan. Cover tightly; heat, stirring occasionally, until thawed. Remove from heat.

Heat oven to 350°. Melt butter in large saucepan; stir in flour, salt and pepper. Cook over low heat, stirring constantly, until smooth and bubbly. Remove from heat; stir in 1 cup broth and the milk. Heat, stirring constantly, until sauce boils. Boil and stir 1 minute. Stir in Base ingredients.

Pour into ungreased baking dish, 10×6×1½ inches, or 1½-quart casserole. Bake uncovered 40 to 45 minutes. Sprinkle snipped parsley on top for added color.

CHICKEN TETRAZZINI

Makes enough for 6 servings.

Cooked Chicken (page 24)

Sauce
¼ **cup butter or margarine**
¼ **cup all-purpose flour**
½ **teaspoon salt**
¼ **teaspoon pepper**
1 **cup whipping cream**
2 **tablespoons sherry, if desired**

Base
7 **ounces hot cooked spaghetti**
1 **can (3 ounces) sliced mushrooms, drained**
½ **cup grated Parmesan cheese**

One hour before serving, remove 1 container Cooked Chicken from freezer. Dip container into very hot water just to loosen. Place frozen block in large saucepan. Cover tightly; heat, stirring occasionally, until thawed. Remove from heat.

Heat oven to 350°. Melt butter in large saucepan; stir in flour, salt and pepper. Cook over low heat, stirring constantly, until smooth and bubbly. Remove from heat; stir in 1 cup broth and the cream. Heat, stirring constantly, until sauce boils. Boil and stir 1 minute. Stir in sherry, spaghetti, chicken and mushrooms.

Pour into ungreased 2-quart casserole. Sprinkle cheese on top. Bake uncovered until bubbly, about 30 minutes. To brown, place briefly under broiler.

Cooking Time

A dish that you cook to freeze and use at a later date should be a little under-cooked; otherwise it may overcook as it reheats. When you prepare a double batch—one to eat and one to freeze—set the freezer batch aside a few minutes before it is fully cooked.

CHICKEN À LA KING

Store no longer than 3 months. Makes enough for 3 meals—4 or 5 servings each.

2 **cans (6 ounces each) sliced mushrooms, drained (reserve ½ cup liquid)**
1 **cup diced green pepper**
1 **cup butter or margarine**
1 **cup all-purpose flour**
2 **teaspoons salt**
½ **teaspoon pepper**
2 **cups light cream**
2½ **cups chicken broth***
4 **cups cut-up cooked chicken**
2 **jars (4 ounces each) pimiento, drained and chopped**

In Dutch oven, cook and stir mushrooms and green pepper in butter 5 minutes. Stir in flour, salt and pepper. Cook over low heat, stirring constantly, until bubbly. Remove from heat; stir in cream, broth and reserved mushroom liquid. Heat, stirring constantly, until sauce boils. Boil and stir 1 minute. Stir in chicken and pimiento; heat until hot. (Can be served immediately on toast, hot rice or in patty shells. 12 to 14 servings.) Divide between three 1-quart freezer containers. Cool quickly. Cover, label and freeze.

■ **45 minutes before serving, remove 1 container Chicken à la King from freezer. Have ready:** toast, hot rice or patty shells.

Dip container of chicken into very hot water just to loosen. Place ½ cup water and frozen block in medium saucepan. Cover tightly; heat over medium-low heat, turning occasionally, until hot and bubbly. Serve on toast, hot rice or in patty shells. (4 or 5 servings.)

*Chicken broth can be made by dissolving 2 chicken bouillon cubes or 2 teaspoons instant chicken bouillon in 2½ cups boiling water.

3-IN-1 FREEZER CHICKEN

Store no longer than 4 months. Makes enough for 3 meals—4 to 6 servings each.

3 broiler-fryer chickens (2½ to 3 pounds each), cut up
1 sprig parsley
1 celery stalk with leaves, cut up
1 carrot, sliced
1 small onion, sliced
1 tablespoon salt
½ teaspoon pepper

Place all ingredients (with giblets) in large kettle. Add enough water to cover (about 3 quarts). Heat until water boils. Reduce heat; cover tightly and simmer until done, about 45 minutes.

Remove meat from broth. Cool quickly. Place pieces of 1 chicken in 2-quart freezer container; refrigerate. Remove skin and meat from remaining chickens. Cut meat into pieces (about 6 cups); refrigerate. Strain broth. Prepare Chicken Gravy (below).

CHICKEN GRAVY

8 cups chicken broth (reserve remaining broth for Egg Drop Soup)
2 cups water
1½ cups all-purpose flour
2 tablespoons salt
1 teaspoon pepper
⅛ teaspoon yellow food color

Spoon off fat from broth. Pour broth into 3-quart saucepan. Shake water and flour in covered jar; stir slowly into broth. Heat, stirring constantly, until gravy boils. Boil and stir 1 minute. Season with salt and pepper. Stir in food color. Cool quickly.

Prepare Chicken Almond Casserole (right), Chicken Pie and Chicken and Dumplings (page 28) as directed and freeze. Prepare Egg Drop Soup to serve today.

For Egg Drop Soup, have ready: remaining chicken broth (4 to 6 cups); ⅛ teaspoon salt; 1 egg, well beaten.

Heat chicken broth and salt until it boils; remove from heat. Stirring constantly, slowly pour egg in a thin stream into broth. If desired, sprinkle sliced green onion on soup. (4 to 6 servings.)

CHICKEN ALMOND CASSEROLE

Store no longer than 4 months. Makes enough for 6 to 8 servings.

4 cups cut-up cooked chicken (see 3-in-1 Freezer Chicken—left)
1 can (4 ounces) mushroom stems and pieces, drained
1 can (5 ounces) water chestnuts, drained and sliced
⅔ cup sliced almonds
1 tablespoon dried sweet bell peppers
2 teaspoons parsley flakes
½ teaspoon salt
2 cups Chicken Gravy (left)

Stir all ingredients into Chicken Gravy. Pour into 2-quart freezer container. Continue to cool quickly if necessary. Cover, label and freeze.

■ **24 hours before serving, remove Chicken Almond Casserole from freezer and place in refrigerator. About 20 minutes before serving, have ready:** ⅓ cup milk; 2 tablespoons sherry; Buttered Bread Crumbs (below).

Heat milk and chicken mixture in 2-quart saucepan over medium heat, stirring occasionally, until hot and bubbly, 10 to 12 minutes. Stir in sherry; heat slightly. Turn into serving dish; sprinkle Buttered Bread Crumbs on top. (Or, can be served on hot cooked rice.)

BUTTERED BREAD CRUMBS

Cook and stir 1 tablespoon butter or margarine and ¼ cup dry bread crumbs over medium heat until crumbs are golden brown, about 5 minutes.

Pictured at right, top to bottom: Chicken and Dumplings (page 28), Chicken Pie (page 28) and Chicken Almond Casserole

CHICKEN PIE

Store no longer than 4 months. Makes enough for 4 or 5 servings.

1 package (10 ounces) frozen
  peas and carrots
1 can (8 ounces) small whole onions,
  drained
1 can (4 ounces) mushroom stems and pieces
2 cups cut-up cooked chicken (see 3-in-1
  Freezer Chicken—page 26)
2 cups Chicken Gravy (page 26)
  Pastry for 9-inch One-crust Pie (page 77)

Rinse frozen peas and carrots with running cold water to remove ice crystals. Stir peas and carrots, onions, mushrooms (with liquid) and chicken into Chicken Gravy. Pour into ungreased 9-inch square foil pan.

Prepare Pastry; roll into 9-inch square. Fold in half; cut slits. Carefully place pastry on mixture; press edges of pastry onto rim of foil pan with fork. Freeze uncovered just until crust is firm, about 1 hour. Remove from freezer. Wrap, label and return to freezer.

■ **1 hour 30 minutes before serving, remove Chicken Pie from freezer and unwrap.** Loosely cover edges with 2- to 3-inch strip of aluminum foil to prevent excessive browning during baking. Bake in 450° oven until crust is brown and mixture is bubbly, about 1 hour 15 minutes. Let set 10 minutes before serving.

Storage Time for Cooked Dishes at 0°

Precooked foods	6 months
with sauce or gravy	3 months

If you want to use a special casserole, but not tie it up in the freezer, do this. Line the casserole with heavy foil and cook the food in it. Cool quickly; freeze till set. Remove dish in foil from casserole and wrap. To heat, unwrap and place in casserole.

CHICKEN AND DUMPLINGS

Store no longer than 4 months. Makes enough for 4 servings.

4 cups Chicken Gravy (page 26)
  Cooked pieces of 1 chicken (see 3-in-1
  Freezer Chicken—page 26)

Pour Chicken Gravy on chicken pieces in freezer container. Continue to cool quickly. Cover, label and freeze.

■ **24 hours before serving, remove chicken and gravy from freezer and place in refrigerator. Forty-five minutes before serving, have ready:** ½ cup milk and ingredients for Dumplings (below).

Heat chicken and gravy, milk and ½ cup water in large skillet over medium heat, stirring occasionally, until hot and bubbly, about 15 minutes.

Prepare dough for Dumplings; drop by tablespoonfuls onto chicken. Cook uncovered 10 minutes. Cover tightly; cook 20 minutes.

DUMPLINGS

1½ cups all-purpose flour*
 2 teaspoons baking powder
 ¾ teaspoon salt
 3 tablespoons shortening
 ¾ cup milk

Measure flour, baking powder and salt into bowl. Cut in shortening until mixture looks like meal. Stir in milk.

*If using self-rising flour, omit baking powder and salt.

CHICKEN-RICE ORANGE

Store no longer than 3 months. Makes enough for 2 meals—4 servings each.

Meat
¼ **cup shortening**
¼ **cup butter or margarine**
½ **cup all-purpose flour**
1 **teaspoon salt**
1 **teaspoon paprika**
¼ **teaspoon pepper**
2 **broiler-fryer chickens (2½ to 3 pounds each), cut up**

Sauce
2 **cups orange juice**
¼ **cup dry sherry or apple juice**
1 **tablespoon brown sugar**
2 **teaspoons salt**

Topping
1 **large onion, thinly sliced**
½ **cup chopped green pepper**
1 **can (6 ounces) sliced mushrooms, drained**

Heat oven to 425°. In oven, melt shortening and butter in 2 standard or foil baking pans, 13×9×2 inches. Mix flour, 1 teaspoon salt, the paprika and pepper. Coat chicken with flour mixture. Place 1 chicken in each baking pan; turn to coat with shortening. Turn skin side up. Bake uncovered 30 minutes. Mix Sauce ingredients in saucepan. Heat until mixture boils; remove from heat and set aside.

For Topping, sprinkle half the onion, the green pepper and mushrooms on each chicken. Pour half the orange sauce on each chicken. Bake uncovered until done, about 30 minutes. Cool quickly. Wrap, label and freeze.

■ **45 minutes before serving, remove 1 pan Chicken-Rice Orange from freezer and unwrap. Have ready:** ingredients for Orange Rice (right).
Heat chicken uncovered in 375° oven until hot, about 40 minutes. Prepare Orange Rice (right). Place rice and chicken on warm platter. Pour orange sauce into a small pitcher and spoon off fat; serve with chicken and rice. If desired, garnish with orange slices. (4 servings.)

ORANGE RICE

1½ **cups boiling water**
1 **cup uncooked regular rice**
⅔ **cup orange juice**
¼ **teaspoon allspice**
1 **teaspoon salt**

Heat oven to 375°. Mix all ingredients thoroughly in ungreased 1- or 1½-quart casserole or in baking dish, 10×6×1½ or 11½×7½×1½ inches. Cover tightly; bake until liquid is absorbed and rice is tender, 25 to 30 minutes.

FRIED CHICKEN

Store no longer than 4 weeks. Makes enough for 2 meals—4 servings each.

Salad oil
2 **cups all-purpose flour**
2 **tablespoons salt**
2 **broiler-fryer chickens (2½ to 3 pounds each), cut up**
4 **eggs, slightly beaten**

Heat oil (¼ inch) in large skillet or electric frypan over medium-high heat. Mix flour and salt. Dip chicken in egg, then coat with flour mixture. Brown chicken, a few pieces at a time, in oil. Reduce heat. Layer chicken skin side down in skillet in the following order: breasts, thighs, drumsticks, backs and wings. Cover tightly; simmer, turning once or twice, until done, 30 to 40 minutes. (If skillet cannot be tightly covered, add 1 to 2 tablespoons water.) After chicken has simmered 25 minutes, uncover to crisp.

Remove chicken from skillet. (Can be served immediately. 8 servings.) Divide in half. Wrap in heavy-duty aluminum foil. Cool quickly. Label and freeze.

■ **50 minutes before serving, remove 1 package Fried Chicken from freezer and open foil wrap.** Place on oven rack. Heat in 375° oven until hot, 45 minutes. (4 servings.)

Note: Chicken normally can be stored for a longer period of time. Fried chicken is best, however, if used within 4 weeks of initial freezing.

BATTER-FRIED FISH

Store no longer than 2 weeks. Makes enough for 6 servings.

1 cup all-purpose flour*
1 teaspoon baking powder
½ teaspoon salt
1 egg
1 cup milk
¼ cup salad oil
2 pounds fish fillets, steaks or pan-dressed
   fish
   Flour

Prepare batter. Measure 1 cup flour, the baking powder, salt, egg, milk and salad oil into a bowl; beat with rotary beater until smooth. If fillets are large, cut into serving pieces. Coat fish with flour, then dip in batter to coat completely.

Heat oil (½ to 1 inch) in large pan or deep skillet. Cook fish in oil until golden brown, about 4 minutes on each side. Cool quickly. Wrap, label and freeze.

■ **About 25 minutes before serving, heat oven to 400°.** Heat Batter-fried Fish on ungreased baking sheet until hot, about 15 minutes.

*If using self-rising flour, omit baking powder and salt.

Storage Time for Fish at 0°

Cod, Yellow Perch, Bluefish, Haddock	9 months
Lake Bass, Flounder, Bluegill, Sunfish	7 to 8 months
Whitefish, Lake Trout, Catfish, Northern Pike, Shrimp	4 to 5 months

Note: Fish frozen in ice, glazed or kept in a freezer at −10° can be stored an additional 1 or 2 months.

SEAFOOD SALAD IN A PUFF BOWL

Store no longer than 3 months. Makes enough for 6 servings.

½ cup water
¼ cup butter or margarine
½ cup all-purpose flour*
⅛ teaspoon salt
2 eggs

Heat oven to 400°. Grease 9-inch glass pie pan. Heat water and butter until mixture boils vigorously. Stir in flour and salt. Beat over low heat until mixture leaves side of pan and forms a ball, about 1 minute. Remove from heat; cool slightly, about 10 minutes. Beat in eggs; beat until smooth and glossy. Spread batter evenly *just* to side of pan. Bake 45 to 55 minutes. Cool at room temperature. (To serve immediately, see below.) Remove from pan. Wrap, label and freeze.

■ **15 minutes before serving, heat oven to 400°. Have ready:** Seafood Salad (below); 2 hard-cooked eggs, sliced; watercress.

Remove puff bowl from freezer and unwrap; place on ungreased baking sheet. Heat in oven about 10 minutes. Cool. Fill with Seafood Salad. Garnish with egg slices and watercress.

*Self-rising flour can be used in this recipe.

SEAFOOD SALAD
2 to 2½ cups cooked shrimp, crabmeat
   or lobster
2 cups thinly sliced celery
½ to ⅔ cup mayonnaise or salad dressing
1 tablespoon minced green onion
½ teaspoon salt
   Dash pepper

Mix seafood and celery. Mix mayonnaise, onion, salt and pepper. Pour on seafood and celery; toss. Cover tightly; chill at least 2 hours.

To Serve Immediately: Have ready: Seafood Salad; 2 hard-cooked eggs, sliced; watercress.

Fill bowl with Seafood Salad. Garnish with egg slices and watercress.

CHEESE SOUFFLÉ

Store no longer than 2 months. Makes enough for 4 servings.

¼ cup butter or margarine
¼ cup all-purpose flour
½ teaspoon salt
¼ teaspoon dry mustard
    Dash cayenne red pepper
1 cup milk
1 cup shredded process American cheese
    (about 4 ounces)
3 eggs, separated
¼ teaspoon cream of tartar

Butter 4-cup soufflé dish. Melt butter in saucepan over low heat. Stir in flour and seasonings. Cook over low heat, stirring constantly, until mixture is smooth and bubbly. Remove from heat; stir in milk. Heat, stirring constantly, until sauce boils. Boil and stir 1 minute. Stir in cheese; heat until cheese is melted and sauce is smooth. Remove from heat.

Beat egg whites and cream of tartar until stiff but not dry; set aside. Beat egg yolks until very thick and lemon colored; stir into cheese mixture. Stir about ¼ of the egg whites into cheese mixture. Gently fold mixture into remaining egg whites.

Carefully pour into soufflé dish. Wrap, label and freeze.

■ **2 hours before serving, heat oven to 325°. Remove Cheese Soufflé from freezer and unwrap.** Make a 4-inch band of triple thickness aluminum foil 2 inches longer than the circumference of soufflé dish; butter one side. Extend depth of dish by securing foil band, buttered side in, around outside top of dish. Bake until knife inserted halfway between edge and center comes out clean, 1½ to 1¾ hours. Serve immediately. Carefully remove foil band and spoon soufflé onto serving plate.

Note: Recipe can be doubled. Pour soufflé into 2 buttered 4-cup soufflé dishes.

MACARONI AND CHEESE

Store no longer than 3 months. Makes enough for 6 to 8 servings.

6 to 7 ounces elbow macaroni
    (about 2 cups)
2 tablespoons butter or margarine
2 tablespoons flour
1¼ teaspoons salt
¼ teaspoon pepper
2 cups milk
2 tablespoons grated onion
3 cups shredded process sharp American
    cheese (about 12 ounces)
1 tablespoon butter or margarine

Cook macaroni as directed on package; place in ungreased 2-quart casserole. Melt 2 tablespoons butter in saucepan over low heat. Stir in flour, salt and pepper. Cook over low heat, stirring constantly, until mixture is smooth and bubbly. Remove from heat; stir in milk. Heat, stirring constantly, until sauce boils. Boil and stir 1 minute. Stir in onion and cheese; heat until cheese is melted and sauce is smooth. Pour sauce on macaroni; dot with 1 tablespoon butter. (To serve immediately, see below.) Cool quickly. Wrap, label and freeze.

■ **65 minutes before serving, remove Macaroni and Cheese from freezer and unwrap.** Bake uncovered in 425° oven until hot and bubbly throughout, about 1 hour.

To Serve Immediately: Heat oven to 375°. Cover; bake 30 minutes. Uncover; bake 15 minutes.

Note: The Macaroni and Cheese can be divided between 2 ungreased 1-quart casseroles or foil pans, 8×8×2 inches. Cool quickly. Wrap, label and freeze. One hour before serving, heat oven to 425°. Remove 1 casserole Macaroni and Cheese from freezer and unwrap. Bake uncovered until hot and bubbly, about 45 minutes. (3 servings.)

Freezer Dinners

Mom's Night Out? Serve a piping hot dinner from freezer to oven to table in 25 to 35 minutes. We have designed our freezer dinners using leftover roasted meats and gravy; frozen, canned or leftover vegetables and a few special surprises that make mom's freezer dinners extra special!

Points to remember in preparing freezer dinners:

1. For ease and quick assembly, we recommend that you save the foil trays from commercially frozen dinners. If you don't have any, use foil broiler pans, cake or pie pans; shape divider compartments of foil to place in these pans. Fill the trays with the desired food, cover tightly with foil, label and freeze.

2. About 35 minutes before serving, heat oven to 450°. Heat frozen dinners in foil-covered commercial foil pans 25 minutes, in foil-covered homemade foil pans 35 minutes. (When heating 2 or more dinners in the same oven, allow 5 minutes longer.) When your dinner includes French fries or potato puffs, fold back foil to expose potatoes. Just before serving, stir gravy; spoon gravy on meat and season with salt.

3. Store no longer than 3 weeks.

4. Recommended portions for freezer dinners:

MEAT

3 ounces roast meats with ⅓ to ½ cup Gravy (page 33), or ½ cup sauce (page 33). (The meat without a gravy or sauce is dry and has a "reheated" taste.)

POTATOES OR RICE

½ cup Mashed Potatoes (below) with 1 teaspoon butter
½ cup frozen French fried potatoes or potato puffs
Instant Rice (below)

Mashed Potatoes

Prepare instant mashed potato puffs as directed on package for desired number of servings except—add 1 tablespoon additional milk for each serving. Cool.

Instant Rice

3 tablespoons uncooked instant rice
¼ cup water
⅛ teaspoon salt
½ teaspoon butter or margarine
Pinch of curry powder, if desired

Place all ingredients in foil pan. Freeze. When heating the frozen dinner, cook rice covered with foil.

VEGETABLES

½ cup frozen vegetables (mixed vegetables, corn, peas or green beans) with ½ teaspoon butter or margarine. Frozen carrots can also be used, if you add 2 tablespoons water.
⅓ to ½ cup canned or leftover vegetables with 2 tablespoons liquid and ½ teaspoon butter or margarine

ACCOMPANIMENTS

2 to 3 tablespoons cranberry sauce, Mustard Sauce (page 33), mint jelly, chutney, fruit pie filling with a pinch of cinnamon. (Place in separate compartment.)

Shape divider compartments of foil.

Arrange foods in compartments.

Mustard Sauce

1 tablespoon butter or margarine
1 tablespoon flour
½ teaspoon salt
¼ teaspoon pepper
1 cup milk
3 tablespoons prepared mustard
1 tablespoon horseradish

Melt butter in small saucepan over low heat. Stir in flour, salt and pepper. Cook over low heat, stirring constantly, until smooth and bubbly. Remove from heat; stir in milk. Heat, stirring constantly, until sauce boils. Boil and stir 1 minute. Stir in mustard and horseradish. Heat until hot. Cool.

About 1 cup.

GRAVY AND SAUCE FOR FROZEN DINNERS

To 1 packet (1¼ ounces) gravy mix, add 1½ cups water
To 1 can (10¾ ounces) gravy, add ¾ cup water
To 1 cup kettle or pan gravy, add ½ cup water
Cherry Sauce (below)

Cherry Sauce

½ cup cherry pie filling
¼ cup water
1 teaspoon lemon juice

Mix all ingredients. Pour on ham. Enough sauce for 2 frozen dinners.

Variations or Substitutions

If you are using large trays, you may have space to try some special treats or you may substitute them for potatoes or meat accompaniments. For a change of pace, try baked muffins, 2 teaspoons Double Chocolate Drops Dough (page 67) or ⅓ to ½ cup canned chocolate or vanilla pudding.

FREEZER DINNERS THAT WE RECOMMEND

Roast Turkey with Gravy
Cranberry Sauce
Buttered Sweet Potatoes
Buttered Green Beans
Blueberry Muffins
Vanilla Pudding

Roast Lamb with Gravy
Chutney or Mint Jelly
Instant Curried Rice
Buttered Mixed Vegetables

Roast Beef with Gravy
Sliced Peaches or Peach Pie Filling with Cinnamon
Twice Baked Potatoes
Buttered Peas

Baked Ham with Cherry Sauce (left)
Shredded Potato Patty
Asparagus
Carrots
Blueberry Muffins or Double Chocolate Drops Dough (page 67)

Roast Veal with Gravy
Buttered Green Beans
Mustard Sauce (left)
French Fried Potatoes

Roast Pork with Gravy
Spiced Crab Apple
Mexicali Corn
Broccoli Spears
Chocolate Pudding

Meat Loaf Slices with Gravy
Buttered Mashed Potatoes
Buttered Carrots
Orange Muffins

Roast Turkey freezer dinner

Roast Beef freezer dinner

Roast Pork freezer dinner

Appetizers and Snacks

INDIVIDUAL HOT SUB SANDWICHES

Store no longer than 1 month. Makes 8 sandwiches.

8 individual French rolls (about
    6 × 2½ inches each)
    Soft butter or margarine
8 slices salami or boiled ham
8 slices mozzarella cheese
8 slices cooked turkey or chicken
½ package (4-ounce size) blue cheese,
    crumbled

Cut rolls horizontally into 3 parts. Spread butter on all cut surfaces. Layer salami slice and cheese slice on bottom part of each roll. Place second part of roll on cheese; top with turkey slice and sprinkle blue cheese on turkey. Cover sandwich with third part of roll. Wrap each sandwich individually in heavy-duty aluminum foil. (To serve immediately, see below.) Label and freeze.

■ **35 minutes before serving, heat oven to 450°.** Remove Individual Hot Sub Sandwiches from freezer; heat wrapped sandwiches on oven rack 30 minutes.

To Serve Immediately: Heat oven to 425°. Heat wrapped sandwiches on oven rack 15 to 20 minutes.

TUNA SALAD SANDWICHES

Store no longer than 2 weeks. Makes 4 sandwiches.

1 can (6½ ounces) tuna, drained
¼ cup finely chopped sweet pickle
⅓ cup salad dressing* or dairy sour cream
¼ teaspoon salt
    Soft butter or margarine
8 slices bread

Mix all ingredients except butter and bread. Spread butter on bread, covering to edges. Spread filling on 4 slices; top each with a second slice. (Can be served immediately.) Place in sandwich bags; wrap each sandwich in heavy-duty aluminum foil, label and freeze.

■ **4 hours before serving, remove Tuna Salad Sandwich(es) from freezer and remove only foil wrap.** Thaw in sandwich bag(s) at room temperature.

*Do not use mayonnaise in this recipe.

VARIATIONS

Shrimp Salad Sandwiches: Substitute 1 can (4½ ounces) shrimp for tuna and use only 6 slices bread. Rinse shrimp; let stand in ice and water 20 minutes before mixing with other ingredients. (3 sandwiches.)

Crab Salad Sandwiches: Substitute 1 can (7½ ounces) crabmeat, drained and cartilage removed, for tuna.

Salmon Salad Sandwiches: Substitute 1 can (7¾ ounces) salmon, drained, for tuna.

For Pepped-up Sandwiches

Freezer-stored herbs or chopped onion add zip to sandwiches. To preserve herbs, wash and drain; wrap in foil or plastic bag. Put into carton or glass jar and store in freezer. Peel, wash and quarter onions; chop, then scald for 1½ minutes. Chill in iced water. Drain, package and freeze immediately.

SPICY RYE ROLLS

Store no longer than 2 weeks. Makes 6 sandwiches.

Butter Mixture
⅓ **cup soft butter**
2 **tablespoons minced onion**
2 **tablespoons prepared mustard**
2 **teaspoons poppy seed**
2 **teaspoons lemon juice**
   Dash cayenne red pepper

Rolls and Filling
6 **rye rolls, split into halves**
6 **slices Swiss cheese (about 6 ounces),**
   cut into halves
6 **slices salami (about 4 ounces)**

Mix Butter Mixture ingredients. Spread Butter Mixture on cut surfaces of rolls. Layer cheese slice, salami slice and cheese slice on each bottom half. Place top half on cheese. Wrap each sandwich in heavy-duty aluminum foil. (To serve immediately, see below.) Label and freeze.

■ **40 minutes before serving, heat oven to 375°.** Remove Spicy Rye Rolls from freezer; heat wrapped rolls on oven rack 35 minutes.

To Serve Immediately: Heat oven to 350° before assembling rolls. Heat wrapped rolls on oven rack 25 minutes.

UNUSUAL SANDWICHES FOR THE FREEZER

Spread butter or margarine on bread slices. Spread one of the Fillings (below) on half of the slices; top with second slice. Cut sandwiches in half. Place in sandwich bags; wrap each in heavy-duty aluminum foil, label and freeze.

■ **4 hours before serving, remove sandwich(es) from freezer and remove only foil wrap.** Thaw in sandwich bag(s) at room temperature.

FILLINGS

CHIPPED BEEF-CREAM CHEESE
1 **package (3 ounces) cream cheese, softened**
1 **package (3 ounces) dried beef**

Spread cream cheese on buttered bread slice; top with dried beef. Store no longer than 3 weeks. Enough for 3 sandwiches.

DEVILED HAM-CHILI SAUCE
1 **can (2¼ ounces) deviled ham**
1 **tablespoon plus 1 teaspoon chili sauce**

Mix ingredients. Store no longer than 3 weeks. Enough for 2 sandwiches.

SARDINES, CAPERS AND CHILI SAUCE
1 **can (3¾ ounces) sardines, drained**
2 **tablespoons chili sauce**
2 **teaspoons capers, chopped**

Mix ingredients. Store no longer than 2 weeks. Enough for 2 sandwiches.

FRANKFURTER-APPLE BUTTER
1 **to 2 tablespoons apple butter**
1 **frankfurter, cut lengthwise into thirds**

Spread apple butter on buttered bread slice; top with frankfurter slices. Store no longer than 3 weeks. Enough for 1 sandwich.

SHRIMP-GREEN OLIVE-CREAM CHEESE
1 **can (4½ ounces) shrimp, rinsed,**
   drained and chopped
1 **package (3 ounces) cream cheese, softened**
2 **or 3 green olives, chopped**
   (2 tablespoons)

Mix ingredients. Store no longer than 2 weeks. Enough for 3 sandwiches.

PEANUT BUTTER-HONEY-DATE
2 **tablespoons peanut butter**
1 **teaspoon honey**
2 **or 3 dates, chopped (1 tablespoon)**

Mix ingredients. Store no longer than 2 weeks. Enough for 1 sandwich.

RIBBON CANAPÉS

Store no longer than 2 months. Makes 1 ribbon loaf (about 5½ dozen 4×1-inch canapés).

Trim crust from 1 unsliced loaf white and 1 unsliced loaf whole wheat sandwich bread. Cut each loaf horizontally into 1-inch slices.

For each ribbon loaf, spread softened butter or margarine on each of 2 slices white and 1 slice whole wheat bread. Prepare 3 Canapé Spreads (pages 36 to 39). Spread ¼ cup of one of the Canapé Spreads on each slice. Assemble loaf, alternating white and whole wheat slices; top with unspread whole wheat slice.

Place on baking sheet and freeze 1 hour. Cut loaf into ½-inch slices; cut each slice into 3 canapés.

VARIATION

Checkerboard Canapés: Cut 4-layer ribbon loaf (above) into ½-inch slices. Spread softened butter or margarine on 1 slice; top with a second slice with the dark strip on top of the light. Press together gently but firmly. Spread softened butter or margarine on second slice; top with a third slice with the light strip on top of the dark. Press together gently but firmly. Cut into 4 slices; cut each slice into 2 canapés.

About 5½ dozen 2×1½-inch canapés.

Do-Ahead Sandwiches

Freeze 1 to 3 weeks' supply of sandwiches. Spread bread slices to the edges with butter or margarine.

Sliced meat, poultry, cheese, cheese spread, peanut butter, salmon and tuna freeze well. Moisten with applesauce, fruit juice or dairy sour cream, not mayonnaise, salad dressing or jelly. Don't use fresh vegetables or boiled egg whites.

Freezer-wrap sandwiches individually. Place sandwich in lunchbox unthawed —it will defrost in 3 to 3½ hours.

FROZEN CANAPÉ TRAY

Store no longer than 2 months. Makes about 8 dozen 1-inch canapés per sandwich loaf.

Trim crust from day-old unsliced loaf white, whole wheat or rye sandwich bread. Cut loaf horizontally into ½-inch slices. Spread softened butter or margarine lightly on each slice; cut into desired shapes. Spread 1 level measuring teaspoonful of one of the canapé spreads (pages 36 to 39) to the edge of each canapé. Use two or more of the following canapé spreads for a tasty and attractive tray. (Can be served immediately.)

Place desired number of canapés on cardboard tray; cover with plastic wrap. Wrap with aluminum foil, label and freeze.

■ **45 minutes before serving, remove Frozen Canapé Tray from freezer and remove aluminum foil.** Let stand at room temperature covered with the plastic wrap.

CREAMY DEVILED HAM

1 can (4½ ounces) deviled ham
1 package (3 ounces) cream cheese, softened
1 tablespoon salad dressing*
1 teaspoon snipped chives
   Stuffed green olive slices

Mix deviled ham, cheese and salad dressing. Stir in chives. Garnish canapés with olive slices.

About 1 cup (enough for 4 dozen 1-inch canapés).

*Do not use mayonnaise in this recipe.

DEVILED HAM AND OLIVE SPREAD

1 can (4½ ounces) deviled ham
2 tablespoons chopped stuffed green olives
1 tablespoon chopped pickled onion
1 teaspoon snipped parsley

Mix all ingredients.

About ½ cup (enough for 2 dozen 1-inch canapés).

CHICKEN-HAM-CHEESE SPREAD

**1 can (5 ounces) boned chicken,
  rinsed and finely chopped**
½ cup finely chopped ham
½ cup grated sharp Cheddar cheese
1 teaspoon salt
  Dash pepper
  Parsley leaves

Mix all ingredients except parsley leaves. Garnish canapés with parsley leaves.

About 1¼ cups (enough for 5 dozen 1-inch canapés).

CHILI HAM SPREAD

1 can (4½ ounces) deviled ham
1 tablespoon salad dressing*
¼ teaspoon onion juice
1 teaspoon minced chili peppers
  Green olive slices

Mix all ingredients except olive slices. Garnish canapés with green olive slices.

About ½ cup (enough for 2 dozen 1-inch canapés).

*Do not use mayonnaise in this recipe.

CREAM CHEESE AND HORSERADISH SPREAD

**1 package (8 ounces) cream cheese,
  softened**
2 tablespoons salad dressing*
1 teaspoon horseradish

Mix cream cheese and salad dressing. Stir in horseradish.

About 1 cup (enough for 4 dozen 1-inch canapés).

*Do not use mayonnaise in this recipe.

CRABMEAT SPREAD

**1 can (7½ ounces) crabmeat, drained and
  cartilage removed**
⅓ cup salad dressing*
1 tablespoon capers

Mix all ingredients. Garnish canapés with additional capers.

About 1 cup (enough for 4 dozen 1-inch canapés).

*Do not use mayonnaise in this recipe.

To make Checkerboard Canapés (page 36), assemble a ribbon loaf from white and whole wheat breads and 3 Canapé Spreads, then slice it ½ inch thick.

Stack 3 ribbon slices, alternating light strips of bread over dark ones to make a checkerboard pattern. Slice again and cut slices in half.

Frozen Canapé Tray (page 36). Assorted canapés are featured here.

SHRIMP-DILL SPREAD

1 can (6¾ ounces) medium shrimp, rinsed,
  drained and finely chopped
⅓ cup salad dressing*
2 teaspoons lemon juice
½ teaspoon dill weed
¼ teaspoon salt
  Parsley leaves

Mix all ingredients except parsley leaves. Garnish canapés with parsley leaves.

About ¾ cup (enough for 3 dozen 1-inch canapés).

*Do not use mayonnaise in this recipe.

CLAM AND CREAM CHEESE SPREAD

1 package (8 ounces) cream cheese,
  softened
1 can (8 ounces) minced clams, rinsed and
  drained
½ teaspoon seasoned salt
¼ teaspoon Worcestershire sauce
¼ teaspoon onion juice
  Ripe olive slices

Mix cream cheese and clams. Stir in remaining ingredients except olive slices. Garnish canapés with ripe olive slices.

About 1¼ cups (enough for 5 dozen 1-inch canapés).

CRABMEAT AND MUSHROOM SPREAD

1 can (7½ ounces) crabmeat, drained
  and cartilage removed
1 can (4 ounces) mushroom stems and
  pieces, drained and finely chopped
3 tablespoons dairy sour cream
¼ teaspoon red pepper sauce
¼ teaspoon horseradish
½ teaspoon salt
  Parsley leaves
  Pimiento slices

Finely chop crabmeat. Mix all ingredients except parsley leaves and pimiento slices. Garnish canapés with parsley leaves and pimiento slices.

About 1¼ cups (enough for 5 dozen 1-inch canapés).

SAVORY SPREAD

1 package (3 ounces) cream cheese,
  softened
1 cup butter or margarine, softened
1 teaspoon prepared mustard
⅛ teaspoon curry powder
½ teaspoon horseradish
¼ teaspoon Worcestershire sauce
¼ teaspoon red pepper sauce
¼ teaspoon onion juice
  Ripe olives
  Pimiento

Mix cheese and butter. Stir in remaining ingredients except olives and pimiento. Garnish canapés with ripe olives and pimiento.

About 1⅓ cups (enough for about 5 dozen 1-inch canapés).

CHICKEN AND MUSHROOM SPREAD

1 can (5 ounces) boned chicken,
  rinsed and finely chopped
1 can (4 ounces) mushroom stems and
  pieces, drained and finely chopped
1½ teaspoons sherry
  Dash cayenne red pepper
  Cocktail onion halves

Mix all ingredients except onion halves. Garnish canapés with cocktail onion halves.

About 1 cup (enough for 4 dozen 1-inch canapés).

LIVERWURST AND MUSHROOM SPREAD

¼ pound liverwurst
1 can (4 ounces) mushroom stems and
  pieces, drained and finely chopped
1 teaspoon chili sauce
  Chopped hard-cooked egg yolk

Mash liverwurst with fork until smooth. Stir in mushrooms and chili sauce. Garnish canapés with chopped hard-cooked egg yolk.

About 1 cup (enough for 4 dozen 1-inch canapés).

KIPPERED HERRING SPREAD

1 can (3¼ ounces) kippered herring, drained
¼ teaspoon vinegar
¼ teaspoon red pepper sauce
  Chopped hard-cooked egg yolk or pickle relish

Mix all ingredients except egg yolk. Garnish canapés with chopped hard-cooked egg yolk or pickle relish.

About ¼ cup (enough for 1 dozen 1-inch canapés).

CHEESE ROLLS

Store no longer than 10 months. Makes 2 dozen appetizers.

1 cup shredded natural Cheddar cheese
¼ cup grated or shredded Parmesan cheese
⅓ cup salad dressing
¼ teaspoon Worcestershire sauce
12 slices fresh soft bread
2 tablespoons butter, melted

Mix cheeses, salad dressing and Worcestershire sauce; set aside. Trim crusts from bread. Roll each slice lengthwise until thin and about 4½×4 inches. Cut slices crosswise in half; spread 1 rounded teaspoonful cheese mixture on each piece. Roll up, beginning at narrow end; secure with wooden picks. Brush rolls with melted butter. (To serve immediately, see below.) Freeze uncovered on ungreased baking sheet until firm, at least 2 hours. Divide rolls among freezer containers. Cover, label and return to freezer.

■ **15 minutes before serving, heat oven to 450°.** Remove Cheese Rolls from freezer; place on ungreased baking sheet. Bake until light brown, about 10 minutes.

To Serve Immediately: Heat oven to 400°. Place rolls on ungreased baking sheet. Bake until light brown, about 10 minutes.

OLIVE-CHEESE BALLS

Store no longer than 3 months. Makes 3 dozen appetizers.

2 cups shredded sharp natural Cheddar cheese
1¼ cups all-purpose flour*
½ cup butter or margarine, melted
36 pimiento-stuffed olives, drained

Mix cheese and flour. Stir in butter until mixture is smooth. (If dough seems dry, work with hands.) Shape dough by level teaspoonfuls around olives. (To serve immediately, see below.) Freeze uncovered on ungreased baking sheet until very firm, at least 2 hours. Place cheese balls in plastic freezer bags. Seal, label and return to freezer.

■ **25 minutes before serving, heat oven to 400°.** Remove Olive-Cheese Balls from freezer; place 2 inches apart on ungreased baking sheet. Bake until hot, about 20 minutes.

To Serve Immediately: Place 2 inches apart on ungreased baking sheet. Cover; chill at least 1 hour. Heat oven to 400°. Bake 15 to 20 minutes.

*Do not use self-rising flour in this recipe.

GUACAMOLE

Store no longer than 1 month. Makes about 2 cups.

2 ripe avocados, peeled and pitted
1 medium onion, finely chopped
1 or 2 small green chilies, finely chopped
1 teaspoon salt
½ teaspoon coarsely ground pepper
½ teaspoon ascorbic acid mixture

Mash avocados. Stir in remaining ingredients; beat until creamy. (To serve immediately, see below.) Pour Guacamole into 1-pint freezer container. Cover, label and freeze.

■ **3 hours before serving, remove Guacamole from freezer; thaw at room temperature. Have ready:** 1 medium tomato, peeled and finely chopped. Just before serving, stir in tomato.

To Serve Immediately: Stir in 1 medium tomato, peeled and finely chopped.

CRAB ROLLS

Store no longer than 6 weeks. Makes 2 dozen appetizers.

 1 can (7½ ounces) crabmeat,
   drained and cartilage removed
¼ cup dairy sour cream
 2 tablespoons chili sauce
¼ cup chopped green onion
½ teaspoon salt
½ teaspoon Worcestershire sauce
12 slices fresh soft bread
 2 tablespoons butter, melted

Mix crabmeat, sour cream, chili sauce, onion, salt and Worcestershire sauce; set aside. Trim crusts from bread. Roll each slice lengthwise until thin and about 4½×4 inches. Cut slices crosswise in half; spread 1 rounded teaspoonful crab mixture on each piece. Roll up, beginning at narrow end; secure with wooden picks. Brush rolls with melted butter. (To serve immediately, see below.) Freeze uncovered on ungreased baking sheet until firm, at least 2 hours. Place rolls in freezer containers. Cover, label and return to freezer.

■ **15 minutes before serving, heat oven to 450°.** Remove Crab Rolls from freezer; place on ungreased baking sheet. Bake until light brown, about 10 minutes.

To Serve Immediately: Heat oven to 400°. Place rolls on ungreased baking sheet. Bake until light brown, about 10 minutes.

ORIENTAL-GLAZED CHICKEN WINGS

Store no longer than 3 weeks.

3 pounds chicken wings (17 or 18)
⅓ cup soy sauce
2 tablespoons salad oil
2 tablespoons chili sauce
¼ cup honey
1 teaspoon salt
½ teaspoon ginger
¼ teaspoon garlic powder
¼ teaspoon cayenne red pepper, if desired

For easier handling as finger food, separate chicken wings at joint before marinating. Mix remaining ingredients; pour on chicken. Cover; refrigerate, turning chicken occasionally, at least 1 hour.

Heat oven to 375°. Remove chicken from marinade; reserve marinade. Place chicken on rack in foil-lined broiler pan. Bake 30 minutes. Brush chicken with reserved marinade. Turn chicken and bake, brushing occasionally with marinade, until tender, about 30 minutes. (Can be served immediately.) Cool quickly. Wrap, label and freeze.

■ **15 minutes before serving, heat oven to 375°.** Remove Oriental-glazed Chicken Wings from freezer and unwrap; place on ungreased baking sheet. Heat until hot, about 10 minutes.

Note: Baked chicken wings can be covered and stored in refrigerator no longer than 24 hours. Heat in 375° oven about 7 minutes.

CHILI CHEESE FRIES

Store no longer than 6 months. Makes about 5 dozen appetizers.

Dough
- **4 cups all-purpose flour***
- **2 teaspoons salt**
- **2 teaspoons baking powder**
- **2 teaspoons chili powder**
- **1 cup milk**
- **2 eggs**
- **½ cup butter or margarine, melted**

Filling
- **¼ cup thinly sliced green onion tops**
- **¼ cup snipped parsley**
- **1 tablespoon butter or margarine**
- **¼ teaspoon salt**
- **¼ teaspoon pepper**
- **½ pound shredded Monterey (Jack) cheese**

Mix flour, 2 teaspoons salt, the baking powder and chili powder. Beat milk and eggs in small bowl; stir into flour mixture. Stir in melted butter. Turn dough onto lightly floured cloth-covered board; knead until smooth, about 4 minutes. Shape into ball. Cover with plastic wrap; set aside for 30 minutes.

Cook and stir onion and parsley in 1 tablespoon butter until onion is tender. Remove from heat; stir in ¼ teaspoon salt, the pepper and cheese.

Divide dough into 4 parts. Roll each part ⅛ inch thick; cut into 3-inch circles. Spoon filling by rounded ½ teaspoonful on center of each circle. Moisten edge of circle; fold dough over filling and press edges with fork to seal securely. (If seal does not hold, reseal on both sides with fork just before frying.)

Heat shortening or oil (1 inch) in large skillet to 400°. Fry Chili Cheese Fries until golden brown on both sides, about 5 minutes; drain. Cool. Place desired number in freezer containers. Cover, label and freeze.

■ **15 minutes before serving, heat oven to 400°.** Remove Chili Cheese Fries from freezer; place on ungreased baking sheet. Heat until hot, about 10 minutes.

*If using self-rising flour, omit 2 teaspoons salt and the baking powder.

ESCARGOTS IN PETIT CHOUX (PUFF SHELLS)

Store no longer than 3 months. Makes 4 dozen puff shells.

- **1 cup water**
- **½ cup butter**
- **1 cup all-purpose flour**
- **4 eggs**

Heat oven to 400°. Heat water and butter until mixture boils vigorously. Stir in flour. Beat over low heat until mixture forms a ball, about 1 minute. Remove from heat. Beat in eggs; beat until smooth. Drop dough by slightly rounded teaspoonfuls onto ungreased baking sheet. Bake 25 to 30 minutes. (To serve half of recipe immediately, see below.) Cut puffs in half; cool. Place puffs on 2 pieces heavy-duty aluminum foil. Wrap, label and freeze.

■ **10 minutes before serving, heat oven to 400°. Have ready:** ingredients for Escargots (below).

Remove 1 package Puff Shells from freezer and open foil wrapper; place on ungreased baking sheet. Heat in oven until warm, about 5 minutes. Or, heat unwrapped frozen puff shells in electric bun warmer 25 minutes. Prepare Escargots. Guests spoon escargots and butter sauce into half of puff shell and top with other half. (2 dozen appetizers.)

ESCARGOTS

- **⅔ cup butter or margarine**
- **1 can (4½ ounces) escargots, rinsed and drained**
- **2 cloves garlic, crushed**
- **1 teaspoon parsley flakes**
- **1 teaspoon finely chopped green onion**
- **⅛ teaspoon pepper**
- **2 tablespoons dry white wine or, if desired, apple juice**

Melt butter in small saucepan. Stir in remaining ingredients; simmer 5 minutes. Serve in chafing dish.

To Serve Immediately: Cut 2 dozen puff shells in half; keep warm. Prepare Escargots (above). Guests spoon escargots and butter sauce into half of puff shell and top with other half. (2 dozen appetizers.)

Salads

FROZEN CHERRY-PINEAPPLE SALAD

Store no longer than 2 months. Makes enough for 12 servings.

1 can (12 ounces) pitted dark sweet cherries, drained (reserve syrup)
1 can (8½ ounces) crushed pineapple, drained (reserve syrup)
2 tablespoons lemon juice
1 package (3 ounces) cherry-flavored gelatin
1 package (3 ounces) cream cheese
½ cup chopped pecans
1 bottle (6 ounces) carbonated cola beverage

Heat ½ cup of the combined reserved syrups and the lemon juice until mixture boils. Pour boiling syrup on gelatin in large bowl; stir until gelatin is dissolved. Cool to room temperature.

Cut cream cheese into small pieces. Stir cheese pieces, fruit, pecans and cola beverage into gelatin mixture. Chill until slightly thickened. Spoon mixture into 12 paper-lined muffin cups. Wrap, label and freeze. Freeze at least 24 hours.

■ 30 minutes before serving, remove Frozen Cherry-Pineapple Salad from freezer. Remove salad from cups; serve on greens as a salad or, if you prefer, serve in sherbet glasses as a dessert.

FROZEN RASPBERRY SALAD

Store no longer than 2 months. Makes enough for 9 to 12 servings.

½ cup boiling water
1 package (3 ounces) raspberry-flavored gelatin
1 package (10 ounces) frozen raspberries, thawed
⅛ teaspoon salt
2 packages (3 ounces each) cream cheese, softened
1 cup dairy sour cream
1 can (16 ounces) whole cranberry sauce

Pour boiling water on gelatin in large bowl; stir until gelatin is dissolved. Stir in raspberries (with syrup). Mix remaining ingredients; stir into gelatin mixture. (Salad will be slightly lumpy.) Pour mixture into baking pan, 8×8×2 or 9×9×2 inches. Cover, label and freeze. Freeze at least 24 hours.

■ 20 minutes before serving, remove Frozen Raspberry Salad from freezer. Let stand at room temperature 10 minutes. Cut salad into serving pieces.

FROZEN COCKTAIL SALAD

Store no longer than 4 weeks. Makes enough for 16 servings.

2 cups dairy sour cream
¾ cup sugar
1 tablespoon plus 1 teaspoon lemon juice
1 can (30 ounces) fruit cocktail, drained
2 medium bananas, cut into ¼-inch slices
½ cup coarsely chopped walnuts
1 jar (10 ounces) maraschino cherries (¾ cup), halved

Mix sour cream, sugar and lemon juice. Stir in fruit cocktail, bananas, walnuts and cherries. Pour mixture into 2 refrigerator trays. Cover, label and freeze. Freeze until firm, at least 24 hours. (Upright or chest freezers will freeze salad in about 2 hours.)

■ 15 minutes before serving, remove Frozen Cocktail Salad from freezer; place in refrigerator. Cut each salad into 8 pieces, 2×2¼ inches. Stemmed red cherries make a bright garnish.

Vegetables

OVEN-FRIED EGGPLANT

Store no longer than 10 weeks. Makes enough for 4 servings.

½ cup seasoned bread crumbs
1 teaspoon salt
1 small eggplant (about 1 pound), pared
1 egg, slightly beaten

Heat oven to 375°. Grease jelly roll pan, 15½×10½×1 inch. Mix crumbs and salt. Cut eggplant into ½-inch slices; cut large slices into halves. Dip eggplant slices in egg, then coat with crumbs; arrange in pan. Bake uncovered 15 minutes; turn and bake 15 minutes longer. (Can be served immediately.) Cool thoroughly. Wrap, label and freeze.

■ **15 minutes before serving, heat oven to 450°.** Remove Oven-fried Eggplant from freezer and unwrap; arrange on ungreased jelly roll pan, 15½×10½×1 inch. Heat until hot, about 8 minutes.

FRENCH FRIED EGGPLANT

Store no longer than 1 month. Makes enough for 4 servings.

1 medium eggplant (about 1½ pounds), pared
⅔ cup milk
½ cup all-purpose flour*
¾ teaspoon baking powder
¼ teaspoon salt

Cut eggplant into ¼-inch slices; cut large slices into halves. Heat fat or oil (1 inch) in large skillet to 375°.

Beat remaining ingredients with rotary beater until smooth. Dip eggplant slices in batter, letting excess drip into bowl.

Fry a few slices at a time in hot fat, turning once, until golden brown; drain. (Can be served immediately.) Cool thoroughly. Wrap, label and freeze.

■ **15 minutes before serving, heat oven to 450°.** Remove French Fried Eggplant from freezer and unwrap; place on ungreased jelly roll pan, 15½×10½×1 inch. Heat until hot, about 8 minutes.

*If using self-rising flour, omit baking powder and salt.

Combine Frozen Vegetables

1 package artichoke hearts, 1 package green peas, 1 tablespoon lemon juice, 1 tablespoon butter.

1 package Chinese pea pods, 1 package carrot nuggets in butter sauce, 2 teaspoons lemon juice.

1 package chopped spinach, 1 package chopped broccoli, 1 tablespoon butter, 1 tablespoon lemon juice.

1 package cut green beans, 1 package cut wax beans, ½ teaspoon savory, 1 tablespoon butter.

Slice a large onion, then separate each slice into rings.

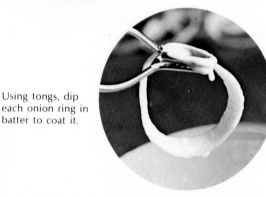

Using tongs, dip each onion ring in batter to coat it.

Drain the fried onion rings on paper towels.

FRENCH FRIED ONION RINGS

Store no longer than 3 months. Makes enough for 3 or 4 servings.

 1 **large Spanish or Bermuda onion**
⅔ **cup milk**
½ **cup all-purpose flour***
¾ **teaspoon baking powder**
¼ **teaspoon salt**

Cut onion into ¼-inch slices; separate into rings. Heat fat or oil (1 inch) in large skillet to 375°.

Beat remaining ingredients with rotary beater until smooth. Dip each onion ring in batter, letting excess drip into bowl.

Fry a few onion rings at a time in hot fat, turning once, until golden brown, about 2 minutes; drain. (Can be served immediately.) Cool thoroughly. Wrap, label and freeze.

■ **15 minutes before serving, heat oven to 350°.** Remove French Fried Onion Rings from freezer and unwrap; place on ungreased baking sheet. Heat 6 or 7 minutes.

*If using self-rising flour, omit baking powder and salt.

Vegetables with a Difference

You can vary the flavor of your vegetables with different seasonings.

Onions: Add a pinch of basil, cayenne pepper or celery seed.

Potatoes: Add a little bit of bay leaf, sage or poppy seed.

Green Beans: Sprinkle lightly with basil, dill, nutmeg or thyme.

Eggplant: Create an interesting flavor with garlic, curry powder, allspice or rosemary.

Corn: Add a little cayenne pepper, chili powder or celery seed.

Squash: Try oregano or rosemary.

TWICE BAKED POTATOES

Store no longer than 2 months. Makes enough for 4 servings.

4 large baking potatoes
 Shortening
⅓ to ½ cup milk
¼ cup butter or margarine, softened
½ teaspoon salt
 Dash pepper
 Shredded Cheddar cheese, if desired

Heat oven to 350°. Rub potatoes with shortening for softer skins. Prick several times with fork to allow steam to escape. Bake until potatoes are soft, 1¼ to 1½ hours.

Cut thin slice from top of each potato; scoop out inside, leaving a thin shell. Mash potato until no lumps remain. Add small amounts of milk, beating after each addition. (Amount of milk needed to make potato smooth and fluffy depends on kind of potatoes.) Add butter, salt and pepper; beat vigorously until potato is light and fluffy.

Fill potato shells with mashed potato; sprinkle cheese on top. (To serve immediately, see below.) Wrap, label and freeze.

■ **45 minutes before serving, heat oven to 400°.** Remove Twice Baked Potatoes from freezer and unwrap; place on ungreased baking sheet. Bake until centers of potatoes are hot, about 40 minutes. (Or, thaw potatoes uncovered at room temperature 1 hour 45 minutes; bake in 400° oven until golden brown, about 20 minutes.)

To Serve Immediately: Increase oven temperature to 400°. Place potatoes on ungreased baking sheet. Bake until golden, about 20 minutes.

GNOCCHI

Store no longer than 3 months. Makes enough for 4 servings.

2½ cups milk
 1 cup white cornmeal
 1 tablespoon butter or margarine
 2 eggs, well beaten
¼ teaspoon salt
 1 tablespoon butter or margarine
¼ to ½ cup grated Parmesan cheese

Butter baking pan, 8×8×2 inches. Heat milk in medium saucepan until small bubbles appear; remove from heat. Sprinkle cornmeal slowly into hot milk, stirring constantly. Cook over medium-high heat, stirring constantly, until very thick (spoon will stand upright in the Gnocchi), about 7 minutes.

Remove from heat. Mix in 1 tablespoon butter, the eggs and salt; beat until smooth. Spread in pan; cool. Refrigerate uncovered at least 2 hours. (Store no longer than 24 hours.)

Cut cornmeal mixture into sixteen 2-inch squares. Arrange squares in buttered baking dish, 10×6 inches, or ovenproof skillet; dot with 1 tablespoon butter and sprinkle cheese on top. (To serve immediately, see below.) Wrap, label and freeze.

■ **40 minutes before serving, remove Gnocchi from freezer and unwrap.** Bake uncovered in 425° oven until golden brown, about 35 minutes.

To Serve Immediately: Heat oven to 425°. Bake uncovered 10 to 12 minutes. Set oven control at broil and/or 550°. Broil Gnocchi with top 2 to 3 inches from heat until golden brown, about 2 minutes.

ASPARAGUS WITH CASHEWS

Makes enough for 3 or 4 servings.

- 1 package (10 ounces) frozen cut asparagus
- ¼ cup cashew nuts
- 2 tablespoons finely chopped onion
- 2 tablespoons butter or margarine

Cook asparagus as directed on package; drain. Cook and stir nuts and onion in butter until golden brown; toss with asparagus.

CLASSIC ASPARAGUS

Makes enough for 3 servings.

- 1 package (10 ounces) frozen asparagus spears
- 1 tablespoon butter or margarine
- 1 tablespoon light cream
- ¼ teaspoon salt
- ¼ teaspoon nutmeg
  Lemon wedges

Cook asparagus as directed on package; drain. Arrange asparagus in serving dish; top with butter, cream, salt and nutmeg. Serve with lemon wedges.

BUTTERED BLACKEYE ASPARAGUS

Makes enough for 8 servings.

Cook 2 packages (10 ounces each) frozen asparagus spears as directed on package; drain. Toss asparagus with ¼ cup soft butter or margarine and ¼ cup sliced pitted ripe olives until butter melts.

GREEN BEANS AND BAMBOO SHOOTS

Makes enough for 4 servings.

- 1 package (9 ounces) frozen cut green beans
- 1 tablespoon salad oil
- ½ cup water
- ¼ cup bamboo shoots, cut into ½-inch pieces or ¼ cup sliced water chestnuts
- ½ teaspoon salt
- ¼ teaspoon sugar
- ¼ teaspoon ginger

Rinse beans with small amount of running cold water to separate and remove ice crystals; drain. Cook and stir beans in oil 2 minutes. Stir in remaining ingredients. Heat until mixture boils; cook until beans are tender, 5 to 8 minutes.

GREEN BEANS IN SOUR CREAM

Makes enough for 3 or 4 servings.

- 1 package (10 ounces) frozen green beans
- 2 tablespoons finely chopped onion
- 2 tablespoons chopped pimiento
  Salt and pepper
- ½ cup dairy sour cream

Cook green beans as directed on package; drain and return to saucepan. Stir in onion, pimiento, salt and pepper; heat. Turn into serving dish; spoon sour cream on top.

SMOKY GREEN BEANS

Makes enough for 6 servings.

Cook 2 packages (9 ounces each) frozen cut green beans as directed on package; drain. Stir in 1 teaspoon smoky salt.

OVEN GREEN BEANS

Makes enough for 4 servings.

- 1 package (9 ounces) frozen cut green beans
- ½ teaspoon seasoned salt
- ¼ cup water
- 1 to 2 tablespoons butter or margarine

Heat oven to 425°. Place frozen beans in ungreased 1½-quart casserole. Sprinkle salt and water on beans; dot with butter. Cover tightly; bake 15 minutes. Separate beans with fork; cover and bake 15 minutes.

ITALIAN GREEN BEANS

Makes enough for 3 or 4 servings.

- 1 package (10 ounces) Italian green beans
- 1 small onion, thinly sliced
- ½ teaspoon salt
- 2 tablespoons oil and vinegar salad dressing

Cook green beans as directed on package except—stir in onion during last 2 minutes; drain. Toss green beans with salt and dressing.

CREOLE LIMA BEANS

Makes enough for 5 servings.

- 1 can (8 ounces) stewed tomatoes
- 1 package (10 ounces) frozen baby lima beans
- ⅔ cup thinly sliced celery
- ¾ teaspoon salt
- ⅛ teaspoon pepper

Heat tomatoes to boiling. Stir in remaining ingredients. Return to boiling; separate beans with fork. Reduce heat; cover tightly and simmer until beans are tender, 5 minutes.

BAKED LIMAS IN CREAM
Makes enough for 4 servings.
- **1 package (10 ounces) frozen baby lima beans**
- **½ cup light cream (20%)**
- **1 teaspoon salt**
- **⅛ teaspoon pepper**

Heat oven to 350°. Place all ingredients in ungreased 1-quart casserole. Cover tightly; bake 30 minutes.

DILLY BROCCOLI
Makes enough for 3 or 4 servings.
- **1 package (10 ounces) frozen chopped broccoli**
- **1 tablespoon butter or margarine**
- **¾ teaspoon dill weed**

Cook broccoli as directed on package; drain. Stir in butter and dill weed.

BROCCOLI WITH MUSTARD SAUCE
Makes enough for 3 servings.
- **1 package (10 ounces) frozen broccoli spears**
- **1 tablespoon butter or margarine**
- **1 tablespoon light cream**
- **½ teaspoon dry mustard**
- **1 teaspoon sugar**
- **⅛ teaspoon pepper**

Cook broccoli as directed on package; drain. Stir in butter. Turn into serving dish. Mix cream, mustard, sugar and pepper; pour on broccoli.

SAVORY BROCCOLI
Makes enough for 3 or 4 servings.
- **1 package (10 ounces) frozen chopped broccoli**
- **1 tablespoon butter or margarine**
- **⅛ teaspoon allspice**

Cook broccoli as directed on package; drain. Stir in butter and allspice.

SWEET AND SOUR BRUSSELS SPROUTS
Makes enough for 3 or 4 servings.
- **1 package (10 ounces) frozen Brussels sprouts**
- **1 tablespoon butter or margarine**
- **1 teaspoon vinegar**
- **1 teaspoon sugar**
- **2 slices bacon, crisply fried and crumbled**

Cook Brussels sprouts as directed on package; drain. Stir in butter, vinegar, sugar and bacon.

BRUSSELS SPROUTS À L'ORANGE
Makes enough for 3 or 4 servings.
- **1 package (10 ounces) frozen Brussels sprouts**
- **3 thin orange slices, cut into wedges**
- **1 tablespoon butter or margarine**
- **1 tablespoon honey**
- **⅛ teaspoon cloves**

Cook Brussels sprouts as directed on package; drain. Stir in orange wedges, butter, honey and cloves.

CARROTS 'N GREEN ONIONS
Makes enough for 3 or 4 servings.
- **1 package (10 ounces) frozen carrots**
- **1 tablespoon butter or margarine**
- **2 green onions, sliced**

Cook carrots as directed on package; drain. Stir in butter and onion.

Buttered Blackeye Asparagus (page 46)

Italian Green Beans (page 46)

Brussels Sprouts à l'Orange

Orange-glazed Carrots

Sweet Corn

Vegetable Medley

ORANGE-GLAZED CARROTS

Makes enough for 3 or 4 servings.

- 1 **package (10 ounces) frozen carrots**
- 1 **tablespoon butter or margarine**
- 1 **tablespoon orange marmalade**
- 2 **tablespoons chopped pecans**

Cook carrots as directed on package; drain. Stir in butter, orange marmalade and pecans.

VEGETABLE COMBINATION

Makes enough for 6 servings.

- 1 **package (10 ounces) frozen cauliflower**
- 1 **package (10 ounces) frozen chopped spinach**
- 1 **tablespoon butter or margarine**
- 1 **tablespoon lemon juice**

Cook cauliflower and spinach separately as directed on packages; drain. Toss cauliflower with spinach; stir in butter and lemon juice. Garnish with lemon slices.

CAULIFLOWER AND TOMATO

Makes enough for 4 or 5 servings.

- 1 **package (10 ounces) frozen cauliflower**
- ⅛ **teaspoon instant minced garlic**
- 1 **tablespoon butter or margarine**
- ½ **teaspoon salt**
- 1 **medium tomato, cut into eighths**
- 1 **tablespoon snipped parsley**
- 2 **tablespoons grated Parmesan cheese**

Cook cauliflower as directed on package; drain and return to saucepan. Add garlic, butter, salt and tomato. Cover tightly; simmer 2 to 3 minutes. Turn into serving dish; sprinkle parsley and cheese on top.

CHILI CORN

Makes enough for 3 or 4 servings.

- 1 **package (10 ounces) frozen whole kernel corn**
- 1 **tablespoon butter or margarine**
- ¼ **teaspoon chili powder**
- ¼ **cup sliced ripe olives**

Cook corn as directed on package; drain. Stir in butter, chili powder and olives.

SWEET CORN

Makes enough for 3 or 4 servings.

- 1 **package (10 ounces) frozen whole kernel corn**
- 1 **tablespoon butter or margarine**
- 1 **tablespoon maple-flavored syrup**

Cook corn as directed on package; drain. Stir in butter and syrup.

VEGETABLE MEDLEY

Makes enough for 6 or 7 servings.

- 1 **can (16 ounces) chop suey vegetables**
- 1 **package (10 ounces) frozen green peas**
- 2 **tablespoons butter or margarine**
- 1 **tablespoon soy sauce**

Drain chop suey vegetables; rinse with running cold water and drain. Cook peas as directed on package except—when peas and water are boiling, stir in chop suey vegetables. Reduce heat; cover tightly and simmer 5 minutes. Drain; stir in butter and soy sauce.

CRUNCHY PEAS

Makes enough for 3 or 4 servings.

1 package (10 ounces) frozen green peas
1 tablespoon butter or margarine
1 can (1¾ ounces) shoestring potatoes

Cook peas as directed on package; drain. Stir in butter and potatoes.

Substitution

½ cup canned French fried onions can be substituted for the potatoes.

CASSEROLED SPINACH

Makes enough for 6 servings.

2 packages (10 ounces each) frozen chopped spinach
1 teaspoon salt
⅛ teaspoon pepper
⅛ teaspoon instant minced garlic
2 teaspoons lemon juice
1 tablespoon flour
2 eggs

Heat oven to 350°. Cook spinach as directed on package except—simmer 3 minutes; drain. Beat remaining ingredients with hand beater in ungreased 1-quart casserole until very well mixed. Stir in spinach. Bake uncovered 25 minutes.

ZESTY SPINACH

Makes enough for 3 or 4 servings.

1 package (10 ounces) frozen leaf spinach
1 tablespoon butter or margarine
2 tablespoons milk
2 teaspoons horseradish

Cook spinach as directed on package; drain. Stir in butter, milk and horseradish.

VEGETABLE SAUCES

Store no longer than 4 months in the freezer (or 2 months in the refrigerator).

Seasoned Butter Pieces

Mix ½ cup butter or margarine softened, and ½ cup all-purpose flour. Stir in one of the following seasonings and 4 or 5 drops yellow food color:

¼ cup grated Parmesan cheese
2 teaspoons chili powder
1 teaspoon garlic powder
¼ cup soy sauce
2 teaspoons chopped parsley flakes
1 teaspoon dill weed
2 tablespoons grated lemon peel and 1 tablespoon lemon juice
2 tablespoons grated orange peel and 1 tablespoon orange juice

Drop mixture by level measuring tablespoonfuls onto waxed paper. Chill until firm, about 1 hour. Freeze or refrigerate in covered container or plastic bag.

Frozen Vegetable with Sauce

Cook 1 package (about 9 ounces) frozen vegetable, using ½ cup water as directed except —2 minutes before vegetable is done, add 2 Seasoned Butter Pieces. Cook 2 minutes; stir gently until sauce is smooth.

Canned Vegetable with Sauce

Drain liquid from 1 can (about 16 ounces) vegetable into saucepan. Heat liquid until it boils; boil until about ½ cup liquid remains. Add vegetable and 2 Seasoned Butter Pieces. Heat over medium heat until vegetable is hot and butter pieces melt. Stir gently until sauce is smooth.

Crunchy Peas

Zesty Spinach

Seasoned Butter Pieces (orange)

Breads

CHEESE SOUFFLÉ BREAD

Store no longer than 6 months. Makes 1 loaf.

  1 package active dry yeast
  ¼ cup warm water (105 to 115°)
  ¼ cup lukewarm milk (scalded then cooled)
  ⅓ cup butter or margarine, softened
  1 egg
  ½ teaspoon salt
  ¼ teaspoon pepper
  ⅔ cup finely shredded Cheddar cheese
  1½ cups all-purpose flour*
    Soft butter or margarine

Dissolve yeast in warm water in large mixer bowl. Add milk, ⅓ cup butter, the egg, salt, pepper, cheese and ½ cup of the flour; mix on low speed, scraping bowl constantly, ½ minute. Beat on medium speed, scraping bowl occasionally, 2 minutes. Stir in remaining flour until dough is smooth. Scrape dough from side of bowl. Cover; let rise in warm place until double, about 30 minutes. (Dough is ready if impression remains when touched.)

Beat dough about 25 strokes. Spread evenly in greased 1-quart casserole. Cover; let rise until double, about 40 minutes.

Heat oven to 375°. Bake until loaf is brown and sounds hollow when tapped, 40 to 45 minutes. Immediately remove bread from casserole; place on wire rack. Brush top of bread with butter.

Cool 1 hour. Wrap in heavy-duty aluminum foil, label and freeze.

■ **4 hours before serving, remove Cheese Soufflé Bread from freezer and unwrap.** Thaw at room temperature at least 3½ hours. Rewrap loaf in foil; heat in 400° oven until warm, 30 minutes. To serve, cut into wedges with serrated knife.

*If using self-rising flour, omit salt.

PUMPERNICKEL RYE BREAD

Store no longer than 9 months. Makes 2 loaves.

  3 packages active dry yeast
  1½ cups warm water (105 to 115°)
  ½ cup molasses
  4 teaspoons salt
  2 tablespoons shortening
  2 tablespoons caraway seed
  2¾ cups rye flour
  1 to 1½ cups all-purpose flour*

Dissolve yeast in warm water in large bowl. Mix in molasses, salt, shortening, caraway seed and rye flour; beat until smooth. Stir in enough white flour to make dough easy to handle.

Turn dough onto lightly floured board. Cover; let stand 10 to 15 minutes. Knead until smooth, about 5 minutes. Place in greased bowl; turn greased side up. Cover; let rise in warm place until double, about 1½ hours.

Punch down dough; round up, cover and let rise again until double, about 50 minutes.

Grease baking sheet; sprinkle cornmeal on greased sheet. Punch down dough; divide in half. Shape each half into round, slightly flat loaf. Place loaves in opposite corners of baking sheet. Cover; let rise 1 hour.

Heat oven to 375°. Bake 30 to 35 minutes. Cool. (Can be served immediately.)

Cool loaves 1½ hours. Wrap in heavy-duty aluminum foil, label and freeze.

■ **2 hours 30 minutes before serving, remove Pumpernickel Rye Bread from freezer.** Thaw in wrapper at room temperature.

*If using self-rising flour, omit salt.

BLUEBERRY COFFEE CAKE

Store no longer than 3 months. Makes 2 cakes—9 to 12 servings each.

      4 cups all-purpose flour*
  1½ cups sugar
      1 tablespoon plus 2 teaspoons
         baking powder
  1½ teaspoons salt
      ½ cup shortening
  1½ cups milk
      2 eggs
      4 cups fresh or frozen blueberries
         Topping (below)
         Confectioners' Glaze (below),
         if desired

Heat oven to 375°. Grease 2 layer pans, 9×1½ inches, or 2 baking pans, 9×9×2 inches. Mix all ingredients except blueberries, Topping and Confectioners' Glaze until moistened; beat vigorously ½ minute. Carefully stir in blueberries. Spread half the batter in each pan; sprinkle Topping on batter. Bake until wooden pick inserted in center comes out clean, 45 to 50 minutes.

Cool slightly. Drizzle Confectioners' Glaze on top. (Can be served immediately.) Cool thoroughly. Wrap, label and freeze.

■ **50 minutes before serving, remove Blueberry Coffee Cake from freezer and unwrap.** Heat uncovered in 350° oven until warm, 45 minutes.

TOPPING

Mix 1 cup sugar, ⅔ cup all-purpose flour, 1 teaspoon cinnamon and ½ cup soft butter.

CONFECTIONERS' GLAZE

Mix 2 cups confectioners' sugar, ¼ cup butter or margarine, softened, and 1 teaspoon vanilla. Stir in ⅓ to ½ cup water, about 2 tablespoons at a time, until glaze is spreading consistency.

*If using self-rising flour, omit baking powder and salt.

BUTTERY STREUSEL COFFEE CAKE

Store no longer than 3 months. Makes 2 cakes—9 to 12 servings each.

      3 cups all-purpose flour*
  1½ cups sugar
      1 tablespoon plus 2 teaspoons
         baking powder
  1½ teaspoons salt
      ½ cup shortening
  1½ cups milk
      2 eggs
         Cinnamon-Nut Filling (below)
         Streusel Topping (below)
         Confectioners' Glaze (left), if desired

Heat oven to 375°. Grease 2 layer pans, 9×1½ inches, or 2 baking pans, 9×9×2 inches. Mix all ingredients except Cinnamon-Nut Filling, Streusel Topping and Confectioners' Glaze until moistened; beat vigorously ½ minute. Spread ⅓ of batter (about 1⅓ cups) in each pan. Sprinkle half the Cinnamon-Nut Filling on the batter in each pan; spread half the remaining batter (about ⅔ cup) in each pan. Sprinkle Streusel Topping on top. Bake until wooden pick inserted in center comes out clean, 30 to 35 minutes.

Cool slightly. Drizzle Confectioners' Glaze on top. (Can be served immediately.) Cool thoroughly. Wrap, label and freeze.

■ **25 minutes before serving, remove Buttery Streusel Coffee Cake from freezer and unwrap.** Heat uncovered in 350° oven until warm, about 20 minutes.

*If using self-rising flour, omit baking powder and salt.

CINNAMON-NUT FILLING

Mix ½ cup brown sugar (packed), ½ cup finely chopped nuts and 2 teaspoons cinnamon.

STREUSEL TOPPING

Mix ½ cup all-purpose flour, 1 cup sugar and ½ cup firm butter until crumbly.

FRUITED LOAF

Store no longer than 9 months. Makes 2 coffee cakes.

Dough
    1 package active dry yeast
    ¾ cup warm water (105 to 115°)
    ½ cup sugar
    ½ teaspoon salt
    3 eggs
    1 egg yolk (reserve white)
    ½ cup butter or margarine, softened
    3½ cups all-purpose flour*
    ½ cup chopped blanched almonds
    ¼ cup cut-up citron
    ¼ cup cut-up candied cherries
    ¼ cup raisins
    1 tablespoon grated lemon peel
    ¼ cup plus 2 tablespoons soft butter

Icing (optional)
    1½ cups confectioners' sugar
    1½ tablespoons milk

Dissolve yeast in warm water in large mixer bowl. Add sugar, salt, eggs, egg yolk, ½ cup butter and 1½ cups of the flour; mix on low speed, scraping bowl constantly, ½ minute. Beat on medium speed, scraping bowl occasionally, about 10 minutes.

Stir in remaining flour, the almonds, citron, cherries, raisins and lemon peel. Scrape dough from side of bowl. Cover; let rise in warm place until double, about 1½ hours.

Beat dough 25 strokes. Cover tightly; refrigerate at least 8 hours. Turn dough onto well-floured board; coat with flour. Divide dough in half; press each half into oval, about 10×7 inches. Spread 3 tablespoons butter on each oval. Fold in half lengthwise; press only folded edge firmly. Place on greased baking sheet. Beat reserved egg white slightly; beat in 1 tablespoon water. Brush loaves with beaten egg white. Let rise until double, 45 to 60 minutes.

Heat oven to 375°. Bake until golden brown, 20 to 25 minutes. Mix confectioners' sugar and milk until smooth. While loaves are warm, frost with Icing; if desired, decorate with almond halves, pieces of citron and cherry halves.

Cool 1 hour. (Can be served immediately.) If frosted and decorated, freeze uncovered 2 hours. Wrap, label and return to freezer.

■ **2 hours before serving, remove Fruited Loaf from freezer; thaw in wrapper at room temperature 1 hour.** Unwrap and thaw 1 hour. (Or, after first hour of thawing, loaf can be sliced and thawed on serving plate 30 minutes.)

*Do not use self-rising flour in this recipe.

Storage Time for Dairy Products at 0°

Butter, Margarine	3 months
Cheese	1½ to 4 months
Ice Cream	less than 1 month
Eggs (prepared)	9 months

Note: Do not freeze milk or cream.

Overwrap butter or margarine in freezer wrap, even if it is already in parchment or a carton.

Keep cheese in unopened first wrapping. Overwrap in freezer wrap. Before eating, thaw in refrigerator; use as soon as possible.

Ice cream keeps better when you overwrap the carton with freezer wrap. In an opened carton, smooth plastic wrap over surface of ice cream.

To freeze egg yolks, break yolks. For each cup of yolks, add either 1 teaspoon salt or 2 tablespoons sugar or 2 tablespoons corn syrup. Stir, but do not beat air in. To freeze egg whites, strain through sieve; do not add anything. To freeze eggs whole, break yolks; mix well with whites, but do not stir air in.

Pictured at right: Blueberry Coffee Cake (page 51), Fruited Loaf, Buttery Streusel Coffee Cake (page 51) and Citron-Anise Loaf (page 55)

Spread the dough with a filling (Apricot-Cherry Filling, page 55, is shown here) and roll up, starting from long side.

After shaping the roll into a ring, cut partway through at 1-inch intervals with scissors. Twist each section on its side.

Filled Rings: The unglazed ring is made with Date Filling (page 55), the glazed one with Apricot-Cherry Filling.

FILLED RINGS

Store no longer than 9 months. Makes 3 rings.

2 cups dairy sour cream
2 packages active dry yeast
½ cup warm water (105 to 115°)
¼ cup butter or margarine, softened
⅓ cup sugar
2 teaspoons salt
2 eggs
  About 6 cups all-purpose flour*
  Fillings (page 55)

Heat sour cream over low heat just until lukewarm. Dissolve yeast in warm water in large bowl. Mix in sour cream, butter, sugar, salt, eggs and 2 cups of the flour; beat until smooth. Stir in enough remaining flour to make dough easy to handle.

Turn dough onto well-floured board; knead until smooth, about 10 minutes. Place in greased bowl; turn greased side up. Cover; let rise in warm place until double, about 1 hour.

Heat oven to 375°. Punch down dough; divide into 3 parts. Roll each part into rectangle, 15×9 inches. Spread a different filling evenly on each rectangle. Roll up, beginning at long side. Pinch edge of dough into roll to seal securely. Stretch roll to make even.

With sealed edge down, shape into ring on lightly greased baking sheet. Pinch ends together. With scissors, make cuts ⅔ of the way through each ring at 1-inch intervals. Turn each section on its side. Bake until golden brown, 15 to 20 minutes. Cool. (Can be served immediately.) Freeze uncovered until firm, about 2 hours. Wrap in heavy-duty aluminum foil, label and return to freezer.

■ **40 minutes before serving, remove Filled Ring from freezer.** Heat wrapped ring in 350° oven 35 minutes. Or, thaw in wrapper at room temperature 2 hours. If desired, drizzle Glaze (page 55) on top.

*If using self-rising flour, omit salt.

FILLINGS

Date Filling (enough for 1 ring)
1 cup chopped dates
¼ cup sugar
⅓ cup water
⅓ cup coarsely chopped nuts

Cook dates, sugar and water over medium heat, stirring constantly, until thickened. Stir in nuts; cool.

Cinnamon-Raisin Filling (enough for 1 ring)
2 tablespoons butter or margarine
½ cup brown sugar (packed)
2 teaspoons cinnamon
½ cup raisins

Spread butter on rectangle; sprinkle sugar, cinnamon and raisins on top.

Apricot-Cherry Filling (enough for 1 ring)
½ cup finely chopped dried apricots
½ cup drained finely chopped
   maraschino cherries

Mix apricots and cherries.

GLAZE

Mix 2 cups confectioners' sugar, ¼ cup butter or margarine, softened, 1 teaspoon vanilla and enough water so glaze is proper consistency to drizzle on rings.

Fresh from the Freezer

With your freezer and a little planning ahead, you can serve fresh rolls and coffee cake at the crack of dawn. When you bake, overwrap sweet rolls individually; wrap 2 slices of coffee cake together. Unwrapped, the separated slices and the rolls will thaw out in a few minutes. Packed lunches, too, will taste fresh when sandwiches are made with frozen bread.

CITRON-ANISE LOAF

Store no longer than 9 months. Makes 2 loaves.

Dough
   2 packages active dry yeast
   ½ cup warm water (105 to 115°)
   ½ cup lukewarm milk (scalded
      then cooled)
   ½ cup sugar
   1 teaspoon salt
   2 eggs
   ½ cup butter or margarine, softened
4½ to 5 cups all-purpose flour*
   ½ cup raisins
   ½ cup cut-up citron
   1 tablespoon anise seed
   2 tablespoons pine nuts, if desired

Glaze
   1 egg
   1 tablespoon water

Dissolve yeast in warm water in large bowl. Mix in milk, sugar, salt, 2 eggs, the butter and 2½ cups of the flour; beat until smooth. Stir in fruit, anise seed, nuts and enough remaining flour to make dough easy to handle.

Turn dough onto lightly floured board; knead until smooth and elastic, about 5 minutes. Place in greased bowl; turn greased side up. Cover; let rise in warm place until double, 1½ to 2 hours.

Punch down dough; divide in half. Shape each half into round, slightly flat loaf. Place loaves in opposite corners of greased baking sheet. Cut a cross ½ inch deep on top of each loaf. Let rise until double, about 1 hour.

Heat oven to 350°. Mix 1 egg and 1 tablespoon water; brush on loaves. Bake 35 to 45 minutes. Cool. (Can be served immediately.)

Cool loaves 1 hour. Wrap in heavy-duty aluminum foil, label and freeze.

■ **2½ hours before serving, remove Citron-Anise Loaf from freezer.** Thaw in wrapper at room temperature. Can be warmed, if desired.

*Do not use self-rising flour in this recipe.

QUICK BUTTERMILK SWEET DOUGH

    2 packages active dry yeast
    ½ cup warm water (105 to 115°)
    1¼ cups buttermilk
    2 eggs
    5½ to 6 cups all-purpose flour*
    ½ cup butter or margarine, softened
    ½ cup sugar
    2 teaspoons baking powder
    2 teaspoons salt

Dissolve yeast in warm water in large mixer bowl. Add buttermilk, eggs, 2½ cups of the flour, the butter, sugar, baking powder and salt; mix on low speed, scraping bowl constantly, ½ minute. Beat on medium speed, scraping bowl occasionally, 2 minutes. Stir in enough remaining flour to make dough easy to handle. (Dough should remain soft and slightly sticky.)

Turn dough onto well-floured board; knead 5 minutes or about 200 turns. Shape dough immediately (no need to let rise) into desired rolls and coffee cakes. Cover; let rise in warm place until double, about 1 hour. Use for your choice of the recipes on pages 56 to 57.

*If using self-rising flour, omit baking powder and salt.

CINNAMON ROLLS

Store no longer than 9 months. Makes 12 rolls.

    ½ recipe Quick Buttermilk Sweet
        Dough (above)
    1 tablespoon butter or margarine,
        softened
    ¼ cup sugar
    1 teaspoon cinnamon
        Confectioners' Icing (right),
        if desired

Roll dough into rectangle, 12×7 inches. Spread butter on dough. Sprinkle sugar and cinnamon on rectangle. Roll up, beginning at long side. Pinch edge of dough into roll to seal securely. Stretch roll to make even; cut into 12 slices.

Place slices slightly apart in greased layer pan, 9×1½ inches. Let rise until double. Heat oven to 375°. Bake 25 minutes. Frost with Confectioners' Icing. (Can be served immediately.)

Cool rolls 1 hour. Freeze uncovered until completely frozen, at least 2 hours. Wrap in heavy-duty aluminum foil, label and return to freezer.

■ **50 minutes before serving, remove Cinnamon Rolls from freezer and place wrapped rolls on oven rack.** Heat in 350° oven until warm, about 45 minutes.

CONFECTIONERS' ICING

Mix ¾ cup confectioners' sugar, 1 tablespoon milk and ½ teaspoon vanilla until smooth.

FROSTED ORANGE ROLLS

Store no longer than 8 months. Makes 12 rolls.

    3 tablespoons butter or margarine,
        softened
    1 tablespoon grated orange peel
    2 tablespoons orange juice
    1½ cups confectioners' sugar
    ½ recipe Quick Buttermilk Sweet
        Dough (left)

Beat butter, orange peel, juice and confectioners' sugar until creamy and smooth. Roll dough into rectangle, 12×7 inches. Spread half the orange filling on dough. Roll up, beginning at long side. Pinch edge of dough into roll to seal securely. Stretch roll to make even; cut into 12 slices.

Place slices slightly apart in greased layer pan, 9×1½ inches. Let rise until double. Heat oven to 375°. Bake 25 to 30 minutes. Spread remaining filling on warm rolls. (Can be served immediately.)

Cool rolls 1 hour. Freeze uncovered until completely frozen, at least 2 hours. Wrap in heavy-duty aluminum foil, label and return to freezer.

■ **50 minutes before serving, remove Frosted Orange Rolls from freezer and place wrapped rolls on oven rack.** Heat in 350° oven until warm, about 45 minutes.

BUTTERSCOTCH-PECAN ROLLS

Store no longer than 8 months. Makes 15 rolls.

½ recipe Quick Buttermilk Sweet Dough
   (page 56)
2 tablespoons butter or margarine,
   softened
¼ cup granulated sugar
2 teaspoons cinnamon
½ cup butter or margarine
½ cup brown sugar (packed)
½ cup pecan halves

Roll dough into rectangle, 15×9 inches. Spread 2 tablespoons butter on dough. Mix granulated sugar and cinnamon; sprinkle on rectangle. Roll up, beginning at long side. Pinch edge of dough into roll to seal securely. Stretch roll to make even. Melt ½ cup butter in baking pan, 13×9×2 inches; sprinkle brown sugar and pecan halves on butter.

Cut roll into 15 slices. Place slices slightly apart in baking pan. Let rise until double. Heat oven to 375°. Bake 25 to 30 minutes. Immediately invert pan onto large tray. Let pan remain a minute so butterscotch drizzles down on rolls. (Can be served immediately.)

Cool rolls 1 hour. Freeze uncovered until completely frozen, at least 2 hours. Wrap in heavy-duty aluminum foil, label and return to freezer.

■ **30 minutes before serving, remove Butterscotch-Pecan Rolls from freezer and place wrapped rolls on oven rack. Heat in 350° oven until warm,** about 25 minutes.

FROSTED CHOCOLATE ROLLS

Store no longer than 9 months. Makes 12 rolls.

3 tablespoons cocoa
3 tablespoons butter or margarine,
   softened
2 tablespoons milk
1½ cups confectioners' sugar
½ recipe Quick Buttermilk Sweet Dough
   (page 56)

Beat cocoa, butter, milk and confectioners' sugar until creamy and smooth. Roll dough into rectangle, 12×7 inches. Spread half the chocolate filling on dough. Roll up, beginning at

long side. Pinch edge of dough into roll to seal securely. Stretch roll to make even; cut into 12 slices.

Place slices slightly apart in greased layer pan, 9×1½ inches. Let rise until double. Heat oven to 375°. Bake 25 to 30 minutes. Spread remaining filling on warm rolls. (Can be served immediately.)

Cool rolls 1 hour. Freeze uncovered until completely frozen, at least 2 hours. Wrap in heavy-duty aluminum foil, label and return to freezer.

■ **50 minutes before serving, remove Frosted Chocolate Rolls from freezer and place wrapped rolls on oven rack. Heat in 350° oven until warm,** about 45 minutes.

HUNGARIAN COFFEE CAKE

Store no longer than 8 months. Makes 1 coffee cake.

   Quick Buttermilk Sweet Dough (page 56)
¾ cup sugar
1 teaspoon cinnamon
½ cup finely chopped nuts
½ cup butter or margarine, melted

Shape 1½-inch pieces of dough into balls. Mix sugar, cinnamon and nuts. Dip balls in butter, then in sugar mixture. Place a single layer of balls so they just touch in well-greased 10-inch tube pan. (If pan has removable bottom, line with aluminum foil.) Top with another layer of balls. Let rise until double.

Heat oven to 375°. Bake 1 hour. (If coffee cake browns too quickly, cover with aluminum foil.) Loosen from pan. Invert pan onto serving plate so butter-sugar mixture can drizzle down over cake. (To serve immediately, break coffee cake apart with 2 forks.)

Cool 1 hour. Wrap in heavy-duty aluminum foil, label and freeze.

■ **8 to 12 hours before serving, remove Hungarian Coffee Cake from freezer; thaw in wrapper at room temperature.** Thirty-five minutes before serving, heat oven to 350°. Heat wrapped coffee cake on oven rack until warm, about 30 minutes.

FLAKY FILLED CRESCENTS

Store no longer than 12 months. Makes 40 crescents.

Dough
- 1 package active dry yeast
- ½ cup warm water (105 to 115°)
- 1 cup lukewarm milk (scalded then cooled)
- 2 tablespoons shortening
- 2 tablespoons sugar
- 1 teaspoon salt
- 1 teaspoon grated lemon peel
- 2 eggs
- 4½ to 5 cups all-purpose flour*

Filling
- 1 cup butter or margarine, softened
- About ½ cup orange marmalade

Sugar Glaze
- 3 tablespoons sugar
- 1 tablespoon water

Dissolve yeast in ½ cup warm water in large bowl. Mix in milk, shortening, 2 tablespoons sugar, the salt, lemon peel, eggs and 2½ cups of the flour; beat until smooth. Stir in enough remaining flour to make dough easy to handle.

Turn dough onto lightly floured board; knead until smooth and elastic, about 5 minutes. Place in greased bowl; turn greased side up. Cover; let rise in warm place until double. Punch down dough. Cover; chill 1 hour.

Punch down dough again. Turn dough onto lightly floured board; roll into rectangle, 20 × 10 inches. Spread ⅓ cup butter on rectangle. Fold rectangle into 3 parts, one on top of the other, making 3 layers; roll out. Repeat 2 times, spreading ⅓ cup butter on rectangle each time. Divide dough in half; chill at least 1 hour. (Chill no longer than 18 hours.)

Shape half the dough at a time (keep other half chilled). Roll each half into rectangle, 20 × 10 inches. Cut lengthwise in half, then crosswise 5 times. Cut each square diagonally into 2 triangles. Spread ½ teaspoon marmalade on each triangle. Roll up, beginning at long side. Place rolls with points underneath on ungreased baking sheet; curve ends to form crescents. Chill 30 minutes.

Heat oven to 425°. Mix 3 tablespoons sugar and 1 tablespoon water; brush rolls with sugar-water mixture. Bake until golden brown and crisp, about 15 minutes. (Can be served immediately.) Cool; divide crescents among 4 pieces heavy-duty aluminum foil. Wrap, label and freeze.

■ **25 minutes before serving, heat oven to 350°.** Remove 1 package Flaky Filled Crescents from freezer; heat wrapped rolls on oven rack until warm, about 20 minutes.

*If using self-rising flour, omit salt.

Flavors for Frozen Rolls and Bread

Buttered rye bread is especially delicious when sprinkled with sesame seed. Cut slices crosswise into 4 strips. Broil 6 inches from heat until seeds are brown, 1½ to 2 minutes.

Brush brown-and-serve rolls with melted butter or margarine, then sprinkle with one of these: snipped chives; parsley flakes; dill weed; garlic salt; onion salt. Bake at 400° until golden brown, 10 to 12 minutes.

Spread cut surfaces of English muffins with soft butter or margarine, then sprinkle with garlic salt and grated Parmesan cheese. Broil 4 inches from heat until golden brown, 5 to 6 minutes.

Cut nut bread into ½-inch slices. Spread with soft butter or margarine. Bake at 400° until light brown, 6 to 8 minutes.

Brush brown-and-serve rolls with melted butter or margarine. Bake at 400° until golden brown, 10 to 12 minutes. Frost hot rolls with confectioners' sugar icing and serve warm.

HONEY HORNS

Store no longer than 9 months. Makes 3 dozen rolls.

Dough
- 2 packages active dry yeast
- ½ cup warm water (105 to 115°)
- ½ cup lukewarm milk (scalded then cooled)
- ½ cup sugar
- 1 teaspoon salt
- 2 eggs
- ½ cup shortening or butter or margarine, softened
- 3¾ to 4½ cups all-purpose flour*

Topping
- ¼ cup honey
- ⅓ cup sugar
- ¼ cup finely chopped nuts
- 3 tablespoons butter or margarine
- ⅛ teaspoon cinnamon

Filling
- ½ cup sugar
- 2 teaspoons cinnamon
- ¼ cup butter or margarine, melted

Dissolve yeast in warm water in large bowl. Mix in milk, ½ cup sugar, the salt, eggs, shortening and 2½ cups of the flour; beat until smooth. Stir in enough remaining flour to make dough easy to handle.

Turn dough onto lightly floured board; knead until smooth and elastic, about 5 minutes. Place in greased bowl; turn greased side up. Cover; let rise in warm place until double, about 1½ hours.

Heat Topping ingredients, stirring frequently, until mixture boils. Cool slightly. Mix ½ cup sugar and 2 teaspoons cinnamon; set aside. Punch down dough. Turn dough onto floured board; divide into 3 parts. Roll each part into 10-inch circle. Spread about 1 tablespoon of the melted butter and 2 tablespoons Topping on each circle; sprinkle about 3 tablespoons sugar-cinnamon mixture on top. Cut each circle into 12 wedges. Roll up, beginning at rounded edges. Place rolls with points underneath in spoke fashion in 3 greased layer pans, 8 or 9×1½ inches; curve ends to form crescents. Let rise in warm place until double, about 45 minutes.

Heat oven to 400°. Bake 10 minutes; remove rolls from oven and spread remaining Topping on top. Bake until golden brown, about 10 minutes. Immediately remove from pans; cool. Wrap in heavy-duty foil, label and freeze.

■ **35 minutes before serving, remove Honey Horns from freezer and place wrapped rolls on oven rack.** Heat in 350° oven until warm, about 30 minutes.

*If using self-rising flour, omit salt.

Break individual Honey Horns from the ring.

Each recipe makes 3 pans of rolls.

BROWN 'N SERVE ROLLS

Store no longer than 2 months. Makes 2 dozen rolls.

 1 package active dry yeast
¾ cup warm water (105 to 115°)
¾ cup lukewarm milk (scalded
    then cooled)
¼ cup sugar
2¼ teaspoons salt
¼ cup shortening
4½ cups all-purpose flour*

Dissolve yeast in warm water in large bowl. Mix in milk, sugar, salt, shortening and 2½ cups of the flour; beat until smooth. Stir in enough remaining flour to make dough easy to handle. Turn dough onto lightly floured board; knead until smooth and elastic, about 5 minutes. Place in greased bowl; turn greased side up. Cover; let rise in warm place until double, about 1½ hours.

Punch down dough; turn onto lightly floured board and divide into 24 pieces. Shape each piece into smooth ball. Place each ball in a greased muffin cup or place balls about 3 inches apart on greased baking sheet. Cover; let rise until almost double, about 45 minutes. Heat oven to 275°. Bake 20 to 30 minutes (do not allow rolls to brown). Remove from pans and cool at room temperature. Wrap, label and freeze.

■ **15 minutes before serving, heat oven to 400°.** Remove rolls from freezer and unwrap; place on ungreased baking sheet. Bake until brown and hot, 7 to 10 minutes.

Note: After rolls are cool, they may be wrapped and refrigerated. Store no longer than 8 days.

*If using self-rising flour, omit salt.

FREEZER FRENCH TOAST

Store no longer than 1 month. Makes enough for 8 servings.

 5 eggs
1¼ cups milk
1½ tablespoons sugar
½ teaspoon salt
16 slices white bread

Heat oven to 500°. Beat eggs, milk, sugar and salt until mixed. Dip bread slices in egg mixture; arrange on buttered baking sheets. Bake until underside is golden brown, about 5 minutes. Turn slices; bake until golden brown, about 2 minutes. (Can be served immediately.) Cool on wire racks. Place in a single layer on baking sheets. Freeze until hard, about 2 hours. Wrap, label and return to freezer.

■ **15 minutes before serving, heat oven to 375°.** Remove Freezer French Toast from freezer and unwrap; place on ungreased baking sheets. Heat until hot, 8 to 10 minutes. Or, small quantities can be heated in a toaster.

Freezer French Toast

Desserts

STRAWBERRY-RHUBARB COBBLER

Store no longer than 2 months. Makes enough for 9 servings.

Base
1 cup all-purpose flour*
¼ cup sugar
⅛ teaspoon baking powder
½ teaspoon salt
⅓ cup butter or margarine

Filling
2 cups fresh strawberries, halved
1 cup thinly sliced rhubarb
¾ cup sugar
3 tablespoons cornstarch
1 teaspoon cinnamon
1 tablespoon lemon juice
1 tablespoon butter or margarine

Heat oven to 400°. Grease baking pan, 9×9×2 inches. Mix flour, ¼ cup sugar, the baking powder and salt. Cut in ⅓ cup butter until mixture is crumbly; press evenly in bottom of pan. Bake until light brown, 8 to 10 minutes. Cool.

Arrange fruit on base. Mix ¾ cup sugar, the cornstarch and cinnamon. Sprinkle sugar mixture and lemon juice on fruit; dot with 1 tablespoon butter. Wrap, label and freeze.

■ **1 hour 15 minutes before serving, remove Strawberry-Rhubarb Cobbler from freezer and unwrap.** Bake uncovered in 400° oven until hot and bubbly throughout, about 40 minutes. Remove from oven; spoon Topping (below) on cobbler. Cool 30 minutes.

TOPPING

Mix 1 tablespoon sugar, 1 teaspoon vanilla and 1 cup dairy sour cream.

*If using self-rising flour, omit baking powder and salt.

FRUIT DESSERT FREEZE

Store no longer than 1 month. Makes enough for 12 servings.

1 package (15.4 ounces) creamy white frosting mix
2 cups whipping cream
1 large banana
1 can (8¾ ounces) crushed pineapple, drained
1 can (11 ounces) mandarin orange segments, drained
⅓ cup halved maraschino cherries, drained
⅓ cup cut-up dates
⅓ cup chopped pecans, if desired
2 tablespoons lemon juice

Chill frosting mix (dry) and whipping cream covered in small mixer bowl at least 1 hour. Beat until soft peaks form. Slice banana into frosting mixture; fold in remaining ingredients. Pour mixture into baking pan, 9×9×2 inches, or 2 refrigerator trays. Wrap, label and freeze. Freeze until firm, at least 4 hours.

ORANGE CHEESECAKE

Store no longer than 1 month. Makes enough for 9 to 12 servings.

Base
1½ cups graham cracker crumbs (about 18 crackers)
3 tablespoons sugar
¼ cup butter or margarine, melted

Topping
1 can (16.5 ounces) vanilla frosting
1 cup creamed cottage cheese
1 cup dairy sour cream
1 can (6 ounces) frozen orange juice concentrate, partially thawed

Mix graham cracker crumbs, sugar and butter. Reserve 3 tablespoons of the crumb mixture; press remaining mixture evenly in bottom of ungreased baking pan, 9×9×2 inches.

Beat Topping ingredients in large mixer bowl until mixed, about 2 minutes; pour on crust. Sprinkle reserved crumbs on top. Wrap, label and freeze. Freeze at least 8 hours.

STRAWBERRY ICE

Store no longer than 1 month. Makes enough for 8 to 10 servings.

- 1 package (3 ounces) strawberry-flavored gelatin
- ½ cup sugar
- 1½ cups boiling water
- 2 packages (10 ounces each) frozen sliced strawberries, partially thawed
- ¼ cup orange juice
- ¼ cup lemon juice

Stir gelatin and sugar in large bowl. Pour boiling water on gelatin mixture; stir until gelatin is dissolved. Stir in remaining ingredients.

Pour into 2 refrigerator trays. Freeze until mushy, about 1 hour. Remove from trays; beat until smooth. Return to trays. Wrap, label and freeze. Freeze until firm, at least 1 hour.

CHERRIES SUPREME

Store no longer than 1 month. Makes enough for 9 servings.

- ½ cup butter or margarine, softened
- ¼ cup brown sugar (packed)
- 1 cup all-purpose flour
- ½ cup chopped pecans
- ½ gallon vanilla ice cream, softened

Heat oven to 400°. Mix butter, sugar, flour and pecans; press evenly in bottom of ungreased baking pan, 9×9×2 inches. Bake until light brown, about 12 minutes. Crumble with spoon. Cool.

Reserve 1 cup of the crumbs; press remaining crumbs evenly in bottom of pan. Pack ice cream on crumbs. Sprinkle reserved crumbs on top. Wrap, label and freeze. Freeze until firm, at least 4 hours.

■ **Just before serving, heat 1 can (21 ounces) cherry pie filling, stirring occasionally.** Stir in 2 tablespoons rum flavoring if desired. Remove Cherries Supreme from freezer and unwrap. Cut into 3-inch squares. Spoon topping on each serving.

FROZEN MOLD GRENADINE

Store no longer than 4 weeks. Makes enough for 6 to 8 servings.

Sauce
- ¼ cup grenadine syrup
- 1 tablespoon orange-flavored liqueur

Ice-cream Mold
- 1 pint vanilla ice cream, slightly softened
- ¼ cup orange-flavored liqueur
- ¾ cup flaked coconut
- 2 tablespoons diced roasted almonds
- 2 teaspoons confectioners' sugar
- ½ cup chilled whipping cream

Mix grenadine syrup and 1 tablespoon liqueur; pour into 5-cup mold. Mix ice cream, ¼ cup liqueur, the coconut, almonds and sugar. Beat cream in chilled bowl until stiff. Fold whipped cream into ice-cream mixture; pour into mold. Cover, label and freeze.

■ **Remove Frozen Mold Grenadine from freezer; invert onto serving plate with a rim.** Dip a cloth in hot water; wring out and place over mold just a few minutes. Lift off mold. Spoon grenadine sauce on each serving.

Delightful Ice-cream Desserts

☐ Warm 1 cup prepared mincemeat in ½ cup cranberry cocktail. Serve warm over vanilla ice cream.

☐ Warm ½ cup honey with ½ cup apricot brandy. (This is especially delicious with coffee ice cream.)

☐ Add 1 cup maple-flavored syrup to ½ cup whole cranberry sauce. Stir and warm; pour over ice cream.

☐ Three ways to vary flavor: Into 1 quart vanilla ice cream, stir 2 teaspoons cinnamon; or ⅓ cup Nesselrode; or 1 tablespoon powdered instant coffee.

CRÊPES

Store no longer than 3 months. Makes 12 crêpes.

1½ **cups all-purpose flour***
 1 **tablespoon sugar**
 ½ **teaspoon baking powder**
 ½ **teaspoon salt**
 2 **cups milk**
 2 **eggs**
 ½ **teaspoon vanilla**
 2 **tablespoons butter or margarine, melted**

Measure flour, sugar, baking powder and salt into bowl. Stir in remaining ingredients. Beat with rotary beater until smooth.

For each crêpe, lightly butter 8-inch skillet; heat over medium heat until butter is bubbly. Pour scant ¼ cup of the batter into skillet; rotate pan immediately until batter covers bottom. Cook until light brown; turn crêpe and brown on other side. Stack crêpes as you remove them from skillet. (To serve immediately, see below.) Cool; keep crêpes covered to prevent drying out. Make 2 stacks of 6 crêpes each, with waxed paper between crêpes. Wrap, label and freeze each stack.

■ **3 hours 10 minutes before serving, remove Crêpes from freezer. Have ready:** applesauce, currant jelly or raspberry jam. Thaw crêpes in wrapper at room temperature about 3 hours.

Heat oven to 325°. Spread applesauce, currant jelly or raspberry jam thinly on crêpes; roll up. Place in ungreased baking dish, 11½ × 7½ × 1½ inches. Heat uncovered 10 minutes. Sprinkle sugar on top.

To Serve Immediately: Spread applesauce, currant jelly or raspberry jam thinly on crêpes; roll up. Sprinkle sugar on top.

*If using self-rising flour, omit baking powder and salt.

CRÊPES SUZETTE

Store no longer than 3 months. Makes enough for 6 servings.

   Crêpes (left)
⅔ **cup butter or margarine**
¾ **teaspoon grated orange peel**
⅔ **cup orange juice**
¼ **cup sugar**

Prepare Crêpes. Stack so first baked side is down when removing from skillet. Cool; keep crêpes covered to prevent drying out.

Heat butter, orange peel, juice and sugar in 10-inch ovenproof skillet, stirring occasionally, until mixture boils. Boil and stir 1 minute. (To serve immediately, see below.) Remove from heat. To assemble Crêpes Suzette, fold crêpes in half, then in half again; place in hot orange sauce and turn once. Arrange crêpes around edge of skillet. Cool. Cover, label and freeze.

■ **65 minutes before serving, heat oven to 350°.** **Have ready:** ⅓ cup brandy; ⅓ cup orange-flavored liqueur.

Remove Crêpes Suzette from freezer. Cover; bake 40 minutes. Uncover; bake until hot and bubbly, about 20 minutes.

Heat brandy and orange-flavored liqueur in small saucepan, but do not boil. Pour warm brandy mixture into center of skillet and ignite. Spoon flaming sauce on crêpes. Place 2 crêpes on each dessert plate; spoon sauce on crêpes.

To Serve Immediately: Have ready: ⅓ cup brandy; ⅓ cup orange-flavored liqueur.

Reduce heat; simmer uncovered. Heat brandy and orange-flavored liqueur in small saucepan, but do not boil. To assemble Crêpes Suzette, fold crêpes in half, then in half again; place in hot orange sauce and turn once. Arrange crêpes around edge of skillet. Pour warm brandy mixture into center of skillet and ignite. Spoon flaming sauce on crêpes. Place 2 crêpes on each dessert plate; spoon sauce on crêpes.

Shape meringue into 6-inch circles on a baking sheet covered with brown paper. If you first draw circles on the paper, it's easy to make the meringue layers uniform.

FROZEN TORTE

Store no longer than 1 month. Makes enough for 9 servings.

4 egg whites
½ teaspoon cream of tartar
1 cup sugar
Mocha Filling (page 65)

Heat oven to 275°. Cover 2 baking sheets with brown paper. Beat egg whites and cream of tartar in large mixer bowl until foamy. Beat in sugar, 1 tablespoon at a time; beat until stiff and glossy. Do not underbeat.

Divide meringue into 3 parts. Place 1 part on 1 baking sheet; shape into 6-inch circle. Shape two 6-inch circles on second baking sheet. Bake 45 minutes. Turn off oven; leave meringue in oven with door closed 1 hour. Remove meringue from oven; cool away from draft.

Fill layers and frost top of torte with Mocha Filling. Decorate with chocolate curls. Freeze uncovered until filling on top is firm, at least

Frozen Torte

3 hours. (Can be served immediately. To cut, dip knife in hot water and wipe after cutting each slice.) Wrap, label and return to freezer.

■ **Remove Frozen Torte from freezer and unwrap.** To cut, dip knife in hot water and wipe after cutting each slice.

Note: This dessert mellows if frozen 1 week or longer.

Fill the baked and cooled meringue layers with Mocha Filling, using it to frost the top of the torte as well. Stack and decorate with chocolate curls before placing torte in the freezer.

MOCHA FILLING

2 packages (about 2 ounces each)
    dessert topping mix
3 tablespoons cocoa
½ cup sugar
2 tablespoons powdered instant coffee

Prepare dessert topping mix as directed on package except—before beating, add cocoa, sugar and instant coffee.

BISCUIT TORTONI

Store no longer than 3 weeks. Makes enough for 8 servings.

⅔ cup cookie crumbs (vanilla
    wafers or macaroons)
¼ cup cut-up candied red cherries
½ cup chopped salted almonds
1 quart vanilla ice cream
    Red and green candied cherries

Line 8 muffin cups with paper baking cups. Mix cookie crumbs, cut-up cherries and almonds. Slightly soften ice cream; fold in crumb mixture. Divide ice-cream mixture among paper-lined muffin cups. Arrange red cherry half and slices of green cherry on each to resemble a flower. Freeze uncovered until firm. Wrap, label and return to freezer.

■ **At serving time, have ready:** 8 clusters seedless green grapes.

Place cups and grape clusters on tiered server.

PUMPKIN COOKIES

Store no longer than 9 months. Makes about 6 dozen cookies.

1½ cups brown sugar (packed)
½ cup shortening
2 eggs
1 can (16 ounces) pumpkin
2¾ cups all-purpose flour*
3 teaspoons baking powder
1 teaspoon cinnamon
½ teaspoon salt
½ teaspoon nutmeg
¼ teaspoon ginger
1 cup raisins
1 cup chopped pecans

Heat oven to 400°. Mix brown sugar, shortening, eggs and pumpkin. Stir in remaining ingredients.

Drop dough by teaspoonfuls about 2 inches apart onto ungreased baking sheet. Bake until light brown, 12 to 15 minutes. Remove immediately from baking sheet; cool. (Can be served immediately.) Wrap, label and freeze.

■ **20 minutes before serving, remove Pumpkin Cookies from freezer and unwrap.** Place on serving plate; thaw uncovered at room temperature.

*If using self-rising flour, omit baking powder and salt.

CHOCOLATE CHIP COOKIES

Store no longer than 6 months. Makes about 7 dozen cookies.

⅔ cup shortening
⅔ cup butter or margarine, softened
1 cup granulated sugar
1 cup brown sugar (packed)
2 eggs
2 teaspoons vanilla
3 cups all-purpose flour*
1 teaspoon soda
1 teaspoon salt
1 cup chopped nuts
2 packages (6 ounces each) semisweet
   chocolate pieces

Heat oven to 375°. Mix shortening, butter, sugars, eggs and vanilla. Stir in the remaining ingredients.

Drop dough by rounded teaspoonfuls 2 inches apart onto ungreased baking sheet. Bake until light brown, 8 to 10 minutes. Cool slightly; remove from baking sheet. (Can be served immediately.) Wrap, label and freeze.

■ **20 minutes before serving, remove Chocolate Chip Cookies from freezer and unwrap.** Place on serving plate; thaw uncovered at room temperature.

*If using self-rising flour, omit soda and salt.

Top row, left to right: Quick Orange Cookies (page 67), Chocolate Oatmeal Cookies (page 68) and Pumpkin Cookies. Bottom row, left to right: Double Chocolate Drops (page 67), Soft Molasses Cookies (page 67) and Chocolate Chip Cookies.

DOUBLE CHOCOLATE DROPS

Store no longer than 2 months. Makes about 6 dozen cookies.

½ cup butter or margarine, softened
1 cup sugar
1 egg
2 ounces melted unsweetened chocolate
    (cool)
⅓ cup buttermilk
1 teaspoon vanilla
1¼ cups all-purpose flour*
½ teaspoon soda
½ teaspoon salt
1 cup chopped nuts
1 package (6 ounces) semisweet
    chocolate pieces
    Chocolate Icing or Browned
    Butter Icing (below)

Mix butter, sugar, egg, chocolate, buttermilk and vanilla. Stir in flour, soda, salt, nuts and chocolate pieces. Cover; chill 1 hour.

Heat oven to 400°. Drop dough by rounded teaspoonfuls 2 inches apart onto ungreased baking sheet. Bake until almost no imprint remains when touched with finger, 8 to 10 minutes. Remove immediately from baking sheet; cool. Frost cookies. (Can be served immediately.) Wrap, label and freeze.

■ **20 minutes before serving, remove Double Chocolate Drops from freezer and unwrap.** Place on serving plate; thaw uncovered at room temperature.

CHOCOLATE ICING

Melt 2 ounces unsweetened chocolate and 2 tablespoons butter or margarine over low heat. Remove from heat; mix in 2 cups confectioners' sugar and about 3 tablespoons water until spreading consistency.

BROWNED BUTTER ICING

Heat ¼ cup butter or margarine over low heat until golden brown. Remove from heat; mix in 2 cups confectioners' sugar, 1 teaspoon vanilla and about 2 tablespoons light cream until spreading consistency.

*If using self-rising flour, omit soda and salt. If using quick-mixing flour, increase buttermilk to ½ cup.

SOFT MOLASSES COOKIES

Store no longer than 2 months. Makes about 6 dozen cookies.

1 cup shortening
1 cup sugar
1 egg
½ cup molasses
¼ cup dairy sour cream
3 cups all-purpose flour*
2 teaspoons soda
1 teaspoon salt
1 teaspoon ginger
1 teaspoon cinnamon

Heat oven to 375°. Mix shortening, sugar, egg and molasses. Stir in remaining ingredients.

Drop dough by teaspoonfuls about 2 inches apart onto ungreased baking sheet. Bake about 8 minutes. Cool slightly; remove from baking sheet. While warm, cookies can be frosted with canned vanilla frosting; cool. (Can be served immediately.) Wrap, label and freeze.

■ **20 minutes before serving, remove Soft Molasses Cookies from freezer and unwrap.** Place on serving plate; thaw uncovered at room temperature.

*If using self-rising flour, omit soda and salt.

QUICK ORANGE COOKIES

Store no longer than 3 months. Makes about 3 dozen cookies.

1 package (14 ounces) orange muffin mix
⅓ cup salad oil
1 egg
2 tablespoons milk

Heat oven to 375°. Mix all ingredients. Drop dough by teaspoonfuls 2 inches apart onto ungreased baking sheet. Flatten slightly with greased glass dipped in sugar. Bake until light brown, 8 to 10 minutes. Remove immediately from baking sheet; cool. (Can be served immediately.) Wrap, label and freeze.

■ **20 minutes before serving, remove Quick Orange Cookies from freezer and unwrap.** Place on serving plate; thaw uncovered at room temperature.

CHOCOLATE OATMEAL COOKIES

Store no longer than 2 months. Makes about 6 dozen cookies.

½ cup shortening
½ cup butter or margarine, softened
1½ cups sugar
1 egg
¼ cup water
1 teaspoon vanilla
1 cup all-purpose flour*
3 cups quick-cooking oats
⅓ cup cocoa
½ teaspoon soda
½ teaspoon salt
1 package (6 ounces) semisweet chocolate pieces

Heat oven to 350°. Mix shortening, butter, sugar, egg, water and vanilla. Stir in remaining ingredients.

Drop dough by rounded teaspoonfuls 1 inch apart onto ungreased baking sheet. Bake until almost no imprint remains when touched with finger, 10 to 12 minutes. Remove immediately from baking sheet; cool. (Can be served immediately.) Wrap, label and freeze.

■ **20 minutes before serving, remove Chocolate Oatmeal Cookies from freezer and unwrap.** Place on serving plate; thaw uncovered at room temperature.

*If using self-rising flour, omit soda and salt.

FRUITED DROPS

Store no longer than 9 months. Makes about 7½ dozen cookies.

1½ cups raisins
1 cup water
¾ cup shortening
1½ cups sugar
2 eggs
3 cups all-purpose flour*
1½ teaspoons salt
1 teaspoon cinnamon
¾ teaspoon baking powder
¾ teaspoon soda
¼ teaspoon allspice
¼ teaspoon nutmeg
¾ cup chopped nuts
½ cup chopped maraschino cherries

Heat oven to 400°. Heat raisins and water, stirring occasionally, until water boils. Boil 5 minutes. Drain; reserve ⅓ cup liquid. Mix shortening, sugar, eggs and reserved liquid. Stir in remaining ingredients, including raisins.

Drop dough by rounded teaspoonfuls 2 inches apart onto ungreased baking sheet. Bake until light brown, 8 to 10 minutes. Remove immediately from baking sheet; cool. (Can be served immediately.) Wrap, label and freeze.

■ **20 minutes before serving, remove Fruited Drops from freezer and unwrap.** Place on serving plate; thaw uncovered at room temperature.

*If using self-rising flour, omit salt, baking powder and soda.

PEANUT BUTTER CHIPPERS

Store no longer than 9 months. Makes about 4 dozen cookies.

  1 can (14 ounces) sweetened condensed milk
  ½ cup creamy peanut butter
  2 cups crushed whole wheat flakes cereal
  1 package (6 ounces) semisweet chocolate pieces

Heat oven to 350°. Mix milk and peanut butter until smooth. Stir in cereal and chocolate pieces.

Drop dough by rounded teaspoonfuls about 2 inches apart onto ungreased baking sheet. Bake until light brown, 10 to 12 minutes. Remove immediately from baking sheet; cool. (Can be served immediately.) Wrap, label and freeze.

■ **20 minutes before serving, remove Peanut Butter Chippers from freezer and unwrap.** Place on serving plate; thaw uncovered at room temperature.

CHOCOLATE ALMOND CHIPS

Store no longer than 2 months. Makes about 4 dozen cookies.

  1 cup butter or margarine, softened
  1 cup sugar
  1 egg
  ½ teaspoon almond extract
  ½ cup roasted diced almonds
  2 cups all-purpose flour
  2 squares (2 ounces) semisweet cooking chocolate, melted

Heat oven to 325°. Grease baking pan, 13×9×2 inches. Mix all ingredients except chocolate; beat on lowest speed of mixer or by hand until dough forms. Spread in pan.

Bake until golden brown, 35 to 40 minutes. Drizzle with chocolate. Cool slightly; cut into 1-inch squares. Cool. (Can be served immediately.) Wrap, label and freeze.

■ **20 minutes before serving, remove Chocolate Almond Chips from freezer and unwrap.** Thaw uncovered at room temperature.

BROWNIES

Store frosted brownies no longer than 2 months, unfrosted brownies no longer than 3 months. Makes 32 cookies.

  4 ounces unsweetened chocolate
  ⅔ cup shortening
  2 cups sugar
  4 eggs
  1 teaspoon vanilla
  1¼ cups all-purpose flour*
  1 teaspoon baking powder
  1 teaspoon salt
  1 cup chopped nuts

Heat oven to 350°. Grease baking pan, 13×9×2 inches. Melt chocolate and shortening in large saucepan over low heat. Remove from heat. Mix in sugar, eggs and vanilla. Stir in remaining ingredients. Spread in pan.

Bake until brownies start to pull away from sides of pan, about 30 minutes. Do not overbake. Cool slightly. If desired, spread your favorite frosting on slightly cooled brownies. Cut into bars, about 2×1½ inches. Cool completely or until frosting is firm. (Can be served immediately.) Wrap, label and freeze.

■ **30 minutes before serving, remove Brownies from freezer and unwrap.** Place on serving plate; thaw uncovered at room temperature.

*If using self-rising flour, omit baking powder and salt.

MIX-QUICK BROWNIES

Store frosted brownies no longer than 2 months, unfrosted brownies no longer than 3 months. Makes 3 or 4 dozen cookies.

Bake fudgy or fudge cake brownies as directed on fudge brownie mix or fudge brownie mix supreme package. Cool. If desired, spread your favorite frosting on cooled brownies. When frosting is firm, cut into 1½-inch squares. Wrap, label and freeze.

■ **30 minutes before serving, remove Mix-Quick Brownies from freezer and unwrap.** Place on serving plate; thaw uncovered at room temperature.

SPICY TOFFEE TRIANGLES

Store no longer than 4 months. Makes 4 dozen cookies.

1 cup butter or margarine, softened
1 cup brown sugar (packed)
1 egg, separated
1 teaspoon vanilla
2 cups all-purpose flour*
¼ teaspoon salt
1 teaspoon cinnamon
1 cup chopped walnuts

Heat oven to 275°. Mix butter, sugar, egg yolk and vanilla. Stir in flour, salt and cinnamon. Spread evenly in ungreased jelly roll pan, 15½×10½×1 inch. Brush dough with unbeaten egg white. Sprinkle walnuts on top; press into dough. Bake 1 hour. While warm, cut into 2½-inch squares, then cut each square diagonally in half. Cool. (Can be served immediately.) Wrap, label and freeze.

■ **20 minutes before serving, remove Spicy Toffee Triangles from freezer and unwrap.** Place on serving plate; thaw uncovered at room temperature.

VARIATIONS

Hawaiian Spice Triangles: Substitute 1 teaspoon ginger for the cinnamon and ¼ cup chopped salted macadamia nuts and ¼ cup flaked coconut for the 1 cup chopped walnuts.

Greek Triangles: Substitute 1 teaspoon ground cardamom for the cinnamon and 1 can (5 ounces) diced roasted almonds for the 1 cup chopped walnuts.

Orange-Chocolate Triangles: Substitute ½ teaspoon cloves and 1 tablespoon grated orange peel for the cinnamon and 2 packages (6 ounces each) semisweet chocolate pieces for the 1 cup chopped walnuts.

*If using self-rising flour, omit salt.

Top row, left to right: Brownies (page 69), Apricot-Cherry Bars (page 71) and Hawaiian Spice Triangles. Bottom row, left to right: Spicy Toffee Triangles, Mix-quick Date Bars (page 71), Mixed Nut Bars (page 71) and Orange-Chocolate Triangles.

MIXED NUT BARS

Store no longer than 6 months. Refrigerate no longer than 2 weeks. Makes 4 dozen cookies.

Base
1 cup butter or margarine, softened
1 cup brown sugar (packed)
1 egg yolk
1 teaspoon vanilla
2 cups all-purpose flour*
¼ teaspoon salt

Topping
1 package (6 ounces) butterscotch pieces
½ cup light corn syrup
2 tablespoons butter or margarine
1 tablespoon water
1 can (13 ounces) salted mixed nuts

Heat oven to 350°. Mix 1 cup butter, the sugar, egg yolk and vanilla. Stir in flour and salt. Press evenly in bottom of ungreased baking pan, 13×9×2 inches. Bake until light brown, about 25 minutes. Cool.

Mix butterscotch pieces, corn syrup, 2 tablespoons butter and the water in saucepan. Cook over medium heat, stirring occasionally, until butterscotch pieces are melted; cool.

Spread butterscotch mixture on cooled base. Sprinkle nuts on top; gently press into topping. Chill until topping is firm, about 1 hour. Cut into 1½-inch squares. (Can be served immediately.) Wrap, label and freeze or cover and refrigerate.

■ **30 minutes before serving, remove Mixed Nut Bars from freezer and unwrap.** Place on serving plate; thaw uncovered at room temperature.

*Do not use self-rising flour in this recipe.

MIX-QUICK DATE BARS

Store no longer than 3 months. Makes 32 cookies.
Bake 1 package (14 ounces) date bar mix as directed; cool. Cut into bars, 2×1 inch. Wrap, label and freeze.

■ **30 minutes before serving, remove Mix-Quick Date Bars from freezer and unwrap.** Place on serving plate; thaw uncovered at room temperature.

APRICOT-CHERRY BARS

Store no longer than 3 months. Makes 2½ dozen cookies.

¼ cup water
2 eggs
¼ cup butter or margarine, softened
¼ cup brown sugar (packed)
1 package (18.5 ounces) yellow cake mix
½ cup drained chopped maraschino cherries
1 cup cut-up dried apricots
  Confectioners' sugar

Heat oven to 375°. Grease and flour jelly roll pan, 15½×10½×1 inch. Beat water, eggs, butter, brown sugar and half the cake mix (dry) until smooth. Stir in remaining cake mix, the cherries and apricots.

Spread evenly in pan. Bake 20 to 25 minutes. Cool thoroughly. Sprinkle confectioners' sugar on top. Cut into bars, 3×1½ inches. (Can be served immediately.) Wrap, label and freeze.

■ **30 minutes before serving, remove Apricot-Cherry Bars from freezer and unwrap.** Place on serving plate; thaw uncovered at room temperature.

RUSSIAN TEACAKES

Store no longer than 6 months. Makes about 4 dozen cookies.

1 cup butter or margarine, softened
½ cup confectioners' sugar
1 teaspoon vanilla
2¼ cups all-purpose flour*
¼ teaspoon salt
¾ cup finely chopped nuts
  Confectioners' sugar

Heat oven to 400°. Mix butter, ½ cup confectioners' sugar and the vanilla. Work in flour, salt and nuts until dough holds together. Shape dough into 1-inch balls; place on ungreased baking sheet.

Bake until set but not brown, 10 to 12 minutes. While warm, roll in confectioners' sugar. Cool. Roll in sugar again. Wrap, label and freeze.

■ **20 minutes before serving, remove Russian Teacakes from freezer and unwrap.** Place on serving plate; thaw uncovered at room temperature.

*Do not use self-rising flour in this recipe.

BRAZILIAN COFFEE COOKIES

Store no longer than 6 months. Makes about 4 dozen cookies.

⅓ cup shortening
½ cup brown sugar (packed)
½ cup granulated sugar
1 egg
1½ teaspoons vanilla
1 tablespoon milk
2 cups all-purpose flour*
½ teaspoon salt
¼ teaspoon soda
¼ teaspoon baking powder
2 tablespoons powdered instant coffee

Heat oven to 400°. Mix shortening, sugars, egg, vanilla and milk. Stir in remaining ingredients. Shape dough into 1-inch balls. (If dough is too soft, chill until easy to handle.) Place about 2 inches apart on ungreased baking sheet. Flatten balls with greased fork dipped in sugar (press only in one direction) or with greased bottom of glass dipped in sugar, until ⅛ inch thick. Bake until light brown, 8 to 10 minutes. Cool. (Can be served immediately.) Wrap, label and freeze.

■ **20 minutes before serving, remove Brazilian Coffee Cookies from freezer and unwrap.** Place on serving plate; thaw uncovered at room temperature.

*If using self-rising flour, omit salt, soda and baking powder.

Storehouse of Cookies

Thoroughly cool baked cookies before freezing them in an airtight container or freezer wrap. Unfrosted cookies store better than frosted cookies. Baked cookies thaw out quickly.

To store rolls of cookie dough, freezer-wrap and freeze. Frozen dough keeps 5 to 6 months. To bake: Slice the frozen dough with a sharp knife.

PECAN CRESCENTS

Store no longer than 3 months. Makes about 3 dozen cookies.

1 packet or 2 sticks pie crust mix
1 cup confectioners' sugar
1 cup ground or very finely chopped pecans
1 egg
1 teaspoon vanilla
Confectioners' sugar

Heat oven to 350°. Mix pie crust mix (dry), 1 cup confectioners' sugar and the pecans. Stir in egg and vanilla; gather dough into ball. Turn dough onto lightly floured cloth-covered board; knead until smooth. Shape into ¾-inch balls. Shape balls into crescents on ungreased baking sheet. Bake until light brown, 10 to 15 minutes. While warm, roll in confectioners' sugar. Cool. Roll in sugar again. Wrap, label and freeze.

■ **20 minutes before serving, remove Pecan Crescents from freezer and unwrap.** Place on serving plate; thaw uncovered at room temperature.

CHINESE ALMOND COOKIES

Store no longer than 3 months. Makes about 3 dozen.

1 packet or 2 sticks pie crust mix
1 cup confectioners' sugar
1 cup ground or very finely chopped almonds
1 egg
3 teaspoons almond extract
Granulated sugar
36 blanched whole almonds

Heat oven to 400°. Mix pie crust mix (dry), confectioners' sugar and almonds. Stir in egg and extract; gather dough into ball. Turn dough onto lightly floured cloth-covered board; knead until smooth. Shape into 1-inch balls; roll in granulated sugar. Flatten balls on ungreased baking sheet until ½ inch thick; gently press an almond in center of each cookie. Bake until edges are light brown, 8 to 10 minutes. Cool. Wrap, label and freeze.

■ **20 minutes before serving, remove Chinese Almond Cookies from freezer and unwrap.** Place on serving plate; thaw uncovered at room temperature.

DELUXE SUGAR COOKIES

Store no longer than 9 months. Makes about 5 dozen 2- to 2½-inch cookies.

   1 cup butter or margarine, softened
1½ cups confectioners' sugar
   1 egg
   1 teaspoon vanilla
   ½ teaspoon almond extract
2½ cups all-purpose flour*
   1 teaspoon soda
   1 teaspoon cream of tartar
      Granulated sugar

Mix butter, confectioners' sugar, egg, vanilla and almond extract. Stir in flour, soda and cream of tartar. Cover; chill 2 to 3 hours.

Heat oven to 375°. Divide dough in half. Turn one half onto lightly floured cloth-covered board; roll until 3/16 inch thick. Cut into desired shapes; sprinkle granulated sugar on cookies. Place on lightly greased baking sheet. Bake until light brown on edges, 7 to 8 minutes. Remove immediately from baking sheet; cool. (Can be served immediately.) Wrap, label and freeze.

■ **20 minutes before serving, remove Deluxe Sugar Cookies from freezer and unwrap.** Place on serving plate; thaw uncovered at room temperature.

*If using self-rising flour, omit soda and cream of tartar.

Sweet Treats from the Freezer

Stored at 0°, most candy stays fresh a year or more. Overwrap with freezer wrap. Marshmallows and chocolate-covered nuts also freeze well.

CINNAMON CRISPIES

Store no longer than 3 months. Makes about 2 dozen crispies.

Dough
   1 cup butter
1½ cups all-purpose flour*
   ½ cup dairy sour cream

Filling
   3 tablespoons sugar
   1 teaspoon cinnamon

Sugar Glaze
   3 tablespoons sugar
   1 tablespoon water

Cut butter into flour with pastry blender. Stir in sour cream until thoroughly mixed. Divide dough in half; wrap each. Chill 8 to 12 hours.

Mix 3 tablespoons sugar and the cinnamon. Turn half of dough onto sugared, well-floured cloth-covered board. Roll into rectangle, 20×7 inches. Sprinkle half the cinnamon-sugar on dough. Roll up tightly, beginning at narrow end; set aside. Roll other half of dough into rectangle, 20×7 inches. Sprinkle remaining cinnamon-sugar on dough. Place loose end of roll on narrow edge of rectangle; pinch edges to seal securely. Continue to roll up tightly; pinch edge of dough into roll to seal securely. Wrap and chill at least 1 hour. Store no longer than 48 hours.

Heat oven to 350°. Cut roll into ¼-inch slices; place slices 2 inches apart on ungreased baking sheet. Mix 3 tablespoons sugar and the water; brush on cookies. Bake until golden brown, 20 to 25 minutes; cool. (Can be served immediately.) Wrap in heavy-duty aluminum foil, label and freeze.

■ **25 minutes before serving, heat oven to 375°.** Remove Cinnamon Crispies from freezer and unwrap. Place on ungreased baking sheet; heat until hot, about 10 minutes.

*Self-rising flour can be used in this recipe. Baking time may be longer.

MIX-QUICK CAKES AND CUPCAKES

Store no longer than 1 month.

Bake 1 package (18.5 ounces) of any of the following cake mixes as directed for cakes or cupcakes:

Yellow cake mix
Devils food cake mix
White cake mix
Cherry chip cake mix (19.5 ounces)
Sour cream chocolate fudge cake mix
Sour cream white cake mix
Milk chocolate cake mix
Lemon cake mix
Banana cake mix

Cool cake on wire rack 1 hour. (Can be frosted and served immediately.) Place on ungreased baking sheet. Freeze uncovered 2 hours. Wrap in aluminum foil, label and return to freezer. (To insure a well-shaped cake, do not stack anything on top of layers during the freezer storage time. Pressure on top of cake causes wrapping to stick to cake.)

■ **1 hour 45 minutes before serving, remove Mix-Quick Cake or Cupcakes from freezer; thaw in wrapper at room temperature 45 minutes.** Remove wrapper carefully to prevent cake from sticking to wrapper; thaw cake uncovered at room temperature 1 hour. Frost and serve.

FROSTED MIX-QUICK CAKE

Store no longer than 2 months.

Prepare 1 package (14.3 or 15.4 ounces) of your favorite creamy-type frosting mix as directed. Frost cooled cake. (Can be served immediately.) Freeze uncovered 2 hours. Wrap (wooden picks are not necessary as frosting is set from preliminary freezing), label and return to freezer.

■ **2 hours 30 minutes before serving, remove Frosted Mix-Quick Cake from freezer and loosen wrapper.** Thaw at room temperature 2 hours. Cake can be sliced at this time although center will be somewhat frosty. Place on serving plates and thaw 30 minutes.

MIX-QUICK ANGEL FOOD CAKE

Store no longer than 6 months.

Bake 1 package (15 or 16 ounces) angel food cake mix as directed. Cool at least 1 hour. Remove from pan. Place cake on ungreased baking sheet. Freeze uncovered 1 hour. Wrap, label and return to freezer.

■ **About 2 hours before serving, remove Mix-Quick Angel Food Cake from freezer; thaw in wrapper at room temperature 45 minutes.** Remove wrapper carefully to prevent cake from sticking to wrapper; thaw cake uncovered at room temperature.

MIX-QUICK GERMAN CHOCOLATE CAKE

Store no longer than 2 months.

Bake 1 package (18.5 ounces) German chocolate cake mix as directed. Cool.

Prepare 1 package (9.9 ounces) coconut-pecan frosting mix as directed. Frost cake. (Can be served immediately.)

Freeze uncovered 2 hours. Wrap, label and return to freezer.

■ **About 1½ hours before serving, remove Mix-Quick German Chocolate Cake from freezer and loosen wrapper so that it does not touch frosting or cake.** Thaw at room temperature 1 hour. Cut cake into serving pieces. Place on serving plate and thaw 30 minutes.

For the Sake of Cake

Cakes do not freeze solid. To prevent crushing, keep your wrapped, frozen cake in a rigid container. It's smart to package cake in family portions or single pieces, which thaw out quickly and are nice for the lunchbox. To store cakes for as long as 4 to 6 months, leave them unfrosted.

OATMEAL SPICE CAKE

Store no longer than 2 months.

1½ cups all-purpose flour*
1 cup quick-cooking oats
1 cup brown sugar (packed)
½ cup granulated sugar
1½ teaspoons soda
1 teaspoon cinnamon
½ teaspoon salt
½ teaspoon nutmeg
½ cup shortening
1 cup water
2 eggs (½ to ⅔ cup)
2 tablespoons dark molasses
Coconut Topping (below)

Heat oven to 350°. Grease and flour baking pan, 13×9×2 inches. Measure all ingredients except topping into large mixer bowl. Mix on low speed, scraping bowl constantly, ½ minute. Beat on high speed, scraping bowl occasionally, 3 minutes. Pour into pan.

Bake until wooden pick inserted in center comes out clean, 35 to 40 minutes; cool slightly. Spread topping on cake. Set oven control at broil and/or 550°. Place top of cake 3 inches from heat. Broil until topping is golden brown and bubbly, 2 to 3 minutes. (Can be served immediately.)

Cool cake 1 hour. Freeze uncovered 2 hours. Wrap, label and return to freezer.

■ **30 minutes before serving, remove Oatmeal Spice Cake from freezer and loosen wrapper.** Thaw at room temperature. (If plastic wrap has been used, place wooden picks at intervals to prevent wrapper from sticking to topping.)

COCONUT TOPPING
¼ cup butter or margarine, melted
⅔ cup brown sugar (packed)
½ cup flaked coconut
½ cup chopped pecans
3 tablespoons light cream

Mix all ingredients.

*If using self-rising flour, omit soda and salt.

BUTTERY FREEZER CAKE

Store no longer than 1 month.

⅔ cup butter or margarine, softened
1¾ cups sugar
2 eggs (⅓ to ½ cup)
1½ teaspoons vanilla
3 cups cake flour or 2¾ cups all-purpose flour*
2½ teaspoons baking powder
1 teaspoon salt
1¼ cups milk
Buttery Frosting (below)

Heat oven to 350°. Grease and flour baking pan, 13×9×2 inches, or two 9-inch or three 8-inch round layer pans. Mix butter, sugar, eggs and vanilla in large mixer bowl until fluffy. Beat on high speed, scraping bowl occasionally, 5 minutes. On low speed, mix in flour, baking powder and salt alternately with milk. Pour into pan(s).

Bake until wooden pick inserted in center comes out clean, oblong 45 to 50 minutes, layers 30 to 35 minutes. Cool. Frost cake with Buttery Frosting. (Can be served immediately.)

Place wooden picks at intervals around top of cake to prevent wrapper from sticking to frosting. Wrap, label and freeze.

■ **2 hours before serving, remove Buttery Freezer Cake from freezer.** Thaw in wrapper at room temperature 1 hour. Remove wrapper; thaw cake uncovered 1 hour. (Or, after the first hour of thawing, cut cake into serving pieces. Place on serving plate and thaw 30 minutes.)

BUTTERY FROSTING
2⅔ cups confectioners' sugar
⅔ cup butter, softened
2 ounces melted unsweetened chocolate (cool)
¾ teaspoon vanilla
2 tablespoons milk

Beat sugar, butter, chocolate and vanilla in small mixer bowl on low speed. Gradually beat in milk until smooth and fluffy.

*If using self-rising flour, omit baking powder and salt.

Best Chocolate Cake can be frozen in the pan in which it was baked; just wrap it well, pan and all.

BEST CHOCOLATE CAKE

Store no longer than 1 month.

    2 cups all-purpose flour* or cake flour
    2 cups sugar
    1 teaspoon soda
    1 teaspoon salt
    ½ teaspoon baking powder
    ¾ cup water
    ¾ cup buttermilk
    ½ cup shortening
    2 eggs (⅓ to ½ cup)
    1 teaspoon vanilla
    4 ounces melted unsweetened
        chocolate (cool)
        Fluffy White Frosting (right)

Heat oven to 350°. Grease and flour baking pan, 13×9×2 inches, or two 9-inch or three 8-inch round layer pans. Measure all ingredients except frosting into large mixer bowl. Mix on low speed, scraping bowl constantly, ½ minute. Beat on high speed, scraping bowl occasionally, 3 minutes. Pour into pan(s).

Bake until wooden pick inserted in center comes out clean, oblong 40 to 45 minutes, layers 30 to 35 minutes. Cool. Frost cake with frosting.

Place cake in cake box. Wrap box, label and freeze. (Frosting will remain soft.)

■ **2 hours before serving, remove Best Chocolate Cake from freezer.** Thaw in box at room temperature 1 hour. Remove cake from box; thaw uncovered 1 hour. (Or, after the first hour of thawing, cut cake into serving pieces. Place on serving plate and thaw 30 minutes.)

FLUFFY WHITE FROSTING

    ½ cup sugar
    ¼ cup light corn syrup
    2 tablespoons water
    2 egg whites (¼ cup)
    1 teaspoon vanilla

Mix sugar, corn syrup and water in small saucepan. Cover tightly; heat over medium heat until mixture boils vigorously. Uncover; boil rapidly, without stirring, to 242° on candy thermometer (or until small amount of mixture spins a 6- to 8-inch thread when dropped from spoon).

While mixture boils, beat egg whites until stiff peaks form. Pour hot syrup very slowly in a thin stream into the beaten egg whites, beating constantly on medium speed. Beat on high speed until stiff peaks form, adding vanilla during last minute of beating.

*If using self-rising flour, omit soda, salt and baking powder.

PASTRY

One-crust Pie
One 8- or 9-inch

1 cup all-purpose flour*
½ teaspoon salt
⅓ cup plus 1 tablespoon shortening or
   ⅓ cup lard
2 to 3 tablespoons cold water

Two 8- or 9-inch

2 cups all-purpose flour*
1 teaspoon salt
⅔ cup plus 2 tablespoons shortening or
   ⅔ cup lard
  4 to 5 tablespoons cold water

Two-crust Pie
One 8- or 9-inch

2 cups all-purpose flour*
1 teaspoon salt
⅔ cup plus 2 tablespoons shortening or
   ⅔ cup lard
  4 to 5 tablespoons cold water

Two 8- or 9-inch

  4 cups all-purpose flour*
  2 teaspoons salt
1½ cups shortening or 1⅓ cups lard
  ⅔ cup cold water

Measure flour and salt into mixing bowl. Cut in shortening thoroughly. Sprinkle water, 1 tablespoon at a time, on flour-shortening mixture, mixing with fork until all flour is moistened and dough almost cleans side of bowl (1 to 2 teaspoons water can be added if needed). Gather dough into ball; turn onto lightly floured cloth-covered board and shape into flattened round. (For 2 One-crust Pies or Two-crust Pie, divide in half and shape into 2 flattened rounds. For 2 Two-crust Pies, divide into 4 parts.) Roll dough with floured stockinet-covered rolling pin 2 inches larger than inverted pie pan. Fold pastry in half, then in half again; unfold and ease into pan.

For One-crust Pie, trim overhanging edge of pastry 1 inch from rim of pan. Fold and roll pastry under, even with pan; flute. Fill and bake as directed in recipe. For Baked Pie Shell, prick bottom and side thoroughly with fork. Bake in 475° oven 8 to 10 minutes.

For Two-crust Pie, turn desired filling into pastry-lined pie pan. Trim overhanging edge of pastry ½ inch from rim of pan. Roll second round of dough. Fold in half, then in half again; cut slits so steam can escape. Place over filling and unfold. Trim overhanging edge of pastry 1 inch from rim of pan. Fold and roll top edge under lower edge, pressing on rim to seal securely; flute. Cover edge of pastry with 2- to 3-inch strip of aluminum foil to prevent excessive browning. Bake as directed in recipe. Remove foil 15 minutes before pie is done.

*If using self-rising flour, omit salt. Pastry made with self-rising flour differs in flavor and texture.

Short of Pie Pans?

If you don't want to tie up your pie pans in the freezer, do this. Line pan with an aluminum foil circle, cut 3 inches larger than the pan. Press foil smoothly into the pan. Proceed as directed in recipe. Freeze pie, and when it is completely frozen, grasp the foil extensions and lift foil and pie from the pan. Overwrap with freezer wrap. Place pie in box or container.

Because frozen pies are bulky, they take up a great deal of freezer space. Solution: Package your own special pie fillings in frozen-food containers. When ready to use, partially thaw in container. Add non-freezable ingredients and pour into pastry-lined pie pans.

FROZEN PASTRY CIRCLES

Store no longer than 2 months.

Use one of the following:
**Pastry for Two 8- or 9-inch
  Two-crust Pies (page 77)**
**4 sticks or 2 packets pie crust mix
  (one 22-ounce-size package or two 11-
  ounce-size packages)**

Prepare pastry as directed for 2 Two-crust Pies. Divide into 4 parts. Roll each part 2 inches larger all around than inverted 8- or 9-inch pie pan.

Stack circles, with waxed paper between, on ungreased baking sheet. Freeze uncovered 1 hour. Wrap stack, label and return to freezer. To prevent breaking, store on flat surface.

■ **Baked Pie Shell or One-crust Baked Pie: 35 minutes before needed, remove 1 Frozen Pastry Circle from freezer; place on pie pan.** Thaw uncovered at room temperature until soft, about 20 minutes. Heat oven to 475°. Ease pastry gently into pan. Trim overhanging edge of pastry 1 inch from rim of pan. Fold and roll pastry under, even with pan; flute. (For One-crust Baked Pie, proceed as directed in recipe.) For Baked Pie Shell, prick bottom and side thoroughly with fork. Bake until light brown, 8 to 10 minutes.

■ **Two-crust Pie: 25 minutes before needed, remove 2 Frozen Pastry Circles from freezer; place one on pie pan and one on flat surface. Have ready:** filling.

Thaw uncovered at room temperature until soft, about 20 minutes. Heat oven to temperature designated in recipe. Ease pastry gently into pan. Trim overhanging edge of pastry ½ inch from rim of pan. Pour filling into pastry-lined pie pan. Fold second circle in half, then in half again; cut slits so steam can escape. Place over filling and unfold. Trim overhanging edge of pastry 1 inch from rim of pan. Fold and roll top edge under lower edge, pressing on rim to seal securely; flute. Bake as directed.

FRESH APPLE PIES

Store no longer than 6 months. Makes 2 pies.

**Pastry for Two 9-inch Two-crust Pies
  (page 77)**

Filling for **1** pie
¾ cup sugar
¼ cup all-purpose flour
½ teaspoon nutmeg
½ teaspoon cinnamon
  Dash salt
**6 cups thinly sliced pared tart apples
  (about 6 medium)**
2 tablespoons butter or margarine

Heat oven to 425°. Prepare pastry. Mix sugar, flour, nutmeg, cinnamon and salt; toss with apples. Turn into pastry-lined pie pan; dot with butter. Repeat for second pie. Cover with top crusts which have slits cut in them; seal securely and flute. Cover edges of pastry with 2- to 3-inch strips of aluminum foil to prevent excessive browning; remove foil 15 minutes before pies are done. Bake until crusts are brown and juice begins to bubble through slits in crusts, 40 to 50 minutes. Cool. (Can be served immediately.)

Cool pies until barely warm, about 2 hours. Freeze uncovered until completely frozen, at least 3 hours. (If you prefer to remove pies from pans for storage, freeze 6 hours. See Note.) Wrap, label and return to freezer.

■ **1 hour 40 minutes before serving, remove Fresh Apple Pie(s) from freezer and unwrap.** (Replace in pan if you have frozen out of pan.) Thaw at room temperature 1 hour. Heat in 375° oven on lowest rack position 35 to 40 minutes.

Note: If you prefer, line pie pans with aluminum foil circles cut 3 inches larger all around than inverted pie pans. After pies are completely frozen, gently lift pies from pans with foil extensions.

FRESH PEAR PIES

Store no longer than 6 months. Makes 2 pies.

**Pastry for Two 9-inch Two-crust Pies
   (page 77)**

Filling for **1** pie
½ **cup sugar**
⅓ **cup all-purpose flour**
½ **teaspoon mace, if desired**
4 **cups sliced pared fresh pears
   (about 7 medium)**
1 **tablespoon lemon juice**
2 **tablespoons butter or margarine**

Heat oven to 425°. Prepare pastry. Mix sugar, flour and mace; toss with pears. Turn into pastry-lined pie pan; sprinkle lemon juice on pears and dot with butter. Repeat for second pie. Cover with top crusts which have slits cut in them; seal securely and flute. Cover edges of pastry with 2- to 3-inch strips of aluminum foil to prevent excessive browning; remove foil 15 minutes before pies are done. Bake until crusts are brown and juice begins to bubble through slits in crusts, 40 to 50 minutes. Cool. (Can be served immediately.)

Cool pies until barely warm, about 2 hours. Freeze uncovered until completely frozen, at least 3 hours. (If you prefer to remove pies from pans for storage, freeze 6 hours. See Note.) Wrap, label and return to freezer.

■ **1 hour 40 minutes before serving, remove Fresh Pear Pie(s) from freezer and unwrap.** (Replace in pan if you have frozen out of pan.) Thaw at room temperature 1 hour. Heat in 375° oven on lowest rack position 35 to 40 minutes.

Note: If you prefer, line pie pans with aluminum foil circles cut 3 inches larger all around than inverted pie pans. After pies are completely frozen, gently lift pies from pans with foil extensions.

CRANBERRY-APPLE PIES

Store no longer than 6 months. Makes 2 pies.

**Pastry for Two 9-inch Two-crust Pies
   (page 77)**

Filling for **1** pie
1¾ **cups sugar**
 ⅓ **cup all-purpose flour**
 3 **cups sliced pared tart apples (2 to 3
    medium)**
 2 **cups fresh cranberries**
 2 **tablespoons butter or margarine**

Heat oven to 425°. Prepare pastry. Mix sugar and flour. In pastry-lined pie pan, alternate layers of apples, cranberries and sugar mixture, beginning and ending with apples; dot with butter. Repeat for second pie. Cover with top crusts which have slits cut in them; seal securely and flute. Cover edges with 2- to 3-inch strips of aluminum foil to prevent excessive browning; remove foil 15 minutes before pies are done. Bake until crusts are brown, 40 to 50 minutes. Cool. (Can be served immediately.)

Cool pies until barely warm, 2 hours. Freeze uncovered until completely frozen, at least 3 hours. (If you prefer to remove pies from pans for storage, freeze 6 hours. See Note.) Wrap, label and return to freezer.

■ **1 hour 40 minutes before serving, remove Cranberry-Apple Pie(s) from freezer and unwrap.** (Replace in pan if you have frozen out of pan.) Thaw at room temperature 1 hour. Heat in 375° oven on lowest rack position 35 to 40 minutes.

Note: If you prefer, line pie pans with aluminum foil circles cut 3 inches larger all around than inverted pie pans. After pies are completely frozen, gently lift pies from pans with foil extensions.

Chill the lemon mixture for the chiffon pie filling in the refrigerator or in a bowl of ice and water until it forms soft mounds when dropped from a spoon.

Lemon Chiffon Pie and Pumpkin Chiffon Pie

LEMON CHIFFON PIE

Store no longer than 1 month.

9-inch Baked Pie Shell (Pastry for One 8- or 9-inch One-crust Pie—page 77)
½ cup sugar
1 envelope unflavored gelatin
4 eggs, separated
⅔ cup water
⅓ cup lemon juice
1 tablespoon grated lemon peel
½ teaspoon cream of tartar
½ cup sugar

Bake pie shell. Mix ½ cup sugar and the gelatin in small saucepan. Beat egg yolks, water and lemon juice; stir into sugar mixture. Cook over medium heat, stirring constantly, just until mixture boils. Stir in peel. Place pan in bowl of ice and water or chill in refrigerator, stirring occasionally, until mixture mounds slightly when dropped from spoon.

Beat egg whites and cream of tartar in large mixer bowl until foamy. Beat in ½ cup sugar, 1 tablespoon at a time; beat until stiff and glossy. Do not underbeat. Fold lemon mixture into meringue; pile into baked pie shell. (To serve today, chill until set, at least 3 hours.)

Freeze uncovered 1½ hours. Place wooden picks at intervals around top of pie to prevent wrapper from sticking to pie. Wrap, label and return to freezer.

■ **1 hour 30 minutes before serving, remove Lemon Chiffon Pie from freezer.** Thaw in wrapper in refrigerator.

VARIATION
Lime Chiffon Pie: Substitute lime juice for the lemon juice and grated lime peel for the lemon peel. Add a few drops green food color to intensify color.

Insert wooden picks around the top of the completed pie, then wrap it for freezing. The picks prevent the wrapper from sticking to the pie.

PUMPKIN CHIFFON PIES

Store no longer than 2 months. Makes 2 pies.

**Two Baked Pie Shells (Pastry for Two 8-
   or 9-inch One-crust Pies—page 77)**
 1 cup brown sugar (packed)
 1 tablespoon plus 1 teaspoon unflavored
   gelatin
 ½ teaspoon salt
 ½ teaspoon ginger
 ½ teaspoon cinnamon
 ½ teaspoon nutmeg
 1 can (16 ounces) pumpkin
 4 eggs, separated
 ⅔ cup milk
 ½ teaspoon cream of tartar
 ⅔ cup granulated sugar

Bake pie shells. Mix brown sugar, gelatin, salt, ginger, cinnamon and nutmeg in medium saucepan. Beat pumpkin, egg yolks and milk; stir into brown sugar mixture. Cook over medium heat, stirring constantly, just until mixture boils. Place pan in bowl of ice and water or chill in refrigerator, stirring occasionally, until mixture mounds slightly when dropped from spoon.

Beat egg whites and cream of tartar in large mixer bowl until foamy. Beat in granulated sugar, 1 tablespoon at a time; beat until stiff and glossy. Do not underbeat. Fold pumpkin mixture into meringue; pile into baked pie shells (3 cups filling for each pie). Garnish with whipped cream if desired. (To serve today, chill until set, at least 3 hours.)

Freeze uncovered 1½ hours. Place wooden picks at intervals around top of pie to prevent wrapper from sticking to pie. Wrap, label and return to freezer.

■ **1 hour 30 minutes before serving, remove Pumpkin Chiffon Pie(s) from freezer.** Thaw in wrapper in refrigerator.

CHOCOLATE PIE DELUXE

Store no longer than 2 months.

    Graham Cracker Crust (below)
**16 large marshmallows or 1½ cups miniature
    marshmallows**
 ½ cup milk
  3 bars (3.5 ounces each) milk chocolate
  **1 envelope (about 2 ounces) dessert
    topping mix or 1 cup chilled whipping
    cream**

Prepare crust. (If you want to remove pie from pan after freezing, line pie pan before pressing in crumbs with aluminum foil circle cut 3 inches larger all around than inverted pie pan.) Heat marshmallows, milk and chocolate over medium heat, stirring constantly, just until marshmallows and chocolate melt. Chill until thickened.

Prepare dessert topping mix as directed on package. (If using whipping cream, beat in chilled bowl until stiff.) Stir marshmallow mixture; fold into whipped topping. Pour into crust. (To serve today, chill until set, at least 8 hours.)

Freeze uncovered until pie is completely frozen, about 3 hours. Gently lift pie from pan with foil extension. Wrap, label and return to freezer.

■ **30 minutes before serving, remove Chocolate Pie Deluxe from freezer.** (Unwrap and replace in pan if you have frozen out of the pan. Rewrap.) Thaw in wrapper at room temperature. If desired, garnish with toasted slivered almonds.

GRAHAM CRACKER CRUST

Heat oven to 350°. Mix 1½ cups graham cracker crumbs (about 20 crackers), 3 tablespoons sugar and ⅓ cup butter or margarine, melted. Press mixture firmly and evenly against bottom and side of 9-inch pie pan. Bake 10 minutes.

After freezing 6 hours, lift pie from pan, using foil extensions.

PECAN PIES

Store no longer than 1 month. Makes 2 pies.

**Pastry for Two 9-inch One-crust Pies
    (page 77)**
  6 eggs
1⅓ cups sugar
  1 teaspoon salt
 ⅔ cup butter or margarine, melted
  2 cups dark or light corn syrup
  2 cups pecan halves or broken pecans

Heat oven to 375°. Prepare pastry. Beat eggs, sugar, salt, butter and syrup with rotary beater. Sprinkle 1 cup pecans evenly in each pastry-lined pie pan. Slowly pour 2⅓ cups filling on pecans in each pan. Bake until filling is set, 40 to 50 minutes. Cool. (Can be served immediately.)

Cool pies 2 hours. Freeze uncovered at least 3 hours. (If you prefer to remove pies from pans for storage, freeze 6 hours. See page 77.) Wrap, label and return to freezer.

■ **20 minutes before serving, remove Pecan Pie(s) from freezer and unwrap.** (Replace in pan if you have frozen out of pan.) Thaw in refrigerator 20 minutes to allow pastry to soften. (Filling is ready for cutting directly from freezer.)

Special Freezer Helps

Plan, Buy and **Use** are the key words for making the most efficient use of your freezer. The more frozen food you keep in stock and use, the more you benefit from owning a freezer.

Plan: Mark your packages with the date that ends the recommended storage period. The way you arrange your food in the freezer can help you to use it in good time, too. Instead of dividing it into meat, vegetables and desserts, you could assign separate freezer areas for food to be used this month, next month, etc. Alternatively, keep a running inventory, storing your packages in the order of "expiration" dates.

Before you set out to restock your freezer, check your calendar for the entertaining you will do in the next month or so. Then plan your purchases to take care of your normal needs, of entertaining, and of some unforeseen circumstances, too.

Buy: With a freezer, you can enjoy the best foods at the lowest prices all the time—if you take advantage of your supermarket's "specials" and of the food that costs less because it is in season. Make sure that the food you buy is in top condition. You may want to prepare a freezer recipe with the food you bought, or package it in smaller portions. Whatever you do with it, get the food into your freezer as soon as you can.

Use: It pays you handsome dividends to label packages accurately before freezing. Labeling directions are on page 85. Every freezer recipe in this book carries its own storage instructions. When you want to freeze food prepared from other recipes, consult the general freezing directions on pages 88 through 90.

Now that the exciting possibility exists, consider the electronic oven—a real complement to your freezer, since it's ideal for frozen food. Frozen food can be defrosted in minutes in the electronic oven. One small note of caution: follow the manufacturer's directions meticulously. You'll find that you need to make changes from your normal packaging and timing procedures.

Happy Freezing!

COOL QUICKLY

Have you noticed how the freezer recipes tell you to cool the food quickly after cooking? The less time this food spends at temperatures between 45° and 140°, the better. If you allow foods to remain at these temperatures for more than 3 or 4 hours, they may not be safe to eat. Remember that in these recipes this time span includes all the time the food remains in this temperature range. So speed the cooling process!

Hot foods can be placed right in the refrigerator provided they don't raise the refrigerator temperature above 45°. A large quantity of hot food should be cooled in a big bowl (or a sink) filled with cold water and ice that almost reach the top of the food container. Replace ice as it melts; freeze the food as soon as it is cool.

WRAP

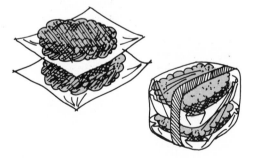

If food is to maintain its high quality in the freezer, it must be stored in wraps or containers which are moisture- and vapor-proof. The containers and wrapping materials that you buy should be designed for the purpose for which you use them. Some are made for the freezer, others for the refrigerator. It's important to use the right type and the right size, so check their labels. When you wrap, press out the air—and wrap tightly. Close packages with tape.

Special tips on wrapping and storage: For easy separation, place freezer wrap between individual patties, chops and small steaks; or wrap them individually and freeze before putting them into a freezer bag. Protect fragile foods with a box; place the freezer-wrapped food in the box, or overwrap the box. Since food expands in freezing, make sure a container has enough room for expansion. When you have to freeze a mixture of solid and liquid food in a container which is too large, fill the space between the food and the lid with crumpled freezer wrap.

There are casseroles now on the market designed to go directly from freezer to oven. Why not splurge a bit and buy some of these?

LABEL

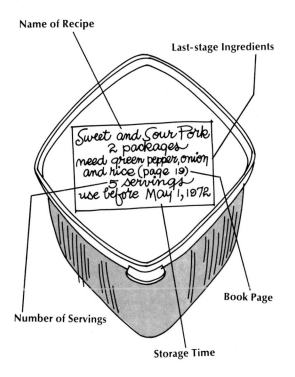

Name of Recipe

Last-stage Ingredients

Sweet and Sour Pork
2 packages
need green pepper, onion
and rice (page 19)
5 servings
use before May 1, 1972

Number of Servings

Storage Time

Book Page

Did you ever look into your freezer and wonder what you'd put into one of the packages or containers there? It's better not to rely on your memory, especially if you make good use of your freezer and keep it well stocked. Label your packages before you put them in the freezer.

What you will need are labels, a grease pencil or a felt-tipped pen, and freezer tape. Keep these handy with your packaging materials so you won't be tempted to smuggle an unlabeled package into the freezer.

Here's the information you'll need to include:
Name of Recipe: Copy its exact title from the cookbook. If you have more than one package from the same recipe, note that on the label.

Last-stage Ingredients: If your recipe calls for additional ingredients after you take the food from the freezer, note this on the label.

Book Page: Copy the number of the page on which your recipe appears. You'll need to refer to that page again later for the instructions which follow the ■ and the **boldface type.**

Number of Servings: Write down the number of servings your package contains. (You'll find the number of servings each recipe provides printed below its title.) Our calculations are based on average servings. If there are hearty eaters in your family, take that into account. Just write down how many servings the package will provide for your hungry crew.

Storage Time: Look at the recommended storage time for your recipe—it's given directly under the title. Now figure out when your package should be used; put that date on your label.

If you leave your package in the freezer beyond the recommended storage time (see pages 88 to 90), your food won't spoil—but it may begin to lose some of its flavor, moisture or texture.

Your Own Recipes and Other Foods: Label them with the same type of information as you put on your Do-Ahead packages. When you freeze meat, note its weight. For your own recipes, write down and keep your own instructions for reheating or last-stage ingredients.

...AND FREEZE

Freezer Types

When it comes to buying a freezer, you will find that you have a choice of three basic types: the refrigerator with a freezer unit; the upright freezer—with shelves from top to bottom; and the freezer chest—with baskets and dividers.

If you are short of floor space or you don't need a great deal of freezer space, the refrigerator-freezer may be your best bet. In a refrigerator-freezer, the storage capacity of your freezer will be between 2 and 10 cubic feet. A model with a freezer unit that is completely insulated from the refrigerator is desirable because such freezers can maintain a constant temperature of 0°. If your freezing compartment does not remain at 0°, the food you store there should be used within a week or two.

You may need the freezer space provided by an upright freezer or a freezer chest. Are you wondering how big a freezer you should buy? In addition to questions of floor space and price, let yourself be guided by the size of your family—allow 5 cubic feet per person—and the amount of preplanning you want to do.

Freezer Temperature

The temperature for freezing and storing food is 0° or lower. At a low temperature (0°), foods freeze faster and there is less breakdown in their cellular structure. Therefore, the foods are more apt to retain true flavor and firm texture.

Chest and upright freezers (and the fully-insulated refrigerator-freezers) are designed to stay at a constant 0° temperature. Be sure the control setting of your freezer is correct—use a freezer thermometer.

Food Freezing

At any one time, freeze only as much food as you can place against a freezing surface. The faster your food freezes, the better it retains flavor and texture. For fast freezing, food packages should be in direct contact with a freezing surface, at least 1 inch apart so the air can circulate. (Once the food is frozen solid, you can stack packages.)

When you want to freeze food in large quantities, guard against a rise of temperature in your freezer. Reduce your freezer temperature to −10° or lower about 24 hours before you put a large amount of unfrozen food into your freezer. This way, your food will be frozen solid in 10 to 12 hours.

It's important that you know exactly what temperature is maintained in your freezer—especially when you're freezing foods. We strongly recommend that you buy a freezer thermometer. Check the thermometer often, and make sure that your freezer actually maintains a temperature of 0° or lower.

Defrosting and Cleaning

Above all, read the manufacturer's instructions carefully.

Unless you have a self-defrosting freezer, defrost it as soon as you see thick frost. Transfer your frozen food to the refrigerator. If necessary, pile frozen foods into a laundry basket and cover with newspapers or a blanket. To speed the defrosting, have an electric fan blow into the freezer, or place pans of warm water in the freezer. Wash with a solution of 3 tablespoons soda to 1 quart water, or with a mild detergent solution. Dry thoroughly before resetting temperature control.

Emergencies

In case of power failure or mechanical defect, *keep the freezer closed.* In a full freezer that is kept at 0°, little or no thawing will take place within the first 12 to 20 hours.

If your freezer might be out of commission for more than a day and you are storing a lot of food, you will want to take action. You can take the contents of your freezer to a frozen food locker. Or you can buy dry ice. Wear heavy gloves when you handle dry ice. Lay cardboard over the packages in your freezer, and place the dry ice on the cardboard; do not place it directly on the packages. A 50-pound block of dry ice will prevent foods from thawing for 2 to 3 days.

GENERAL RECOMMENDATIONS FOR FREEZER STORAGE

Let this 3-page section of general instructions be your guide when you want to freeze food prepared from your own recipes—or purchased products. There's no need to consult these pages when you freeze recipes from this book. Each Do-Ahead recipe has its own specific storage instructions—these have been thoroughly tested.

Appetizers

Storage Time: 1 to 2 months

Recommendations: It is best to freeze hors d'oeuvres and pastry before baking.
Deep-fried appetizers—such as the Chili Cheese Fries on page 41—can be frozen after frying and then reheated in the oven.

Meat, Poultry, Fish

Storage Times: See pages 9, 19, 23, 24 and 30.

Recommendations: Freeze fresh meat, poultry and fish as promptly as possible. One way to freeze cleaned fish is in a waterproof container; cover the fish with water and freeze.

If you thaw meat, poultry or fish before cooking, start cooking them while they are still chilled. Frozen roasts require 1/3 to 1/2 more than their normal cooking time. For small roasts, the additional cooking time will be closer to 1/3, for large roasts, closer to 1/2.

Cooked meat in sauce and leftover roasts freeze very well, as a rule; if possible, they should be slightly undercooked before freezing.

Cooked dishes can be taken from the freezer and heated without thawing. Heat in the oven (use the instructions for Swiss Steak, page 14, as a guide), or place in a skillet and add a little water (see the Pepper Steak instructions, page 13).

We don't recommend that you freeze fried meat, poultry or fish, since these fried foods will often develop a rancid or warmed-over flavor. Sometimes, however, fried foods can be frozen. Take a look at the recipes for Sweet and Sour Pork (page 19), Fried Chicken (page 29), and Batter-fried Fish (page 30). Note that their recommended storage times are very short.

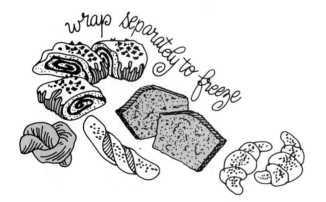

Main Dishes

Storage Time: About 3 months

Recommendations: In adapting your own recipe to freezer storage, find a Do-Ahead recipe that closely resembles your own. Base the preparations for freezing, the storage time, heating and completing of your recipe on the instructions for the Do-Ahead recipe. Check through the Do-Ahead recipes for ingredients that are added just before serving, and observe the same procedure; those ingredients do not freeze well. In preparing your main dish, work according to the food temperature rules on page 84, and remember to reheat your dish quickly.

Fruits and Vegetables

Storage Times:

Citrus Fruits . . . . 3 to 4 months
Other Fruits . . . . 1 year
Vegetables . . . . 1 year

Recommendations: Let your produce man advise you on the varieties that freeze best; new varieties—developed specifically for freezing—will be available before long. Freeze fruit and vegetables at the peak of their ripeness. For good freezing instructions, check the booklet that came with your freezer, the United States Department of Agriculture or a local university.

Breads

Storage Times:

Quick Breads . . . . 2 to 3 months
Yeast Breads . . . . 9 months

Recommendations: Bake breads before freezing; breads baked after freezing will be smaller and tougher. Overwrap the bread you buy if it is to stay in the freezer for more than one week. To thaw at room temperature, keep breads wrapped—at least in the beginning. To thaw and heat breads in the oven, set oven at 350°; heating time will vary with size. For quick thawing, freeze rolls or nut bread or coffee cake slices individually wrapped. Check the recipes on pages 50 to 60 for standard instructions for thawing or heating bread or coffee cakes.

Cakes

Storage Times:

Frosted . . . . .1 to 2 months
Unfrosted . . . . .4 to 6 months

Recommendations: Freeze frosted cakes without wrapping; freezer wrap them as soon as they are firm. To prevent crushing, place cake in box; overwrap box. Frostings that freeze well (not all of them do) are given in recipes in this book. Confectioners' sugar and fudge frostings freeze particularly well.

Cookies

Storage Times:

Frosted . . . . .2 to 3 months
Unfrosted . . . . .9 to 12 months

Recommendations: Nearly all cookies—baked or unbaked—can be frozen. For specific storage times, look through the recipes on pages 66 to 73. When you freeze several cookie varieties in the same container, the least storable cookie should set the storage time. Freeze frosted cookies uncovered until they are firm; then wrap. For additional freezing suggestions, see the notes on page 72.

Pies and Pastry

Storage Times:

Chiffon Pies . . . . .1 month
Other Pies .4 months
Pastry . . . . .4 months

Recommendations: To prevent soggy crusts, bake pies before freezing. Empty pie shells can be frozen unbaked; then they should *not* be thawed before baking. Do not try to freeze custard or cream pies or pies with a meringue topping. To thaw chiffon pies, leave them wrapped in the refrigerator for 1½ hours. Thawing and heating directions for double-crust pies appear in recipes on pages 78 and 79. To heat a pie that is in a pan made of aluminum foil, place a baking sheet under the pie pan for browning.

Your Refrigerator: Short-Term Planning

Your Refrigerator: Short-Term Planning

Your refrigerator is an old friend, one you probably take for granted. But it can serve as one of the best kitchen helpers you could have. In the following pages, you'll find recipes for food you can prepare ahead of time and store in the refrigerator. Some of these recipes can be prepared one day ahead; others—for foods that will keep longer, such as salads, yeast rolls and cookies—can wait in your refrigerator for 2 days or more.

Before serving time, look up the serving instructions which follow this symbol—■; they are in **boldface type** toward the end of the recipe. If you store your prepared food in an ovenproof pan or baking dish, you'll be able to transfer it directly from the refrigerator to the oven.

Your refrigerator—which should be set at 40° or lower—is less effective than your freezer in stopping all bacterial activity. We therefore recommend the following safeguards:

1 Buy fresh food of top quality.

2 As soon as you get home from the grocery store, put foods that require cold storage in your refrigerator.

3 Prepare the food you bring home as soon as you can, and be sure that everything which comes in contact with it is spotless.

4 Refrigerate the food you prepare as soon as possible. Hot foods may be immediately placed in the refrigerator provided the food does not raise the refrigerator's temperature above 45°. With large quantities, place the container of hot food in a large bowl or a basin filled with cold water and ice. This cooling mixture of ice and water should almost reach the top of your food container. Renew the ice as it melts; refrigerate food as soon as possible.

5 Be sure to serve the food within the recommended storage period. This information is listed at the top of every recipe.

Pictured on the preceding page:
Marinated Roast Beef (page 97)

Meats and Main Dishes

STROGANOFF HAMBURGERS

Store no longer than 48 hours. Makes enough for 8 sandwiches.

Base
1 pound ground beef
3 tablespoons instant chopped onion

Sauce
⅓ cup chili sauce
2 tablespoons flour
1 tablespoon prepared mustard
½ teaspoon salt
¼ teaspoon pepper

Cook and stir meat and onion until meat is brown. Spoon off fat. Stir in Sauce ingredients; simmer uncovered about 5 minutes. Cover and refrigerate.

■ **About 10 minutes before serving, have ready:** 1 cup dairy sour cream; 8 hamburger buns, split and toasted; 8 slices tomato; lettuce leaves.

Stir sour cream into hamburger mixture; heat until hot. Serve in buns with tomato slices and lettuce.

ROAST BEEF HASH

Store no longer than 48 hours. Makes enough for 3 or 4 servings.

2 cups finely chopped cooked beef
2 cups finely chopped cooked potato
2 tablespoons grated onion
¼ cup beef gravy
1 teaspoon salt

Mix all ingredients; spread in ungreased 8-inch foil pie pan or layer cake pan, 8 × 1½ inches. Cover and refrigerate.

■ **25 minutes before serving, heat oven to 400°.** Bake Roast Beef Hash uncovered until hot, about 20 minutes.

MEAT LOAF AND GRAVY DUET

Store no longer than 24 hours. Makes enough for 6 to 8 servings.

2 pounds ground beef
1 envelope (about 1½ ounces) onion soup mix
1 can (10½ ounces) condensed cream of mushroom soup

Place 24 × 18-inch piece of heavy-duty aluminum foil in baking pan, 9 × 9 × 2 inches. Mix meat and onion soup mix; turn onto foil and shape into loaf. Spread mushroom soup on loaf. Fold foil loosely over meat. Bake in 350° oven 1 hour. (To serve immediately, bake 20 minutes longer.) Cool quickly. Spoon off fat, rewrap and refrigerate.

■ **About 45 minutes before serving, cook Meat Loaf and Gravy Duet in 350° oven until done.**

POCKET STEW

Store no longer than 24 hours. Makes enough for 4 servings.

1½ pounds ground beef
4 slices Bermuda or Spanish onion
4 cooked pared medium potatoes
4 medium carrots, cut into julienne strips
1½ teaspoons salt
⅛ teaspoon pepper

Shape meat into 4 patties, each about 3 inches in diameter and 1 inch thick. Place patties on 25 × 18-inch piece of heavy-duty aluminum foil. Top each patty with an onion slice and a potato. Arrange carrots *around* meat. Season with salt and pepper. Fold foil over potatoes and carrots, seal foil securely and refrigerate.

■ **About 55 minutes before serving, place Pocket Stew on ungreased baking sheet. Bake in 400° oven until carrots are tender, about 45 minutes.**

Note: If you wish to serve individual portions, divide ingredients among 4 foil packets.

STUFFED GREEN PEPPERS

Store no longer than 24 hours. Makes enough for 6 servings.

Peppers
6 large green peppers
5 cups water
1 teaspoon salt

Filling
1 pound ground beef
2 tablespoons chopped onion
1 teaspoon salt
⅛ teaspoon garlic salt
1 cup cooked rice
1 can (15 ounces) tomato sauce

Cut thin slice from stem end of each pepper. Remove seeds and membranes. Heat water and 1 teaspoon salt until water boils. Cook peppers in boiling water 5 minutes; drain.

Cook and stir meat and onion in medium skillet until onion is tender. Spoon off fat. Stir in salt, garlic salt, rice and 1 cup of the tomato sauce; heat until hot.

Heat oven to 350°. Lightly stuff each pepper with ½ cup meat mixture. Stand peppers upright in ungreased baking dish, 8×8×2 inches. Reserve ⅓ cup tomato sauce; pour remaining sauce on peppers. (To serve immediately, see below.) Cover tightly; bake 30 minutes. Refrigerate peppers and reserved tomato sauce.

■ **45 minutes before serving, heat oven to 350°.** Pour reserved tomato sauce on peppers. Bake uncovered 35 minutes.

To Serve Immediately: Cover tightly; bake 45 minutes. Pour reserved tomato sauce on peppers. Bake uncovered 15 minutes.

CHOW MEIN CASSEROLE

Store no longer than 24 hours. Makes enough for 4 or 5 servings.

1 pound ground beef
¾ cup chopped celery
3 tablespoons instant minced onion
½ cup uncooked converted rice
½ teaspoon salt
1 can (10½ ounces) condensed chicken with rice soup
1 can (4 ounces) mushroom stems and pieces, drained
2 tablespoons soy sauce
1 tablespoon brown sugar
1 teaspoon butter or margarine

Cook and stir meat, celery and onion until meat is brown. (To serve immediately, see below.) Spoon off fat. Stir in remaining ingredients. Pour into greased 2-quart casserole. Cover and refrigerate.

■ **1½ hours before serving, stir 1¼ cups boiling water into casserole.** Cover tightly; bake in 350° oven 30 minutes. Stir casserole; bake uncovered 50 minutes.

To Serve Immediately: While browning meat, pour 1¼ cups boiling water on rice and salt in greased 2-quart casserole and cover. Stir meat mixture into rice; bake covered in 350° oven 30 minutes. Stir casserole; bake uncovered 30 minutes.

To Store Meat and Poultry

Wrap loosely. For 1 or 2 days, meat and poultry can stay in their original wrap. Place them in the coldest part of your refrigerator.

Recommended Storage Time:
1 to 2 days: Ground beef, chicken, turkey, giblets, liver, cooked meat.

2 to 4 days: Roasts, steaks, chops, ham, frankfurters, cold cuts.

7 days: Bacon.

SPINACH MEAT ROLL

Store no longer than 24 hours. Makes enough for 8 servings.

Filling
1 package (10 ounces) frozen leaf spinach

Meat Mixture
2 pounds ground beef
2 eggs
¼ cup catsup
¼ cup milk
¾ cup soft bread crumbs (about 1 slice bread)
½ teaspoon salt
¼ teaspoon pepper
¼ teaspoon oregano

Filling
1 teaspoon salt
1 package (3 ounces) smoked sliced ham

Roll up the meat and filling, using foil to lift.

Thaw frozen spinach quickly by rinsing spinach with running hot water to separate and remove ice crystals; drain. Mix Meat Mixture ingredients. On 18×15-inch piece of aluminum foil, pat meat mixture into rectangle, 12×10 inches.

Arrange spinach evenly on meat mixture, leaving ½-inch margin around edges. Sprinkle the 1 teaspoon salt on spinach; arrange ham on top. Carefully roll up meat, beginning at narrow end and using foil to lift meat. Press edges and ends of roll to seal. Place on rack in ungreased baking pan, 13×9×2 inches. (To serve immediately, see below.) Cover with plastic wrap and refrigerate.

Overlap the cheese triangles on top of the baked roll.

■ **1 hour 35 minutes before serving, have ready:** 3 slices mozzarella cheese, cut diagonally into halves.

Bake Spinach Meat Roll uncovered in 350° oven 1½ hours. Overlap cheese triangles on roll; bake just until cheese begins to melt, about 5 minutes. (Center of meat roll may be slightly pink due to ham.) Nice served with chili sauce.

To Serve Immediately: Have ready: 3 slices mozzarella cheese, cut diagonally into halves.

Bake Spinach Meat Roll uncovered in 350° oven 1 hour 15 minutes. Overlap cheese triangles on roll; bake just until cheese begins to melt, about 5 minutes.

Spinach Meat Roll

CABBAGE PATCH STEW

Store no longer than 48 hours. Makes enough for 4 to 6 servings.

    1 pound ground beef
    2 medium onions, thinly sliced
 1½ cups coarsely chopped cabbage
    ½ cup diced celery
    1 can (16 ounces) tomatoes
 1½ teaspoons garlic salt
    1 teaspoon salt
    1 teaspoon marjoram
    ⅛ teaspoon pepper

Cook and stir meat in Dutch oven until light brown. Spoon off fat. Add onion, cabbage and celery; cook and stir until vegetables are light brown. Stir in tomatoes and seasonings. Cover tightly; simmer 15 minutes. (To serve immediately, see below.) Cool quickly. Cover and refrigerate.

■ **30 minutes before serving, have ready:** 1 can (15½ ounces) kidney beans; instant mashed potato puffs (enough for 4 servings).

Stir in beans (with liquid); heat until mixture boils. Simmer uncovered 15 to 20 minutes. Prepare potato puffs as directed on package. Top stew with potatoes.

To Serve Immediately: Have ready: 1 can (15½ ounces) kidney beans; instant mashed potato puffs (enough for 4 servings).

Stir in beans (with liquid); heat until mixture boils. Simmer uncovered 15 to 20 minutes. Prepare potato puffs as directed on package. Top stew with potatoes.

Pour marinade on beef in plastic bag. Place bag in shallow dish and refrigerate.

Marinated Roast Beef

MARINATED ROAST BEEF

Store no longer than 24 hours. Makes enough for 12 to 14 servings.

Meat

3- to 4-pound sirloin tip beef roast

Marinade

1 bottle (12 ounces) beer or 1½ cups apple cider
⅓ cup salad oil
1 teaspoon salt
¼ teaspoon garlic powder
¼ teaspoon pepper

Pierce meat about 20 times with fork. Place meat in plastic bag or shallow baking dish. Mix 1 cup of the beer and remaining Marinade ingredients; pour on meat. (Reserve remaining beer.) Fasten bag securely or cover dish with plastic wrap. Refrigerate meat, turning occasionally, at least 12 hours.

■ **About 2 hours before serving, place Marinated Roast Beef fat side up on rack in open shallow roasting pan or baking dish. Have ready:** 1 loaf (1 pound) French bread, cut into 1-inch slices.

Insert meat thermometer so tip is in center of thickest part of meat and does not rest in fat. Roast in 325° oven until thermometer registers 160°, about 2 hours.

Place meat on warm platter. Remove drippings from pan, leaving brown particles. Return ¼ cup drippings to pan. Stir in 1 cup water, the reserved ½ cup beer and 1½ teaspoons salt. Heat until mixture boils. Place thin slices of beef on slices of French bread; top with juices.

Add water and beer to drippings from the roast; scrape brown particles from pan.

STEAK CONTINENTAL

Store no longer than 24 hours. Makes enough for 4 to 6 servings.

Meat
2-pound beef round steak, ¾ inch thick

Marinade
3 tablespoons soy sauce
1 tablespoon salad oil
1 tablespoon tomato paste
1 teaspoon salt
½ teaspoon pepper
½ teaspoon oregano
⅛ teaspoon instant minced garlic

Place meat on large piece of plastic wrap. Mix Marinade ingredients; brush both sides of meat with marinade. Fold wrap over meat and seal securely. Refrigerate at least 5 hours. (Flavor improves with longer storage.)

■ **About 15 minutes before serving, set oven control at broil and/or 550°.** Broil Steak Continental with top 3 inches from heat until rare, 5 to 6 minutes on each side, or until medium, 7 to 8 minutes on each side. Cut into ⅛-inch slices.

Tender Treatment

Cuts such as beef round steak, sirloin tip steak, beef flank steak, pork blade steak or pork arm steak need to be tenderized before they can be broiled. A marinade will tenderize these cuts; it will also add flavor (which these meats lack because they have so little fat).

After meat has been broiled, cut it diagonally across the grain into thin slices. Use a very sharp knife.

Marinades are ideal for tenderizing somewhat tough roasts, too (see pages 97, 102 and 105).

OLD-FASHIONED BEEF STEW

Store no longer than 48 hours. Makes enough for 6 servings.

Meat
½ **cup all-purpose flour***
1 **teaspoon salt**
¼ **teaspoon pepper**
2 **pounds beef stew meat, cut into 1-inch pieces**
2 **tablespoons shortening**
6 **cups water**

Vegetables
3 **medium potatoes, pared and cut into 1-inch cubes**
1 **medium turnip, cut into 1-inch cubes**
4 **carrots, cut into 1-inch slices**
1 **green pepper, cut into strips**
1 **cup sliced celery (1-inch pieces)**
1 **medium onion, diced (about ½ cup)**

Seasonings
1 **tablespoon salt**
2 **beef bouillon cubes**
1 **bay leaf**

Mix flour, 1 teaspoon salt and the pepper. Coat meat with flour mixture. Melt shortening in large skillet. Brown meat thoroughly.

Add water; heat until water boils. Reduce heat Cover tightly; simmer 2 hours. Stir in vegetables and seasonings. Cover and simmer until vegetables are tender, about 30 minutes.

If desired, thicken stew. Shake 1 cup water and 2 to 4 tablespoons flour in covered jar; stir slowly into stew. Heat, stirring constantly, until stew boils. Boil and stir 1 minute. (Can be served immediately.) Cover and refrigerate.

■ **15 minutes before serving, heat Old-fashioned Beef Stew over medium-high heat.**

VARIATION

Chicken Stew: Substitute 3- to 4-pound stewing chicken, cut up, for the stew meat and chicken bouillon cubes for the beef bouillon cubes. Increase first cooking period to 2½ hours; skim fat from broth before adding vegetables.

*If using self-rising flour, decrease 1 teaspoon salt to ½ teaspoon.

PORK AND SQUASH IN FOIL

Store no longer than 24 hours.

For each serving:
1 **pork chop, 1 inch thick**
⅛ **teaspoon salt**
   Dash pepper
½ **acorn squash**
1 **tablespoon brown sugar**
1 **tablespoon honey**
1 **tablespoon butter or margarine**

Trim excess fat carefully from meat. Place chop on 18×12-inch piece of heavy-duty aluminum foil. Season with salt and pepper.

Fill hollow of squash with brown sugar, honey and butter; place squash cut side up on chop. Fold foil over squash and seal securely. Place foil package on baking sheet. Bake in 400° oven 45 minutes. (To serve immediately, bake until meat is done and squash is tender, about 15 minutes longer.) Refrigerate.

■ **About 1 hour before serving, bake in 400° oven until meat is done and squash is tender.**

Note: If preparing more than 1 chop, be sure to wrap each individually. This separate packaging is especially convenient for serving 1 portion at a time—when family members are eating at different times, for instance. Or for a person eating alone.

SPARERIBS AND SAUERKRAUT

Store no longer than 24 hours. Makes enough for 4 servings.

1 **can (29 ounces) sauerkraut**
¼ **cup brown sugar (packed)**
2 **unpared apples, cut into eighths**
3 **to 4 pounds spareribs, cut into serving pieces**

Mix sauerkraut (with liquid), sugar and apple pieces in open shallow roasting pan; top with spareribs, meaty side up. Cover tightly; bake in 325° oven 1 hour. Uncover; bake 30 minutes. (To serve immediately, spoon off fat and bake until done, about 20 minutes.) Cool quickly. Cover and refrigerate.

■ **About 30 minutes before serving, spoon off fat from Spareribs and Sauerkraut. Bake uncovered in 325° oven until done.**

SPICY PORK STEAKS

Store no longer than 24 hours. Makes enough for 3 or 4 servings.

Meat
1¾ to 2 pounds pork steaks, ¾ inch thick

Marinade
½ cup orange juice
3 tablespoons brown sugar
3 tablespoons vinegar
1 teaspoon salt
½ teaspoon dry mustard
¼ teaspoon ginger
2 tablespoons catsup

Place meat in plastic bag or shallow glass dish. Mix Marinade ingredients; pour on meat. Fasten bag securely or cover dish with plastic wrap. Refrigerate at least 8 hours.

■ **About 1 hour before serving, remove Spicy Pork Steaks from marinade; reserve marinade.** Place meat in open shallow roasting pan or baking dish. Bake uncovered in 350° oven 15 minutes; pour ¼ cup of reserved marinade on meat. Bake 30 minutes; turn meat and pour on another ¼ cup marinade. Bake until tender, about 15 minutes.

SWEET AND SOUR PORK

Store no longer than 24 hours. Makes enough for 5 or 6 servings.

Sweet and Sour Pork (page 19)
2 medium green peppers, cut into 1-inch pieces
1 medium onion, cut into ½-inch pieces
4 cups hot cooked rice

Prepare Sweet and Sour Pork as directed except—refrigerate 1 package pork cubes and 1 container sauce.

Heat pork cubes on ungreased baking sheet in 400° oven until hot, about 7 minutes. Heat ¼ cup water and the sauce in large saucepan until mixture boils. Stir in green pepper and onion; cover tightly and simmer 5 minutes. Just before serving, stir pork cubes into sauce. Serve on rice.

PORK TENDERLOIN BAKE

Store no longer than 48 hours. Makes enough for 6 servings.

Meat
2 pork tenderloins (10 to 12 ounces each)

Marinade
1 can (13½ ounces) crushed pineapple, drained (reserve ¼ cup syrup)
¼ cup dry sherry or apple juice
2 tablespoons soy sauce
2 tablespoons chili sauce
¼ teaspoon red food color
1 teaspoon salt
2 cloves garlic, crushed
1 green onion, cut into thick slices
2 slices ginger root, smashed

Glaze
1 cup honey

Place meat in plastic bag or shallow glass dish. Mix pineapple and reserved syrup with remaining ingredients except honey; pour on meat. Fasten bag securely or cover dish with plastic wrap. Refrigerate meat, turning occasionally, at least 2 hours.

■ **About 1½ hours before serving, remove Pork Tenderloin Bake from marinade; reserve marinade.** Place meat on rack in open shallow baking pan or dish. Roast in 325° oven 30 minutes. Mix reserved marinade and honey; pour on meat. Bake until done, 30 to 60 minutes. Cut meat diagonally across grain into ¼-inch slices.

Apricot Ham Buffet can be served hot, as pictured, as well as cold.

APRICOT HAM BUFFET

Store no longer than 24 hours. Makes 15 to 18 servings.

5- to 7-pound fully cooked boneless ham
1 tablespoon prepared mustard
1 jar (12 ounces) apricot preserves
1 can (30 ounces) apricot halves, drained
   Whole cloves

Place meat fat side up on rack in open shallow roasting pan. Insert meat thermometer so tip is in center of thickest part of meat and does not rest in fat. Roast in 325° oven 1 hour 45 minutes. Heat mustard and apricot preserves in small saucepan over low heat until preserves are melted; keep warm.

Remove meat from oven. Trim excess fat carefully from meat; brush meat evenly with half the apricot glaze. Bake until thermometer registers 130°, about 20 minutes. Remove meat from oven. Fasten apricots on meat with whole cloves. Carefully brush top with remaining warm apricot glaze. Bake 10 minutes. (Can be served immediately.) Cover and refrigerate.

■ **About 10 minutes before serving, place ham on platter.** Serve cold.

Pour the marinade over the meat, cover and refrigerate, turning occasionally.

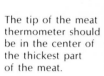

The tip of the meat thermometer should be in the center of the thickest part of the meat.

Luau Roast—a patio feast

LUAU ROAST

Store no longer than 24 hours. Makes enough for 10 servings.

Meat
4-pound boned pork shoulder

Marinade
½ cup pineapple juice
½ cup salad oil
½ cup dark corn syrup
¼ cup lime juice
1 small clove garlic, crushed
2 tablespoons brown sugar
1 tablespoon prepared mustard
1 tablespoon soy sauce
2 teaspoons salt
1 teaspoon ground coriander
½ teaspoon ginger

Trim excess fat carefully from meat. Place meat in glass bowl, plastic bag or shallow baking dish. Mix Marinade ingredients; pour on meat. Fasten bag securely or cover dish with plastic wrap. Refrigerate meat, turning occasionally, at least 8 hours.

■ **About 2½ hours before serving, remove Luau Roast from marinade; reserve marinade.** Place meat fat side up on rack in open shallow baking pan or dish. Insert meat thermometer so tip is in center of thickest part of meat and does not rest in fat. Roast in 325° oven, basting occasionally with reserved marinade, until thermometer registers 170°, about 2½ hours.

BAKED HAM WITH SPINACH STUFFING

Store no longer than 24 hours. Makes enough for 4 to 6 servings.

Filling
1 package (10 ounces) frozen chopped
  spinach
¼ cup diced celery
1 can (4 ounces) mushroom stems
  and pieces, drained
2 tablespoons chopped onion
2 tablespoons salad oil
¼ teaspoon salt
⅛ teaspoon pepper

Meat
2 fully cooked ham slices, ½ inch thick
  (about 1½ pounds)
1 tablespoon butter or margarine, melted

Cook spinach as directed on package; drain. Cook and stir celery, mushroom and onion in oil until celery is tender. Stir in spinach, salt and pepper.

Place 1 slice meat in ungreased shallow baking dish. Spread spinach mixture on meat; top with second slice and brush top with butter. Cover with aluminum foil and refrigerate.

■ **65 minutes before serving, have ready:** 1 envelope (1½ ounces) white sauce mix; 1 tablespoon horseradish, well drained; 1 tablespoon prepared mustard; ⅛ teaspoon nutmeg.

Bake ham covered in 325° oven 30 minutes. To make Horseradish Sauce, prepare white sauce mix as directed on package. Stir in horseradish, mustard and nutmeg. Uncover meat; bake 30 minutes. Serve with Horseradish Sauce.

POTATO DOGS

Store no longer than 24 hours. Makes enough for 5 servings.

  Instant mashed potato puffs (enough for 4
  servings)
2 tablespoons parsley flakes
2 tablespoons instant chopped onion
1 teaspoon prepared mustard
1 pound frankfurters (about 10)

Prepare potato puffs as directed on package. Stir in parsley, onion and mustard. Cut frankfurters lengthwise, being careful not to cut completely through. Arrange cut side up on ungreased baking sheet; spread potato mixture on frankfurters. (To serve immediately, see below.) Cover with plastic wrap and refrigerate.

■ **About 10 minutes before serving, set oven control at broil and/or 550°.** Broil Potato Dogs with tops 5 inches from heat until potatoes are golden brown, 8 to 10 minutes. Garnish with cherry tomatoes or tomato wedges.

To Serve Immediately: Set oven control at broil and/or 550°. Broil frankfurters with tops 5 inches from heat until potatoes are golden brown, 5 to 8 minutes. Garnish with cherry tomatoes or tomato wedges.

LASAGNE

Store no longer than 24 hours. Makes enough for 8 to 10 servings.

Prepare Lasagne as directed on page 20 except —cover and refrigerate instead of freezing. One hour 5 minutes before serving, heat oven to 350°. Remove Lasagne from refrigerator and unwrap. Bake uncovered until hot and bubbly, 55 to 60 minutes.

BAKED SAUSAGE RING

Store no longer than 24 hours. Makes enough for 8 servings.

 2 pounds bulk pork sausage
 2 eggs, beaten
 1½ cups dry bread crumbs
 ¼ cup parsley flakes
 1 tablespoon instant minced onion

Heat oven to 350°. Lightly grease 6-cup ring mold. Mix all ingredients. Press into mold. Bake uncovered 20 minutes. Spoon off fat. Cover and refrigerate immediately.

■ **About 40 minutes before serving, have ready:** ¾ cup applesauce; 2 teaspoons vinegar or lemon juice; ½ teaspoon horseradish.

Bake Baked Sausage Ring uncovered in 350° oven 25 to 30 minutes. After ring has baked 15 minutes, heat applesauce, vinegar and horseradish.

Remove Baked Sausage Ring from oven; pour off fat. Turn onto warm platter; top with applesauce mixture. Very pretty garnished with orange-slice twists and parsley.

To Store Cheese

Store soft cheeses (such as Camembert, cream cheese and cottage cheese) tightly covered. Cottage cheese keeps for 3 to 5 days; other soft cheeses keep for 2 weeks.

Harder cheeses (such as Swiss, Cheddar or Parmesan) will keep for several months. Store them unopened in their original wrappers. After opening, wrap them tightly with foil or plastic wrap.

LAYERED HAM DINNER

Store no longer than 24 hours. Makes enough for 4 to 6 servings.

Base
 1 package (9 ounces) frozen cut green beans

Sauce
 1 can (10½ ounces) condensed cream of celery soup
 ¼ cup mayonnaise
 1 tablespoon prepared mustard

Base and Topping
 2 packages (3 or 4 ounces each) thinly sliced cooked ham
 1 cup shredded Cheddar cheese
 ¼ cup dry bread crumbs

Rinse beans with small amount of running cold water to separate and remove ice crystals; drain. Place beans in ungreased 1½-quart casserole.

Mix soup, mayonnaise and mustard; spoon half the sauce on beans. Top with meat; spoon remaining sauce on meat. Sprinkle cheese and crumbs on sauce. (To serve immediately, see below.) Cover and refrigerate.

■ **50 minutes before serving, heat oven to 350°.** Bake Layered Ham Dinner uncovered until hot and bubbly, about 40 minutes.

To Serve Immediately: Bake uncovered in 350° oven until hot and bubbly, about 25 minutes.

LEG O' LAMB BARBECUE

Store no longer than 24 hours. Makes enough for 6 to 8 servings.

   4- to 5-pound leg of lamb
   2 small cloves garlic, peeled and slivered
   ½ cup red wine vinegar
   ⅓ cup salad oil
   ⅓ cup brown sugar (packed)
   2 tablespoons tarragon leaves
   1 teaspoon salt
   2 green onions (with tops), cut into 2-inch
      slices
   1 can (8 ounces) tomato sauce

Cut 4 or 5 small slits in meat with tip of sharp knife; insert garlic slivers in slits. Place meat in large plastic bag or shallow glass dish. Mix remaining ingredients except tomato sauce; pour on meat. Fasten bag securely or cover dish with plastic wrap. Refrigerate meat, turning occasionally, at least 8 hours.

■ **About 3 hours before serving, remove meat from marinade; reserve marinade.** Place meat fat side up on rack in open shallow roasting pan or baking dish. Insert meat thermometer so tip is in center of thickest part of meat and does not touch bone or rest in fat. Roast in 325° oven 2 hours. Mix reserved marinade and tomato sauce. Remove meat from oven; brush meat with some of the tomato glaze. Bake, brushing several times with remaining glaze, until thermometer registers 175 to 180°, about 30 minutes. Remove garlic slivers before serving.

HEARTY LAMB SHANKS

Store no longer than 24 hours. Makes enough for 4 servings.

   4 lamb shanks (about 12 ounces each)
   1½ cups buttermilk
   2 tablespoons instant minced onion
   1 teaspoon salt
   ¾ teaspoon ginger
   ¾ teaspoon ground coriander
   ½ teaspoon celery seed
   ½ teaspoon pepper

Arrange meat in ungreased baking dish, 11½×7½×1½ inches. Mix remaining ingredients; pour on meat. Cover and refrigerate, turning meat occasionally, at least 8 hours.

■ **About 2½ hours before serving, heat oven to 350°.** Bake Hearty Lamb Shanks covered 2 hours. Uncover; bake until tender, about 30 minutes.

ORIENTAL VEAL CASSEROLE

Store no longer than 24 hours. Makes enough for 5 or 6 servings.

   1 pound boneless veal,* cut into 1-inch cubes
      Flour
   2 tablespoons shortening
   1½ cups sliced celery
   2 small onions, chopped
   1 can (10½ ounces) condensed cream of
      chicken soup
   1 can (10½ ounces) condensed cream of
      mushroom soup
   1 soup can water
   2 to 3 tablespoons soy sauce
   ½ cup uncooked regular rice

Heat oven to 325°. Coat meat with flour. Melt shortening in large skillet. Brown meat in shortening. Stir in remaining ingredients.

Pour into ungreased 3-quart casserole. Cover tightly; bake 1 hour. (To serve immediately, bake 30 minutes longer.) Cover and refrigerate immediately.

■ **1 hour before serving, heat oven to 325°.** Bake Oriental Veal Casserole uncovered 50 minutes. If desired, sprinkle chopped cashews on top and serve with soy sauce.

*1 pound lean pork shoulder, cut into 1-inch cubes, can be substituted for the veal.

MEXICALI CHICKEN

Store no longer than 24 hours. Makes enough for 4 or 5 servings.

Chicken
  2 tablespoons salad oil
  2½- to 3-pound broiler-fryer chicken, cut up

Sauce
  1 bottle (7 ounces) spicy sauce for tacos
  ½ cup water
  1 teaspoon salt
  ½ teaspoon oregano
  ¼ teaspoon instant minced garlic
  ¼ cup instant minced onion

Topping
  2 cups shredded Cheddar cheese
  (about 8 ounces)

Heat oil in large skillet or electric frypan. Brown chicken in oil over medium heat about 15 minutes. Spoon off fat. Mix Sauce ingredients; pour on chicken. Reduce heat; cover tightly and simmer until chicken is done, about 30 minutes.

Place chicken in ungreased baking pan, 9×9×2 inches, or ovenproof serving dish. Sprinkle cheese on top. Cover and refrigerate.

■ **40 minutes before serving, heat oven to 400°.** Bake Mexicali Chicken covered 10 minutes. Uncover; bake 20 minutes.

Note: If spicy sauce for tacos is not available, mix 1 can (8 ounces) tomato sauce, 1 teaspoon chili powder, 5 drops red pepper sauce and 2 tablespoons vinegar or lemon juice. Omit water.

To Store Stuffing

When you get poultry ready the day before you cook it, refrigerate the stuffing ingredients (not mixed) separately from the bird. Stuff the bird just before you cook it. With leftovers, too, remove the stuffing from the bird and refrigerate meat and stuffing separately. Use leftovers within 2 or 3 days.

SKILLET COQ AU VIN

Store no longer than 24 hours. Makes enough for 4 servings.

Meat and Vegetables
  ½ cup all-purpose flour*
  1 teaspoon salt
  ¼ teaspoon pepper
  3- to 3½-pound broiler-fryer chicken, cut up
  6 slices bacon
  6 small onions
  ½ pound mushrooms, sliced

Bouquet Garni
  ½ teaspoon thyme leaves
  1 bay leaf
  2 large sprigs parsley

Carrots and Broth
  4 carrots, halved
  1 teaspoon instant chicken bouillon
  1 cup hot water
  1 cup red Burgundy
  1 clove garlic, crushed
  ½ teaspoon salt

Mix flour, 1 teaspoon salt and the pepper; coat chicken with flour mixture. Cook bacon in large skillet until crisp; remove bacon from skillet and drain. Brown chicken in bacon fat over medium heat.

Push chicken to one side of skillet. Cook and stir onions and mushroom in other side of skillet until mushroom is tender, about 5 minutes. Drain off fat.

To prepare Bouquet Garni: Tie thyme leaves, bay leaf and parsley in cheesecloth or place in tea ball.

Crumble bacon; stir in bacon, Bouquet Garni and remaining ingredients.

Cover tightly; simmer until done, about 1 hour. Remove Bouquet Garni. Spoon off fat. (Can be served immediately.) Cover and refrigerate.

■ **About 20 minutes before serving, spoon off fat.** Heat Skillet Coq au Vin until mixture boils. Cover and simmer 10 minutes. Garnish each bowl with sprig of parsley.

*If using self-rising flour, decrease 1 teaspoon salt to ½ teaspoon.

JAMBALAYA

Store no longer than 24 hours. Makes enough for 6 or 7 servings.

2½- to 3-pound broiler-fryer chicken, cut up
3 teaspoons salt
¼ teaspoon pepper
8 pork sausage links
2 cans (16 ounces each) stewed tomatoes
1 large clove garlic, minced
¼ teaspoon thyme
⅛ to ¼ teaspoon cayenne red pepper

Place chicken in Dutch oven. Add enough water to cover chicken. Season with salt and pepper. Heat until water boils. Reduce heat; cover tightly and simmer 45 minutes.

Remove chicken from broth; set aside. Strain broth; reserve 2 cups. Brown sausage in large pan or Dutch oven. Spoon off fat; reserve 2 tablespoons. Return reserved fat to pan. Add chicken; stir in reserved broth and remaining ingredients. (To serve immediately, see below.) Cover and refrigerate.

■ **About 35 minutes before serving, have ready:** 1 cup uncooked regular rice; snipped parsley.

Heat Jambalaya until mixture boils; stir in rice. Cover and simmer 25 minutes. Serve in large bowl; sprinkle parsley on top.

To Serve Immediately: Have ready: 1 cup uncooked regular rice; snipped parsley.

Heat Jambalaya until mixture boils; stir in rice. Cover and simmer 25 minutes. Serve in large bowl; sprinkle parsley on top.

CHICKEN CASSEROLE

Store no longer than 24 hours. Makes enough for 6 servings.

Base
   1 **package (10 ounces) frozen chopped broccoli**

Sauce
   ¼ **cup butter or margarine**
   ¼ **cup all-purpose flour**
   1½ **teaspoons salt**
   ¼ **teaspoon pepper**
   ½ **teaspoon lemon pepper**
   1 **cup chicken broth**
   2 **cups milk**

Base
   7 **ounces spaghetti, cooked and drained**
   2 **cups cut-up cooked chicken or turkey**
   1 **can (3 ounces) sliced mushrooms, drained**
   ½ **cup sliced ripe olives**
   ½ **cup dry bread crumbs**
   1 **tablespoon butter or margarine, melted**

Rinse frozen broccoli with small amount of running cold water to separate and remove ice crystals; drain. Melt ¼ cup butter in large saucepan over low heat. Stir in flour and seasonings. Cook over low heat, stirring constantly, until mixture is smooth and bubbly.

Remove from heat; stir in broth and milk. Heat, stirring constantly, until sauce boils. Boil and stir 1 minute. Stir in spaghetti, chicken, broccoli, mushrooms and olives.

Pour into ungreased baking dish, 8×8×2 inches. Toss crumbs in melted butter; sprinkle crumbs on top. (Can be baked immediately.) Cover and refrigerate.

■ **About 1½ hours before serving, heat oven to 350°.** Bake Chicken Casserole covered 45 minutes. Uncover; bake until hot and bubbly, about 25 minutes.

TURKEY DIVAN

Store no longer than 24 hours. Makes enough for 5 servings.

Base
   2 **packages (10 ounces each) frozen broccoli spears**

Sauce
   ¼ **cup butter or margarine**
   ¼ **cup all-purpose flour**
   1½ **cups chicken broth***
   2 **tablespoons sherry, if desired**
   ⅛ **teaspoon nutmeg**
   ½ **cup whipping cream, whipped**
   ½ **cup grated Parmesan cheese**

Base and Topping
   5 **large slices cooked turkey or chicken breast (about ¾ pound)**
   ½ **cup grated Parmesan cheese**

Cook broccoli as directed on package except— simmer only 3 minutes; drain. Melt butter in medium saucepan over low heat. Stir in flour. Cook over low heat, stirring constantly, until smooth and bubbly. Remove from heat; stir in chicken broth. Heat until sauce boils. Boil and stir 1 minute. Remove from heat; stir in sherry and nutmeg. Gently fold in whipped cream and ½ cup cheese.

Arrange broccoli in ungreased baking dish, 11½×7½×1½ inches; top with turkey. Pour sauce on meat. Sprinkle ½ cup cheese on top. (To serve immediately, see below.) Cover and refrigerate.

■ **About 55 minutes before serving, heat oven to 350°.** Bake Turkey Divan uncovered until hot, about 45 minutes.

To Serve Immediately: Set oven control at broil and/or 550°. Broil with top of dish 3 to 5 inches from heat until cheese is golden brown.

*Chicken broth can be made by dissolving 2 chicken bouillon cubes or 2 teaspoons instant chicken bouillon in 1½ cups boiling water, or use canned chicken broth.

FISH BAKE

Store no longer than 24 hours. Makes enough for 6 servings.

  2 pounds fresh or frozen cod, pike, pollack
    or flounder fillets
  ¼ cup all-purpose flour
  2 teaspoons salt
  ¼ teaspoon pepper
  1 teaspoon dill weed
  1 cup milk
  2 cups croutons
  ¼ cup butter or margarine, melted

If fish is frozen, thaw. Heat oven to 350°. Cut fish into serving pieces. Mix flour, salt and pepper. Coat fish with flour mixture. Arrange fish in single layer in ungreased baking dish, 13½×9×2 inches. Sprinkle dill weed on fish; pour milk on top. Bake uncovered 45 minutes. Toss croutons with butter; sprinkle on fish. (To serve immediately, bake 10 minutes longer.) Cover and refrigerate.

■ **40 minutes before serving, heat oven to 350°.** Bake Fish Bake uncovered 30 minutes. Garnish with lemon slices and parsley.

For Best Results

Thaw frozen fish in its original wrapping under cold running water. Measure other ingredients while fish thaws. Combine it with other ingredients while still chilled. Work quickly; refrigerate immediately. Clean fresh-caught fish at once. Refrigerate or put on ice immediately.

PIKE FIESTA

Store no longer than 24 hours. Makes enough for 2 or 3 servings.

  1 pound fresh or frozen walleye pike fillets
  1½ teaspoons salt
  ¼ teaspoon pepper
  1 small onion, thinly sliced
  1 tomato, peeled and cut into
    ½-inch slices
  1 tablespoon lime juice
  1 tablespoon salad oil
  1 tablespoon snipped parsley
  8 pitted ripe olives

If fish is frozen, thaw. Arrange fish in ungreased baking dish, 8×8×2 inches. Season with salt and pepper. Cover fish with onion and tomato slices; sprinkle lime juice, salad oil and parsley on onion and tomato. Top with olives. (Can be baked immediately.) Cover and refrigerate.

■ **About 55 minutes before serving, heat oven to 375°.** Bake Pike Fiesta covered 30 minutes. Uncover; bake until fish flakes easily with fork, about 15 minutes. Garnish with lime wedges.

SOY HALIBUT STEAKS

Store no longer than 48 hours. Makes enough for 4 to 6 servings.

  2 pounds fresh or frozen halibut
    steaks (about 6)
  3 tablespoons soy sauce
  1 teaspoon ginger
  ½ teaspoon garlic powder
  2 teaspoons sugar
  1 teaspoon grated lemon peel
  ¼ cup fresh lemon juice
  ¼ cup water

If fish is frozen, thaw. Arrange fish in single layer in shallow dish. Mix remaining ingredients; pour on steaks. Cover and refrigerate.

■ **About 20 minutes before serving, set oven control at broil and/or 550°.** Arrange Soy Halibut Steaks on broiler rack; reserve marinade for basting. Broil steaks with tops about 3 inches from heat until brown, 4 to 6 minutes. Brush with reserved sauce; turn and brush again. Broil until fish flakes easily with fork, 4 to 6 minutes. Garnish with parsley and lemon slices, if desired.

SHRIMP INTERNATIONALE

Store no longer than 24 hours. Makes enough for 5 or 6 servings.

Base

12 ounces frozen cleaned raw shrimp

Marinade

½ cup creamy Italian salad dressing
1 tablespoon soy sauce
1 teaspoon parsley flakes

Vegetables and Seasoning

2 tablespoons salad oil
1 medium onion, diced
¼ cup chopped green pepper
¼ pound fresh mushrooms, trimmed and sliced, or 1 can (2 ounces) mushroom stems and pieces, drained
1 tablespoon soy sauce

Base

2 cups cooked rice
1 can (8¾ ounces) crushed pineapple, drained

Rinse frozen shrimp with running cold water to remove ice glaze. Place shrimp on 18×12-inch piece of heavy-duty aluminum foil. Mix salad dressing, 1 tablespoon soy sauce and the parsley flakes; pour on shrimp. Wrap shrimp securely in the foil and refrigerate.

Heat oil in large skillet or electric frypan. Cook and stir onion, green pepper and mushroom in oil until onion is tender. Remove from heat; stir in 1 tablespoon soy sauce, the rice and pineapple. Place mixture in ungreased 1-quart casserole. (To serve immediately, see right.) Cover and refrigerate.

■ **55 minutes before serving, have ready:** cabbage leaves; ⅓ cup slivered almonds; lime wedges.

Bake rice mixture covered in 375° oven 15 minutes; place foil package of shrimp on baking sheet in oven. Bake until rice is hot and shrimp are tender, about 30 minutes.

Line salad bowl with cabbage leaves. Stir almonds into rice mixture; spoon into bowl. Top with shrimp and sauce; garnish with lime wedges.

To Serve Immediately: Have ready: cabbage leaves; ⅓ cup slivered almonds; lime wedges.

Bake foil package of shrimp on baking sheet and rice mixture covered in 375° oven 25 minutes.

Line salad bowl with cabbage leaves. Stir almonds into rice mixture; spoon into bowl. Top with shrimp and sauce; garnish with lime wedges.

HOT SHRIMP AND MACARONI SALAD

Store no longer than 24 hours. Makes enough for 4 to 6 servings.

1 package (8 ounces) macaroni and Cheddar dinner
1 can (4½ ounces) shrimp, rinsed and drained
½ cup chopped celery
¼ cup chopped gherkins
2 hard-cooked eggs, chopped

Cook macaroni and Cheddar dinner as directed on package. Stir in remaining ingredients. (To serve immediately, heat, stirring occasionally.) Cover and refrigerate.

■ **About 15 minutes before serving, stir in ¼ cup water.** Cover Hot Shrimp and Macaroni Salad tightly; heat over medium heat, stirring occasionally, until hot, about 12 minutes.

About Quantities

Shrimp: 2 cans (4½ ounces each) medium shrimp = 1 package (12 ounces) frozen cleaned shrimp.

To Make 2 Cups of Cooked Rice: Bring ⅔ cup regular rice, ½ teaspoon salt and 1⅓ cups water to a boil, stirring occasionally. Reduce heat; cook tightly covered for 14 minutes. Remove from heat; fluff with fork. Cover and let stand for 5 to 10 minutes.

BAKED AVOCADO-CRABMEAT SALADS

Store no longer than 24 hours. Makes enough for 6 servings.

Salad
1 can (7½ ounces) crabmeat, drained and cartilage removed
2 hard-cooked eggs, chopped
¼ cup finely chopped sweet pickle or pickle relish
⅓ cup salad dressing or dairy sour cream
¼ teaspoon salt
⅛ teaspoon red pepper sauce

Base and Topping
3 ripe avocados
½ cup shredded Swiss cheese

Mix all ingredients except avocados and cheese. Cut unpeeled avocados lengthwise into halves; remove pits. Place avocados cut side up in ungreased baking dish, 9×9×2 inches. Fill each half with ⅓ cup crabmeat salad; sprinkle cheese on salad. (Can be baked immediately.) Cover with plastic wrap and refrigerate.

■ **30 minutes before serving, heat oven to 400°.** Bake salads uncovered until hot and bubbly, about 20 minutes.

Baked Avocado-Crabmeat Salad

CRAB SHELLS

Store no longer than 24 hours. Makes enough for 8 servings.

Filling
1 can (6½ ounces) crabmeat, drained and cartilage removed
2 tablespoons chopped pimiento
1 hard-cooked egg, chopped
1 tablespoon chopped onion
⅓ cup chopped celery
½ teaspoon salt
⅓ cup mayonnaise

Pastry
2 cups all-purpose flour*
1 teaspoon salt
⅔ cup plus 2 tablespoons shortening
4 to 5 tablespoons cold water

Mix Filling ingredients. Refrigerate. Prepare Pastry: Measure flour and 1 teaspoon salt into bowl. Cut in shortening thoroughly. Sprinkle in water, 1 tablespoon at a time, mixing until all flour is moistened and dough almost cleans side of bowl (1 to 2 teaspoons water can be added if needed). Gather dough into a ball; divide in half.

Roll each half into 11-inch circle and cut into eight 4-inch circles. Place 2 tablespoons crabmeat mixture on each of 8 pastry circles. Moisten edge with water; cover with a remaining circle. Press edge with tines of fork to seal securely. Fit Crab Shells into ungreased baking shells; prick top crusts several times. Place shells on baking sheet. (To serve immediately, bake uncovered in 425° oven 20 to 25 minutes.) Cover with plastic wrap and refrigerate.

■ **40 minutes before serving, heat oven to 425°.** Bake Crab Shells uncovered 30 minutes. Turn each baked Crab Shell over in baking shell so lines will show on the pastry.

*If using self-rising flour, omit salt from Pastry. Pastry made with self-rising flour differs in flavor and texture.

Spoon half the flaked salmon onto the cucumber slices.

Jellied Salmon Loaf

JELLIED SALMON LOAF

Store no longer than 24 hours. Makes enough for 8 servings.

Gelatin
- **2 envelopes unflavored gelatin**
- **½ cup cold water**
- **1½ cups boiling water**
- **¼ cup lemon juice**
- **1 tablespoon vinegar**
- **2 teaspoons salt**

Base
- **1 cup chopped celery**
- **½ medium cucumber, chopped**
- **½ medium cucumber, thinly sliced**
- **2 cans (16 ounces each) red salmon, drained, flaked and boned**

Sauce
- **¾ cup dairy sour cream**
- **½ green pepper, finely chopped**
- **2 teaspoons snipped parsley**
- **2 teaspoons snipped chives**
- **½ teaspoon salt**
- **Dash pepper**

Sprinkle gelatin on cold water to soften. Stir boiling water gradually into gelatin; stir until gelatin is dissolved. Mix in lemon juice, vinegar and salt; cool.

In another bowl, mix celery and chopped cucumber. Arrange cucumber slices in bottom of loaf pan, 9×5×3 inches. Layer half the salmon, the cucumber-celery mixture and remaining salmon on slices.

Pour gelatin on salmon. Chill until set. Mix Sauce ingredients. Cover and refrigerate.

■ **Just before serving, loosen Jellied Salmon Loaf from mold; invert onto serving plate.** Garnish as you wish. Serve sauce with salad.

Loosen the salmon loaf around the edges; dip the pan into hot water to unmold.

TUNA MACARONI SALAD

Store no longer than 48 hours. Makes enough for 4 servings.

Base
1 cup elbow macaroni, cooked and drained
1 can (9¼ ounces) tuna, drained
2 tablespoons chopped red onion
1 to 2 tablespoons chopped radish
½ cup chopped green pepper

Dressing
½ cup mayonnaise
½ teaspoon dry mustard
½ teaspoon salt
¼ teaspoon pepper
1 tablespoon lemon juice

Mix Base ingredients. Mix Dressing ingredients; pour dressing on macaroni mixture and toss. Cover and chill at least 3 hours. (Can be served immediately.)

■ **Just before serving, line large bowl with greens or place lettuce cups on plate.** Fill with Tuna Macaroni Salad.

CREAMY TUNA CHEESE MOLD

Store no longer than 48 hours. Makes enough for 4 servings.

1 envelope unflavored gelatin
⅓ cup cold water
½ cup boiling water
¾ cup diced celery
¼ cup minced onion
¼ cup chopped green pepper
1 can (9¼ ounces) tuna, drained
½ teaspoon salt
½ teaspoon lemon pepper
½ cup shredded sharp Cheddar cheese
⅓ cup mayonnaise

Sprinkle gelatin on cold water to soften. Stir boiling water gradually into gelatin; stir until gelatin is dissolved. Mix in remaining ingredients. Pour salad into 4-cup mold. Cover and chill until firm. (Can be served immediately.)

■ **Just before serving, loosen Creamy Tuna Cheese Mold from mold; invert onto serving plate.** Garnish with greens.

TUNA CASSEROLE

Store no longer than 24 hours. Makes enough for 4 to 6 servings.

Sauce
- 1 envelope (1½ to 2 ounces) white sauce mix
- 1 tablespoon peanut butter

Base
- 1 cup elbow macaroni, cooked and drained
- 2 cans (6½ ounces each) tuna, drained
- 1 can (4 ounces) mushroom stems and pieces
- ¼ cup chopped green pepper
- ½ cup sliced pitted ripe olives
- 1 to 1½ teaspoons seasoned salt
- ¼ teaspoon oregano
- ¼ teaspoon pepper

Topping
- 1 cup shredded Cheddar cheese (about 4 ounces)

Prepare 1 cup medium white sauce as directed on sauce mix package. Stir in peanut butter. Mix in macaroni, tuna, mushrooms (with liquid) and remaining ingredients except cheese. Pour into ungreased 1½-quart casserole. Sprinkle cheese on top. (To serve immediately, bake uncovered in 350° oven 30 minutes.) Cover and refrigerate.

■ **50 minutes before serving, heat oven to 350°.** Bake Tuna Casserole covered 30 minutes. Uncover; bake 10 minutes.

"Just Enough" Macaroni

To Make 1 Cup of Cooked Elbow Macaroni: Drop ½ cup elbow macaroni and ½ teaspoon salt into 1½ cups of rapidly boiling water. Bring water to a rapid boil once more. Cook for 3 minutes, stirring constantly. Cover pan tightly and remove from heat. Let the pan stand covered for 10 minutes. Drain. Rinse macaroni with cold water.

BAKED BEANS

Store no longer than 5 days. Makes enough for 6 to 8 servings.

- 1 pound dried navy or pea beans (about 2 cups)
- ¼ pound salt pork (without rind)
- 1 medium onion, sliced
- ¼ cup brown sugar (packed)
- 3 tablespoons molasses
- ¼ teaspoon dry mustard
- ⅛ teaspoon pepper

Place beans in large saucepan. Add enough water to cover beans. Heat until water boils. Boil 2 minutes. Remove from heat; cover and set aside 1 hour. To keep beans covered with water, add small amount of water if necessary. Simmer uncovered until tender, about 1 hour. (Do not boil or beans will burst.) Drain beans; reserve liquid.

Heat oven to 300°. Cut salt pork into several pieces; layer salt pork, beans and onion in ungreased 2-quart bean pot or casserole. Mix 1 cup of the reserved liquid, the sugar, molasses, mustard and pepper; pour on beans. Add enough of the remaining reserved liquid (or water) to almost cover beans. Cover tightly; bake, stirring occasionally, 2 hours. Uncover; bake 1½ hours. Cool slightly. Cover and refrigerate.

■ **15 minutes before serving, place 1 can (8 ounces) tomato sauce and Baked Beans in large skillet.** Cook over medium heat, stirring occasionally, until bubbly, about 15 minutes.

LIMA-MEATBALL STEW

Store no longer than 24 hours. Makes enough for 6 servings.

  1 cup dried large lima beans
4½ cups water
  ½ cup water
  3 tablespoons flour
  1 can (16 ounces) whole tomatoes
  1 cup sliced celery
  3 medium carrots, cut into 2-inch pieces
  ½ cup chopped onion
  1 tablespoon salt
  ¼ teaspoon pepper
  1 bay leaf
  1 container frozen Mini Meatballs
     (page 10)

Heat beans and 4½ cups water to boiling in Dutch oven. Boil uncovered 2 minutes. Remove from heat; cover and set aside 1 hour. Do not drain.

Heat oven to 375°. Mix ½ cup water and the flour; stir into beans. Heat, stirring occasionally, until mixture boils and thickens. Stir in vegetables, salt, pepper and bay leaf. Heat until mixture boils. Cover tightly; bake 1½ hours. Add frozen meatballs. (To serve immediately, cover and bake until meatballs are hot, about 1 hour.) Cover and refrigerate.

■ **40 minutes before serving, heat oven to 375°.** Bake Lima-Meatball Stew covered until meatballs are hot, about 30 minutes.

Tomorrow's Sandwiches

When you make sandwiches the night before, always butter bread right to edges, so other fillings won't soak in. Wrap whole sandwich in plastic bag or wrap. Close tightly. Wrap greens and tomato slices separately. A few tasty combinations: sliced beef and sliced radishes on English muffins; lunch meat and sliced olives on corn muffins.

HEARTY SANDWICH LOAF

Store no longer than 24 hours. Makes enough for 6 servings.

Bread
  1 loaf (1 pound) unsliced white bread
     (about 8 inches long)

Butter Mixture
  ½ cup soft butter or margarine
  3 tablespoons instant minced onion
  3 tablespoons prepared mustard
  1 tablespoon poppy seed
  1 tablespoon lemon juice
     Dash cayenne red pepper

Filling
12 slices Swiss cheese
12 thin slices luncheon meat

Carefully trim crust from top of bread. Make 6 diagonal cuts at equal intervals from top of loaf almost to bottom. Mix butter, onion, mustard, poppy seed, lemon juice and cayenne red pepper. Reserve 3 tablespoons butter mixture. Spread remaining butter mixture into cuts.

Alternate 2 cheese slices and 2 meat slices in *each* cut, allowing each to stick out slightly at top and sides of loaf. Spread reserved butter mixture on top and sides of loaf. (To serve immediately, see below.) Wrap in heavy-duty aluminum foil and refrigerate.

■ **1 hour before serving, heat oven to 350°.** Place wrapped Hearty Sandwich Loaf on ungreased baking sheet; open foil. Bake 30 minutes. Cover loaf with foil; bake until hot, about 20 minutes. To serve, slice through each diagonal cut between meat slice and bread.

To Serve Immediately: Place loaf on lightly greased baking sheet. Bake in 350° oven 15 minutes. Cover loaf with foil; bake 10 minutes.

SPICY CHEESE PIE

Store no longer than 24 hours. Makes enough for 4 to 6 servings.

Pastry

1 cup all-purpose flour*
½ teaspoon salt
⅓ cup plus 1 tablespoon shortening
2 to 3 tablespoons cold water

Egg and Cheese Mixture

4 eggs
¼ cup milk
½ cup diced salami
½ cup diced pepperoni
2 cups shredded mozzarella cheese (about 8 ounces)
½ teaspoon basil
½ teaspoon oregano
¼ teaspoon pepper

Tomato Sauce

2 tablespoons chopped onion
2 tablespoons chopped green pepper
1 tablespoon butter or margarine
1 can (8 ounces) tomato sauce
1 teaspoon salt
¼ teaspoon pepper

Prepare Pastry: Measure flour and ½ teaspoon salt into bowl. Cut in shortening thoroughly. Sprinkle in water, 1 tablespoon at a time, mixing until all flour is moistened and dough almost cleans side of bowl (1 to 2 teaspoons water can be added if needed). Gather dough into a ball. Roll into circle 2 inches larger than inverted 8-inch pie pan on lightly floured cloth-covered board. Fold pastry in half, then in half again; place in pan with point in center and unfold. Trim overhanging edge of pastry 1 inch from rim of pan. Fold and roll pastry under, even with pan; flute. Cover pastry-lined pie pan with plastic wrap and refrigerate.

Mix Egg and Cheese Mixture ingredients. Cover and refrigerate.

Cook and stir onion and green pepper in butter until onion is tender. Stir in tomato sauce, 1 teaspoon salt and ¼ teaspoon pepper. Cover saucepan and refrigerate.

■ **About 50 minutes before serving, place pastry-lined pie pan on oven rack.** Pour egg and cheese mixture into pie pan. Bake in 425° oven until light brown, 35 to 40 minutes. Let stand 5 minutes before cutting. After pie has baked 25 minutes, heat Tomato Sauce. Spoon sauce on wedges of pie.

*If using self-rising flour, omit salt from Pastry. Pastry made with self-rising flour differs in flavor and texture.

EGGS FLORENTINE CASSEROLE

Store no longer than 24 hours. Makes enough for 4 to 6 servings.

Base

2 packages (10 ounces each) frozen chopped spinach
2 tablespoons minced onion
2 tablespoons lemon juice
½ cup shredded Cheddar cheese
8 hard-cooked eggs, sliced

Sauce

3 tablespoons butter or margarine
3 tablespoons flour
½ teaspoon salt
½ teaspoon dry mustard
¼ teaspoon pepper
2¼ cups milk

Topping

½ cup dry bread crumbs
1 tablespoon butter or margarine, melted

Cook spinach as directed on package; drain. Stir in onion and lemon juice. Spread spinach in ungreased baking dish, 8×8×2 inches. Sprinkle cheese on spinach; top with egg slices.

Melt 3 tablespoons butter in saucepan over low heat. Stir in flour and seasonings. Cook over low heat, stirring constantly, until smooth and bubbly. Remove from heat; stir in milk. Heat, stirring constantly, until Sauce boils. Boil and stir 1 minute. Pour on eggs.

Toss crumbs with melted butter; sprinkle crumbs on sauce. (To serve immediately, heat oven to 400°; bake uncovered 20 minutes.) Cover and refrigerate.

■ **40 minutes before serving, heat oven to 400°.** Bake Eggs Florentine Casserole uncovered 30 minutes.

QUICHE LORRAINE

Store no longer than 24 hours. Makes enough for 6 main-dish servings (8 appetizer servings).

Pastry
  1 cup all-purpose flour*
  ½ teaspoon salt
  ⅓ cup plus 1 tablespoon shortening
  2 to 3 tablespoons cold water

Base
  12 slices bacon (about ½ pound), crisply fried and crumbled
  1 cup shredded natural Swiss cheese (4 ounces)
  ⅓ cup minced onion

Egg Mixture
  4 eggs
  2 cups whipping cream or light cream
  ¾ teaspoon salt
  ¼ teaspoon sugar
  ⅛ teaspoon cayenne red pepper

Pour the egg mixture into the pie pan on the oven rack.

Bake the quiche until a knife inserted 1 inch from the edge comes out clean.

Prepare Pastry: Measure flour and ½ teaspoon salt into bowl. Cut in shortening thoroughly. Sprinkle in water, 1 tablespoon at a time, mixing until all flour is moistened and dough almost cleans side of bowl (1 to 2 teaspoons water can be added if needed). Gather dough into a ball. Roll into circle 2 inches larger than inverted 9-inch pie pan on lightly floured cloth-covered board. Fold pastry in half then in half again; place in pan with point in center and unfold. Trim overhanging edge of pastry 1 inch from rim of pan. Fold and roll pastry under, even with pan; flute.

Sprinkle bacon, cheese and onion in pastry-lined pie pan. Cover with plastic wrap and refrigerate. Beat eggs slightly; beat in remaining ingredients. Cover and refrigerate.

■ **1 hour 15 minutes before serving, place pastry-lined pie pan on oven rack.** Stir egg mixture and pour into pie pan. Bake in 425° oven 15 minutes. Reduce oven temperature to 300°; bake until knife inserted 1 inch from edge comes out clean, about 45 minutes longer. Let stand 10 minutes before cutting.

*If using self-rising flour, omit salt from Pastry. Pastry made with self-rising flour differs in flavor and texture.

Quiche Lorraine

Appetizers

BEEF TERIYAKI KABOBS

Store no longer than 48 hours.

1 pound beef sirloin steak or beef round steak, 1¼ inches thick
¼ cup soy sauce
¼ cup water
2 tablespoons honey
¼ teaspoon garlic salt
¼ teaspoon allspice
⅛ teaspoon ginger

Trim fat and bone from meat; cut meat into 1¼-inch strips. Cut each strip into ¼-inch pieces. Mix remaining ingredients; pour on meat in glass bowl. Cover and refrigerate at least 1 hour.

■ **20 minutes before serving, set oven control at broil and/or 550°. Have ready:** 2 bunches green onions. Trim green tops from onions; cut onions into 1-inch pieces. Reserve marinade; alternate 3 pieces meat and 2 pieces onion on each skewer.

Broil kabobs with tops 3 to 4 inches from heat, brushing occasionally with reserved marinade, 3 to 4 minutes on each side. To serve, spoon small amount reserved marinade on meat.

Note: 1 pound white chicken meat, cut into 1×1×¼-inch pieces, can be substituted for meat.

To Charcoal-grill: Cook kabobs on hibachi over hot coals, turning frequently, 10 to 15 minutes. Use a hibachi in a ventilated place—a fireplace with the draft open, near an open window or outdoors. Judge hot coals with a grill thermometer or hold your hand, palm toward the heat, near the grid. If you have to withdraw your hand in less than three seconds, the coals are hot (about 400°).

DEVILED EGGS

Store no longer than 24 hours. Makes enough for 6 servings.

6 hard-cooked eggs
½ teaspoon salt
½ teaspoon dry mustard
¼ teaspoon pepper
3 tablespoons salad dressing, vinegar or light cream (20%)

Cut peeled eggs lengthwise into halves. Slip out yolks; mash with fork. Mix in seasonings and salad dressing. Fill whites with egg yolk mixture, heaping it lightly. Arrange on large serving plate. (Can be served immediately.) Cover plate with plastic wrap and refrigerate.

VARIATIONS

Catsup-flavored Deviled Eggs: Decrease salt to ¼ teaspoon and substitute ¼ cup plus 1 tablespoon catsup for the salad dressing.

Deviled Eggs with Olives: Decrease salt to ¼ teaspoon, omit dry mustard and mix ¼ cup finely minced ripe olives and ⅛ teaspoon curry powder into egg yolk mixture.

Zesty Deviled Eggs: Decrease salt to ¼ teaspoon and mix one of the following into the egg yolk mixture:

½ cup finely shredded process American cheese
2 tablespoons snipped parsley
1 teaspoon horseradish

To Store Eggs

Refrigerate eggs right after you buy them. Use them within a week.

Leftover egg whites will keep in the refrigerator in a covered jar 7 to 10 days. Cover leftover yolks with water and store in a covered jar for 2 to 3 days.

MARINATED SHRIMP

Store no longer than 1 week.

1½ teaspoons salt
1 package (12 ounces) frozen cleaned raw shrimp
1 cup oil and vinegar salad dressing
1 bay leaf, crushed

Heat 2 cups water and the salt to boiling. Add shrimp; heat until water boils. Cook until shrimp are tender, 1 to 2 minutes; rinse quickly with running cold water to cool.

Mix shrimp, salad dressing and bay leaf. Cover and refrigerate at least 2 hours. (Can be served immediately.)

Note: Two cans (4½ ounces each) medium shrimp, rinsed and drained, can be substituted for the cleaned raw shrimp.

SPICED PEACHES

Store no longer than 8 days. Makes 1 quart.

1 can (29 ounces) peach halves, drained
1½ cups honey
½ cup vinegar
3 three-inch cinnamon sticks
3 whole cloves

Place peach halves in 1-quart jar. Heat remaining ingredients until syrup boils. Pour on peaches; cool. Cover and refrigerate at least 8 hours.

VARIATIONS

Spiced Apricots: Substitute 1 can (30 ounces) apricot halves, drained, for the peach halves.

Spiced Pears: Substitute 1 can (29 ounces) pear halves, drained, for the peach halves; ½ to 1 teaspoon red or green food color can be added to sauce. Pears will be fully colored in 12 hours.

Spiced Pineapple: Substitute 1 can (30 ounces) pineapple chunks, drained, for the peach halves.

CUCUMBER SOUP

Store no longer than 48 hours. Makes enough for 6 servings.

  2 medium cucumbers
  ¼ cup buttermilk
  1 teaspoon salt
  ⅛ teaspoon pepper
  1 teaspoon instant minced onion
1¼ cups buttermilk

Pare one of the cucumbers; cut both cucumbers into ¾-inch slices. Reserve six of the unpared slices for garnish; wrap in plastic wrap and refrigerate.

Pour ¼ cup buttermilk into blender; add half the cucumber slices. Beat on high speed until smooth. Add remaining cucumber slices, the salt, pepper and onion. Beat until smooth, about 1 minute. Stir in remaining buttermilk. Cover and refrigerate at least 2 hours. (Can be served immediately.)

■ **At serving time, garnish each serving of Cucumber Soup with a reserved cucumber slice.**

RUBY CONSOMMÉ

Store no longer than 4 days. Makes enough for 8 servings.

2 cans (10½ ounces each) beef
  consommé
1 cup tomato juice
1 cup water

Mix consommé, tomato juice and water; heat through. (Can be served immediately.) Cover and refrigerate.

■ **At serving time, heat Ruby Consommé or serve cold.** Garnish with cucumber or radish slices, if desired.

BORSCH

Store no longer than 24 hours. Makes enough for 4 servings.

1 can (10½ ounces) condensed beef broth
  (bouillon)*
1 can (16 ounces) shoestring beets
1 cup shredded cabbage
2 tablespoons minced onion
1 teaspoon sugar
1 teaspoon lemon juice

Heat broth, beets (with liquid), cabbage, onion and sugar until mixture boils. Reduce heat; simmer uncovered 5 minutes. Stir in lemon juice. Cover and chill. (Can be served immediately.)

■ **At serving time, top each serving of Borsch with a spoonful of dairy sour cream.**

*Beef broth can be made by dissolving 2 beef bouillon cubes or 2 teaspoons instant beef bouillon in 1¾ cups boiling water.

VICHYSSOISE

Store no longer than 3 days. Makes enough for 8 servings (½ cup each).

  1 small onion, grated
  3 chicken bouillon cubes
  1 cup water
  ¼ teaspoon salt
  ½ cup milk
1¼ cups instant mashed potato puffs
1½ cups milk

Heat onion, bouillon cubes, water and salt in large saucepan until mixture boils. Reduce heat; cover tightly and simmer 10 minutes. Remove from heat; stir in ½ cup milk. Mix in potato puffs with fork; beat until fluffy. Stir in 1½ cups milk gradually; heat just until soup boils. Cover and chill thoroughly.

■ **5 minutes before serving, have ready:** 1 cup light cream (20%); snipped chives or watercress.

Stir cream into soup with fork; beat vigorously. Serve in small cups or bowls; sprinkle snipped chives on top.

GOLDENROD EGG DIP

Store no longer than 48 hours. Makes 2 cups.

6 hard-cooked eggs, finely chopped
⅓ cup mayonnaise or salad dressing
2 tablespoons pickle relish
1 tablespoon butter or margarine, softened
2 teaspoons lemon juice
1 teaspoon prepared mustard
1 teaspoon salt
½ teaspoon instant minced onion
¼ teaspoon red pepper sauce
⅛ teaspoon pepper

Mix all ingredients. Cover and refrigerate. Chill at least 2 hours. (Can be served immediately.) Stir before serving.

PIQUANT DIP

Store no longer than 48 hours. Makes 2 cups.

Mix 2 cups dairy sour cream and 1 envelope (about .7 ounce) of your favorite salad dressing mix (Parmesan, garlic-cheese or blue cheese) or 1 envelope (about 1½ ounces) spaghetti sauce mix. Cover and refrigerate. Chill at least 1 hour. (Can be served immediately.) Stir before serving.

DILL WEED DIP

Store no longer than 3 days. Makes about 1½ cups.

1 cup dairy sour cream
½ cup mayonnaise or salad dressing
1 tablespoon dill weed
1 teaspoon seasoned salt

Mix all ingredients. Cover and refrigerate. Chill at least 1 hour. (Can be served immediately.)

TEMPTING TUNA DIP

Store no longer than 24 hours. Makes 2 cups.

1 package (3 ounces) cream cheese, softened
1 cup dairy sour cream
1 can (6½ ounces) tuna, drained and flaked
¼ cup chopped stuffed olives
2 tablespoons snipped chives
2 teaspoons horseradish
1 teaspoon Worcestershire sauce
¼ teaspoon salt

Mix cream cheese and sour cream until smooth. Stir in remaining ingredients. Cover and refrigerate. Chill at least 2 hours. (Can be served immediately.) Stir before serving.

BAVARIAN DIP

Store no longer than 48 hours. Makes about 1 cup.

3 tablespoons liverwurst
1 cup dairy sour cream
2 tablespoons sweet pickle relish

Mash liverwurst with fork. Mix in sour cream gradually until smooth. Stir in pickle relish. Cover and refrigerate. Chill at least 1 hour. (Can be served immediately.)

GARLIC CHEESE DIP

Store no longer than 5 days. Makes about 2½ cups.

2 cups creamed cottage cheese
1 medium clove garlic, crushed
⅓ cup chopped olives
1 tablespoon milk

Mix all ingredients. Cover and refrigerate. Chill at least 3 hours. (Can be served immediately.) Stir before serving.

NEAPOLITAN DIP

Store no longer than 3 days. Makes about 1 cup.

2 tablespoons milk
2 packages (3 ounces each) cream cheese, softened
2 tablespoons chili sauce
2 tablespoons grated Parmesan cheese
½ teaspoon oregano leaves
1 teaspoon horseradish

Stir milk gradually into cream cheese. Mix in remaining ingredients. Cover and refrigerate. Chill at least 1 hour. (Can be served immediately.) Stir before serving.

LIVERWURST SPREAD

Store no longer than 48 hours. Makes about 1½ cups.

½ pound liverwurst
1 tablespoon sweet pickle relish
¼ cup mayonnaise or salad dressing
1 tablespoon catsup
1 teaspoon prepared mustard
  Dash Worcestershire sauce

Mash liverwurst with fork; mix in remaining ingredients. Press plastic wrap onto surface of spread and refrigerate. Chill at least 3 hours. (Can be served immediately.)

■ Serve Liverwurst Spread with rye crackers, pumpernickel or other thinly sliced dark bread.

CHEESE APPLE

Store no longer than 5 days.

1 jar (5 ounces) pasteurized process sharp American cheese spread
1 jar (5 ounces) pasteurized Neufchâtel and blue cheese spread
1 package (3 ounces) cream cheese, softened
  Garlic salt
  Worcestershire sauce
  Paprika

Beat all ingredients except paprika in small mixer bowl on low speed just until smooth. Cover and chill at least 8 hours. (Can be served immediately.)

■ Just before serving, shape cheese mixture into ball. Sprinkle paprika on piece of waxed paper; roll cheese ball in paprika to coat. Mold ball into apple shape by making small depression for stem end. If you like, insert a clove and a small leaf. Serve with crackers or snacks.

SALMON PARTY BALL

Store no longer than 4 days. Makes enough for about 12 servings (3 cups).

1 package (8 ounces) cream cheese, softened
1 can (16 ounces) salmon, drained and flaked
1 tablespoon lemon juice
1 tablespoon grated onion
¼ teaspoon liquid smoke
¼ teaspoon salt

Mix all ingredients. Cover and chill at least 8 hours.

■ At serving time, have ready: ½ cup chopped walnuts or pecans, 3 tablespoons snipped parsley and crackers.

Mix nuts and parsley. Shape salmon mixture into ball; roll in nut mixture. Serve with crackers.

Salads

COTTAGE-LIME SALAD

Store no longer than 3 days. Makes enough for 10 servings.

3 cups boiling water
2 packages (3 ounces each) lime-flavored
  gelatin
1 cup pineapple juice
1 teaspoon vinegar
½ teaspoon salt
2 cups creamed cottage cheese
1 teaspoon minced onion
1 teaspoon minced green pepper
½ cup coarsely chopped cucumber
½ cup coarsely chopped celery

Pour boiling water on gelatin in large bowl; stir until gelatin is dissolved. Stir in pineapple juice, vinegar and salt. Pour 1 cup of gelatin mixture into 8-cup ring mold. Chill until firm.

While bottom layer chills, chill remaining mixture until thickened slightly but not set; beat with rotary beater until light and fluffy. Mix in remaining ingredients; pour on gelatin layer in mold. Chill until firm; cover. (Can be served immediately.)

CRUNCHY CARROT-PINEAPPLE SALAD

Store no longer than 48 hours. Makes enough for 8 servings.

1 can (8½ ounces) crushed pineapple
½ cup water
1 package (3 ounces) orange-flavored
  gelatin
1 cup miniature marshmallows
½ cup diced celery
½ cup shredded carrot
⅓ cup chopped nuts
½ cup frozen dessert topping (thawed)
½ cup mayonnaise or salad dressing

Heat pineapple (with syrup) and water until mixture boils. Pour boiling mixture on gelatin in bowl; stir until gelatin is dissolved. Chill until thickened slightly but not set. Mix in remaining ingredients including pineapple; pour into 4-cup mold or 8 individual molds. Chill until firm; cover. (Can be served immediately.)

■ **5 minutes before serving, unmold Crunchy Carrot-Pineapple Salad and garnish with salad greens.**

Note: This recipe can be doubled.

Tips for Molded Salads

To determine the size of a mold, fill it with water; then pour the water into a large measuring cup. Some molds may be marked: 2 cups=1 pint; 4 cups=1 quart.

When a recipe specifies that gelatin should be "thickened slightly," it means that the gelatin should be just about the consistency of liquid egg whites. If you want to speed up the thickening process, you can place the gelatin mixture in a bowl of ice and water. Remove the mixture from the ice-filled bowl just when it starts to thicken. If the gelatin has become too set, soften it over hot water.

Pour the orange mixture over the slightly-thickened raspberry layer in the mold. A lime layer comes next.

Unmold by wrapping a hot, damp towel carefully around the mold. Lift off the mold.

Ribbon Mold

RIBBON MOLD

Store no longer than 3 days. Makes enough for 9 to 12 servings.

Raspberry Layer
- **1 cup boiling water**
- **1 package (3 ounces) raspberry-flavored gelatin**
- **1 package (10 ounces) frozen raspberries**

Orange Layer
- **1 cup boiling water**
- **1 package (3 ounces) orange-flavored gelatin**
- **1 package (8 ounces) cream cheese, softened**
- **1 can (11 ounces) mandarin orange segments**

Lime Layer
- **1 cup boiling water**
- **1 package (3 ounces) lime-flavored gelatin**
- **1 can (8½ ounces) crushed pineapple**

Raspberry Layer: Pour boiling water on raspberry-flavored gelatin in large bowl; stir until gelatin is dissolved. Stir in frozen raspberries. Chill until thickened slightly but not set; pour into 8-cup mold or 9×9×2-inch baking pan. Chill until almost firm.

Orange Layer: Pour boiling water on orange-flavored gelatin in large bowl; stir until gelatin is dissolved; stir gradually into cream cheese. Chill until thickened slightly but not set. Mix in orange segments (with syrup); pour evenly on raspberry layer. Chill until almost firm.

Lime Layer: Pour boiling water on lime-flavored gelatin in large bowl; stir until gelatin is dissolved. Stir in pineapple (with syrup). Chill until thickened slightly but not set; pour evenly on orange layer. Chill until firm; cover. (Can be served immediately.)

■ **At serving time, unmold Ribbon Mold or cut into pieces.**

CRANBERRY FRUIT MOLD

Store no longer than 3 days. Makes enough for 6 to 8 servings.

¾ cup boiling water
1 package (3 ounces) raspberry-flavored gelatin
1 can (8¼ ounces) seedless grapes
1 can (8½ ounces) pineapple tidbits
1 can (16 ounces) whole cranberry sauce
½ cup nuts, coarsely chopped

Pour boiling water on gelatin in large bowl; stir until gelatin is dissolved. Stir in grapes (with syrup), pineapple tidbits (with syrup) and cranberry sauce. Chill until thickened slightly but not set.

Stir in nuts. Pour mixture into 5-cup mold or 8 to 10 individual molds. Chill until firm; cover. (Can be served immediately.) Serve with your favorite fruit salad dressing.

CREAMY CUCUMBER SALAD

Store no longer than 24 hours. Makes enough for 6 to 8 servings.

5 medium cucumbers
¾ cup boiling water
1 package (3 ounces) lime-flavored gelatin
3 tablespoons vinegar
1 teaspoon onion juice
½ cup mayonnaise or salad dressing
½ cup dairy sour cream

Pare cucumbers; shred and drain thoroughly. Measure 2 cups. Pour boiling water on gelatin in large bowl; stir until gelatin is dissolved. Stir in vinegar, onion juice, mayonnaise, sour cream and cucumber; pour into 4- or 5-cup mold. Chill in refrigerator until firm; cover. (Can be served immediately.)

■ **At serving time, unmold Creamy Cucumber Salad onto crisp salad greens; garnish as desired.**

Note: Drain shredded cucumber in sieve, pressing out liquid with spoon.

GOLDEN APRICOT MOLD

Store no longer than 5 days. Makes enough for 8 servings.

1 can (30 ounces) apricot halves, drained (reserve syrup)
¼ cup vinegar
1 teaspoon whole cloves
4-inch stick cinnamon
1 package (3 ounces) orange-flavored gelatin

Cut apricot halves into fourths; place in 4-cup mold or 8 individual molds. Heat reserved syrup, vinegar and spices until mixture boils. Reduce heat; simmer uncovered 10 minutes. Remove spices. Add enough hot water to hot syrup mixture to measure 2 cups. Pour on gelatin in bowl; stir until gelatin is dissolved. Pour gelatin mixture on apricots. Chill until firm; cover. (Can be served immediately.)

■ **5 minutes before serving, unmold 4-cup mold onto salad greens or individual molds onto slices of jellied cranberry sauce.**

BEET AND HORSERADISH MOLD

Store no longer than 3 days. Makes enough for 6 to 8 servings.

1 cup boiling water
1 package (3 ounces) lemon-flavored gelatin
1 can (16 ounces) diced beets, drained (reserve 1 cup liquid)
¾ cup chopped celery
2 tablespoons chopped green onion
2 tablespoons cream-style horseradish

Pour boiling water on gelatin in large bowl; stir until gelatin is dissolved. Stir in reserved beet liquid, the beets, celery, onion and horseradish. Chill until thickened slightly but not set; pour into 4-cup mold or 6 to 8 individual molds. Chill until firm; cover. (Can be served immediately.)

■ **At serving time, unmold Beet and Horseradish Mold on salad greens and serve with mayonnaise.**

MACARONI FRUIT SALAD

Store no longer than 24 hours. Makes enough for 4 to 6 servings.

1½ cups uncooked macaroni rings
 1 tablespoon cornstarch
 1 tablespoon sugar
 1 can (30 ounces) fruit cocktail, drained
    (reserve ½ cup syrup)
 2 tablespoons lemon juice
 1 cup frozen dessert topping (thawed)
 ¼ cup maraschino cherries, cut into halves

Cook macaroni rings as directed on package; drain. Mix cornstarch and sugar in saucepan. Gradually stir in reserved fruit cocktail syrup and the lemon juice. Cook over medium heat, stirring constantly, until mixture thickens and boils. Boil and stir 1 minute; stir into hot macaroni rings. Cover and chill at least 4 hours.

Fold dessert topping, fruit cocktail and cherries into macaroni rings. (Can be served immediately.) Cover and refrigerate.

■ **At serving time, stir Macaroni Fruit Salad.** If desired, serve on greens.

BRIGHT BEAN SALAD

Store no longer than 24 hours. Makes enough for 4 servings.

 1 medium carrot
 1 can (15½ ounces) French-style green
    beans, drained
 2 tablespoons chopped onion
 ⅛ teaspoon salt
 3 tablespoons oil and vinegar salad dressing

Cut carrot into 1-inch lengths; chop in blender, watching carefully. (Or carrot can be finely chopped by hand.) Mix all ingredients. Cover and refrigerate at least 4 hours. (Can be served immediately.)

Note: 1 package (9 ounces) frozen French-style green beans, cooked and drained, can be substituted for the canned beans.

FRUIT 'N CHEESE SLAW

Store no longer than 48 hours. Makes enough for 6 to 8 servings.

 4 cups shredded cabbage (about ½ head)
 ⅓ cup crumbled blue cheese (about 2
    ounces)
 ½ cup dairy sour cream
 ¼ cup salad dressing or mayonnaise
 ½ teaspoon seasoned salt

Toss cabbage and cheese. Mix sour cream, salad dressing and salt. Pour mixture on cabbage mixture and toss. (To serve immediately, see below.) Cover and refrigerate.

■ **10 minutes before serving, have ready:** 1 or 2 apples. Cut unpared apples into slices (2 cups), then cut into narrow strips. Toss with cabbage mixture.

Note: To chop or crumble blue cheese, freeze first. It is easier to handle and remains in separate pieces.

To Serve Immediately: Cut 1 or 2 unpared apples into slices (2 cups), then cut into narrow strips. Toss with cabbage mixture.

BRUSSELS AND CARROT SALAD

Store no longer than 48 hours. Makes enough for 6 to 8 servings.

 ½ cup oil and vinegar salad dressing
 1 package (10 ounces) frozen Brussels
    sprouts
 1 can (16 ounces) sliced carrots, drained

Heat salad dressing and Brussels sprouts in covered saucepan until dressing boils. Reduce heat; simmer covered 8 minutes. Add carrots; cook until Brussels sprouts are tender. Turn into serving dish. Cover and refrigerate at least 6 hours; stir occasionally. (Can be served immediately.)

MARINATED CUCUMBER SALAD

Store no longer than 48 hours. Makes enough for 4 to 6 servings.

- **1 medium cucumber**
- **1 small onion**
- **½ cup vinegar**
- **½ cup water**
- **2 tablespoons sugar**
- **¼ teaspoon salt**

Run tines of fork lengthwise down side of unpared cucumber. Thinly slice cucumber and onion into glass bowl. Mix vinegar, water, sugar and salt; pour on cucumber and onion slices. Cover and refrigerate at least 2 hours. (Can be served immediately.)

■ **At serving time, have ready:** crisp salad greens. Drain vegetables. Serve on salad greens.

ITALIAN MUSHROOM-BEAN SALAD

Store no longer than 24 hours. Makes enough for 4 or 5 servings.

- **1 package (10 ounces) frozen baby lima beans**
- **8 mushrooms, trimmed and sliced**
- **4 green onions, chopped**
- **2 tablespoons snipped parsley**
- **½ teaspoon salt**
- **½ teaspoon oregano**
- **¼ cup oil and vinegar salad dressing**

Cook lima beans as directed on package; drain. Mix beans and remaining ingredients. Cover and refrigerate at least 4 hours. (Can be served immediately.)

■ **At serving time, pimiento strips or a twisted orange slice add a colorful garnish.**

Marinated Cucumber Salad, Brussels and Carrot Salad (page 126) and Italian Mushroom-Bean Salad

Cook almonds and sugar together until the sugar melts and coats the almonds.

Mandarin Salad

TOMATO MARINADE

Store no longer than 48 hours. Makes enough for 6 to 8 servings.

      8 to 12 tomato slices, ¾ inch thick, or
           peeled small tomatoes
      1 cup olive oil or salad oil
      ⅓ cup wine vinegar
      2 teaspoons oregano leaves
      1 teaspoon salt
      ½ teaspoon pepper
      ½ teaspoon dry mustard
      2 cloves garlic, crushed
           Minced green onion
           Snipped parsley

Arrange tomatoes in baking dish, 8×8×2 inches. Shake oil, vinegar, oregano leaves, salt, pepper, mustard and garlic in tightly covered jar; pour on tomatoes. Sprinkle onion and parsley on tomatoes. Cover and refrigerate at least 3 hours; spoon dressing on tomatoes occasionally. (Can be served immediately.)

■ **At serving time, have ready:** crisp lettuce leaves. Arrange Tomato Marinade on lettuce; drizzle some of the dressing on top.

Note: Tomato Marinade is pictured on page 16 as an accompaniment to Braised Beef on Rice.

Add mandarin oranges and dressing to the greens, fasten the bag and shake.

MANDARIN SALAD

Store no longer than 24 hours. Makes enough for 4 to 6 servings.

Dressing
½ **teaspoon salt**
   Dash pepper
2 **tablespoons sugar**
2 **tablespoons vinegar**
¼ **cup salad oil**
   Dash red pepper sauce
1 **tablespoon snipped parsley**

Salad
¼ **cup sliced almonds**
1 **tablespoon plus 1 teaspoon sugar**
¼ **head lettuce**
¼ **head romaine**
1 **cup chopped celery**
2 **green onions (with tops), thinly sliced**

Shake Dressing ingredients in tightly covered jar; refrigerate.

Cook almonds and 1 tablespoon plus 1 teaspoon sugar over low heat, stirring constantly, until sugar is melted and almonds are coated. Cool and break apart. Store at room temperature.

Tear lettuce and romaine into bite-size pieces (about 4 cups). Place greens in plastic bag; add celery and onion. (To serve immediately, see below.) Fasten bag securely and refrigerate.

■ **5 minutes before serving, pour dressing into bag; add 1 can (11 ounces) mandarin orange segments, drained.** Fasten bag securely and shake until greens and oranges are well coated. Add almonds and shake.

To Serve Immediately: Do not refrigerate Dressing or Salad ingredients.

Vegetables

HERB BARLEY CASSEROLE

Store no longer than 24 hours. Makes enough for 4 to 6 servings.

- ¾ cup uncooked barley
- 1 medium onion, thinly sliced
- 1 tablespoon instant beef bouillon
- 1 tablespoon butter or margarine
- ¼ teaspoon rosemary leaves
- 2 cups boiling water

Heat oven to 400°. Mix all ingredients in ungreased 1½-quart casserole. Cover tightly; bake 45 minutes. (To serve immediately, continue baking until liquid is absorbed and barley is tender, about 15 minutes.) Cover and refrigerate.

■ **35 minutes before serving, heat oven to 400°.** Stir ½ cup water into Herb Barley Casserole. Cover tightly; bake until barley is tender, about 30 minutes.

TRADITIONAL SWEET-SOUR RED CABBAGE

Store no longer than 48 hours. Makes enough for 6 servings.

- 4 slices bacon
- ¼ cup brown sugar (packed)
- 2 tablespoons flour
- 1 teaspoon salt
- ⅛ teaspoon pepper
- ½ cup water
- ¼ cup vinegar
- 5 cups shredded red cabbage (about 1 medium head)
- 1 small onion, sliced

Fry bacon in large skillet until crisp. Remove bacon; pour off all but 1 tablespoon fat. Stir sugar, flour, salt and pepper into fat until smooth. Stir in remaining ingredients.

Cover tightly; heat until mixture boils. Reduce heat; cook, stirring occasionally, 25 to 30 minutes. Crumble bacon on top. (Can be served immediately.) Cover and refrigerate.

■ **15 minutes before serving, heat Traditional Sweet-Sour Red Cabbage covered over medium heat, stirring occasionally, until hot.**

Green Salad Tips

Select crisp fresh greens; avoid those with rusty-looking tips. Wash and drain greens thoroughly. Store in refrigerator in plastic bag or in vegetable crisper; use within a week.

To make a do-ahead green salad, break up washed and dried greens 24 hours before you want to serve the salad. Store greens in a plastic bag. Just before serving, add salad dressing to bag, close and shake until greens are coated. Chopped green pepper, carrots or zucchini add interest to a salad—they can be stored with the torn greens.

SWEET CARROT STICKS

Store no longer than 48 hours. Makes enough for 6 servings.

8 to 10 large carrots
2 tablespoons butter or margarine
½ teaspoon salt
Dash pepper

Heat oven to 400°. Cut each carrot lengthwise into 4 parts; place on double thickness heavy-duty aluminum foil. Dot with butter and sprinkle salt and pepper on top. Wrap carrots securely in the foil. Bake 1 hour. (To serve immediately, see below.) Refrigerate.

■ **35 minutes before serving, heat oven to 400°. Have ready:** ¼ cup brown sugar (packed).

Bake carrots 25 minutes. Sprinkle sugar on carrots (heat of carrots will melt sugar).

To Serve Immediately: Have ready: ¼ cup brown sugar (packed).

Bake 10 minutes longer. Sprinkle sugar on carrots.

VARIATION

Herb-seasoned Carrots: Sprinkle carrots lightly with dill weed or thyme leaves before wrapping; omit brown sugar.

GOLDEN SQUASH BAKE

Store no longer than 24 hours. Makes enough for 6 to 8 servings.

6 cups cut-up pared Hubbard squash
2 tablespoons butter or margarine
1 cup dairy sour cream
½ cup finely chopped onion
1 teaspoon salt
¼ teaspoon pepper

Place squash in saucepan with small amount of boiling salted water (½ teaspoon salt to 1 cup water). Cover tightly and cook until tender, about 15 minutes. Drain squash thoroughly. Mash squash; stir in remaining ingredients. Mound mixture into ungreased 1-quart casserole. Cover and refrigerate.

■ **50 minutes before serving, heat oven to 350°.** Bake Golden Squash Bake uncovered until heated through, about 45 minutes.

About Vegetables

Most vegetables (except root vegetables) should be refrigerated to help preserve freshness and nutrients. Store cleaned vegetables in crisper or plastic bags.

If you buy green peas or limas in the pod, store them in the refrigerator that way. Use within 2 days.

Carrots without tops stay fresh longer than those with tops.

Sweet potatoes, winter squash, eggplant, rutabagas and onions should be stored at about 60°—not in refrigerator.

CELERY BAKE

Store no longer than 24 hours. Makes enough for 4 to 6 servings.

4 cups ¼ inch diagonally sliced celery
1 jar (2 ounces) sliced pimiento, drained and chopped
1 can (8 ounces) water chestnuts, drained and sliced
1 can (10½ ounces) condensed cream of chicken soup or condensed cream soup of your choice
¼ cup water
½ teaspoon salt

Cook celery in 1 inch boiling salted water (½ teaspoon salt to 1 cup water) in tightly covered saucepan 5 minutes; drain. Mix all ingredients in ungreased 1½-quart casserole. (Can be baked immediately.) Cover and refrigerate.

■ **55 minutes before serving, heat oven to 350°.** Cover and bake Celery Bake until hot, 45 minutes. Stir before serving; garnish with salted nuts.

MASHED RUTABAGAS WITH GREEN PEAS

Store no longer than 24 hours. Makes enough for 4 to 6 servings.

1 large or 2 medium rutabagas (about 2 pounds)
  Instant mashed potato puffs (enough for 2 servings)
½ teaspoon salt
  Dash pepper

Cut rutabaga into ½-inch cubes or 2-inch pieces. Heat 1 inch salted water (½ teaspoon salt to 1 cup water) until water boils. Add rutabaga. Cover tightly; heat until water boils. Cook until tender, 15 to 20 minutes; drain.

Prepare potato puffs as directed on package for 2 servings except—omit milk and butter. Combine rutabaga and potato. Add salt and pepper; mash. Spoon rutabaga mixture into ungreased 1-quart casserole. (To serve immediately, cook 1 package [10 ounces] frozen green peas as directed on package; drain. Make indentation in center of rutabaga mixture; fill with peas.) Cover and refrigerate.

■ **50 minutes before serving, heat oven to 350°. Have ready:** 1 package (10 ounces) frozen green peas.

Heat rutabaga mixture covered 40 minutes. Cook peas as directed on package; drain. Make indentation in center of rutabaga mixture; fill with peas.

POTATO PATTIES

Store no longer than 3 days. Makes enough for 4 to 6 patties.

Prepare instant mashed potato puffs as directed on package for 4 servings except—decrease water to 1 cup; use ⅓ cup milk and add ½ teaspoon instant minced onion. Shape potato into patties; coat with flour. Cover and refrigerate.

■ **10 minutes before serving, cook Potato Patties in butter over medium heat until golden brown, about 3 minutes per side.**

GOLDEN BAKED POTATOES

Store no longer than 24 hours. Makes enough for 4 to 6 servings.

½ cup cornflake crumbs
1 teaspoon salt
4 to 6 medium potatoes, pared
2 tablespoons butter or margarine, melted

Heat oven to 375°. Mix cornflake crumbs and salt. Brush potatoes with butter, then coat with crumbs. Arrange in ungreased baking pan, 9×9×2 inches. Bake uncovered 1 hour. (To serve immediately, bake until potatoes are tender, 15 minutes longer.) Cover and refrigerate.

■ **35 minutes before serving, heat oven to 375°.** Bake Golden Baked Potatoes uncovered until tender, 25 minutes.

ELEGANT HASH BROWNS

Store no longer than 24 hours. Makes enough for 4 to 6 servings.

1 package (5.5 ounces) hash brown potatoes with onions
½ cup chopped green onion
1 cup shredded sharp Cheddar cheese (about 4 ounces)
½ teaspoon salt
3 tablespoons butter or margarine

Cover potato with boiling water; let stand 5 minutes. Drain thoroughly. Layer ½ each of potato, onion and cheese in ungreased baking dish, 8×8×2 inches, or shallow 8-inch baking dish. Season with half the salt; dot with half the butter. Repeat with remaining ingredients. (To serve immediately, bake covered in 350° oven 20 minutes. Uncover; bake 10 minutes.) Cover with aluminum foil; refrigerate.

■ **45 minutes before serving, heat oven to 350°.** Bake Elegant Hash Browns covered 20 minutes. Uncover; bake until cheese is melted and potato is golden brown, 15 minutes.

Pictured at right, top to bottom: Elegant Hash Browns, Golden Baked Potatoes and Caramel-glazed Sweet Potatoes (page 134)

CHEESE POTATOES

Store no longer than 48 hours. Makes enough for 6 to 8 servings.

Prepare instant mashed potato puffs as directed on package for 8 servings except—omit butter. After stirring in potato puffs, stir in 1 jar (5 ounces) pasteurized process sharp American cheese spread or flavored pasteurized Neufchâtel cheese spread (the latter is now available with a wide variety of added flavor sparkers, i.e., pineapple, pimiento, relish).

Turn potato into ungreased 1½-quart casserole. (To serve immediately, bake uncovered in 350° oven until hot, 15 to 20 minutes.) Cover and refrigerate.

■ **About 45 minutes before serving, heat oven to 350°.** Bake Cheese Potatoes uncovered until hot, 40 minutes.

CRISPY POTATOES

Store no longer than 24 hours. Makes enough for 4 to 6 servings.

Cook 4 to 6 unpared medium potatoes in 1 inch boiling salted water (½ teaspoon salt to 1 cup water) in tightly covered saucepan until tender, 30 to 35 minutes; drain. Cool.

Heat fat or oil (1 inch) to 375°. Peel potatoes; cut into 4 pieces. Fry in hot fat, turning once, until golden brown, 5 to 7 minutes; drain. (Can be served immediately. Season with salt.) Cover and refrigerate.

■ **25 minutes before serving, heat oven to 400°.** Heat Crispy Potatoes on ungreased baking sheet 15 minutes. Season with salt.

LEMONY POTATOES

Store no longer than 24 hours. Makes enough for 4 to 6 servings.

4 large potatoes, pared and cut into ½-inch cubes (about 4 cups)
¼ cup butter or margarine, melted
2 teaspoons salt
1 teaspoon grated lemon peel
¼ teaspoon nutmeg
¼ teaspoon coarsely ground pepper
3 tablespoons lemon juice
1 green onion (with top), chopped

Cook potato in 1 inch boiling salted water (½ teaspoon salt to 1 cup water) in tightly covered saucepan just until tender; drain. Mix remaining ingredients; toss with potato. Spoon on 20×14-inch piece of double thickness heavy-duty aluminum foil. Wrap potato securely in the foil. (To serve immediately, let stand at room temperature 1 hour. Bake in 350° oven 20 minutes.) Refrigerate.

■ **50 minutes before serving, heat oven to 350°.** Bake Lemony Potatoes 40 minutes.

CARAMEL-GLAZED SWEET POTATOES

Store no longer than 48 hours. Makes enough for 4 servings.

1 can (17 ounces) vacuum-pack sweet potatoes
½ teaspoon salt
⅓ cup caramel ice-cream topping

Mash sweet potatoes and salt. Mound in ungreased 1-quart casserole; drizzle with caramel topping. (To serve immediately, see below.) Cover and refrigerate.

■ **45 minutes before serving, heat oven to 350°.** Heat Caramel-glazed Sweet Potatoes uncovered until hot, 40 minutes.

To Serve Immediately: Heat oven to 350°. Heat uncovered until hot, 30 minutes.

Breads

CINNAMON-APPLE TOAST

Store no longer than 24 hours. Makes enough for 6 servings.

½ cup sugar
¾ teaspoon cinnamon
2 tablespoons soft butter or margarine
6 slices bread, toasted
1 jar (16½ ounces) chunky applesauce
⅓ cup raisins

Butter baking pan, 13×9×2 inches. Mix sugar and cinnamon; sprinkle 2 tablespoons cinnamon-sugar into pan. Spread butter on toast; arrange buttered side up in pan. Sprinkle 2 tablespoons cinnamon-sugar on toast. Mix applesauce and raisins; spread on toast. Sprinkle remaining cinnamon-sugar on applesauce. Cover and refrigerate.

■ **45 minutes before serving, heat oven to 350°.** Bake Cinnamon-Apple Toast uncovered 35 minutes.

FRIED CORNMEAL MUSH

Store no longer than 2 weeks. Makes enough for 9 servings.

1 cup cornmeal
1 cup cold water
3 cups boiling water
1 teaspoon salt

Grease loaf pan, 9×5×3 or 8½×4½×2 inches. Mix cornmeal and cold water in saucepan. Stir in boiling water and salt. Cook, stirring constantly, until mixture thickens and boils. Cover tightly; cook over low heat 10 minutes. Spoon cornmeal mush into pan. Cover and refrigerate.

■ **About 10 minutes before serving, invert pan to unmold cornmeal mush. Have ready:** 2 tablespoons butter or margarine; flour; syrup or jelly.

Cut loaf into ½-inch slices. Melt butter in large skillet. Coat slices with flour; brown on each side in skillet. Serve hot with syrup and, if desired, with bacon, ham or sausage.

To Store Fruits

Fruits will not ripen in the refrigerator. Once ripe, however, most of them stay at their best when refrigerated. Try to use them up soon, since they are fragile.

Berries should be refrigerated whole, and cleaned just before serving. Use within 1 or 2 days.

Wrap ripe pineapples tightly to prevent their odor from permeating other refrigerated foods.

Canned fruits can be stored in the already-opened (but covered) can in the refrigerator.

Orange juice can be kept covered in the refrigerator for several days with little loss of Vitamin C.

CONTINENTAL BRUNCH TOAST

Store no longer than 24 hours. Makes enough for 6 or 7 servings.

½ loaf (1-pound size) French bread
3 eggs
⅓ cup granulated sugar
½ teaspoon cinnamon
  Dash salt
1½ cups milk
2 tablespoons raisins
2 tablespoons brown sugar

Butter baking pan, 9×9×2 inches. Into pan, tear bread into 1- to 1½-inch pieces, each with a little crust (about 8 cups). Beat eggs, granulated sugar, cinnamon and salt; stir in milk and raisins. Pour egg mixture on bread pieces; sprinkle brown sugar on top. (To serve immediately, see below.) Cover and refrigerate.

■ **1 hour 10 minutes before serving, heat oven to 325°.** Bake Continental Brunch Toast uncovered until crust is golden brown, about 1 hour. Serve warm.

Note: For 8 to 10 servings, double amounts of all ingredients except French bread. Bake in buttered baking pan, 13×9×2 inches.

To Serve Immediately: Heat oven to 325°. Bake uncovered until crust is golden brown, 50 to 55 minutes. Serve warm.

RAISED FLAPJACKS

Store no longer than 24 hours. Makes about twenty 4-inch pancakes.

1 package active dry yeast
¼ cup warm water (105 to 115°)
1 egg
1⅓ cups milk
2 cups buttermilk baking mix

Dissolve yeast in warm water in large bowl. Add remaining ingredients; beat with rotary beater until smooth. Cover and refrigerate at least 8 hours. (Can be cooked immediately.)

■ **20 minutes before serving, heat griddle.** (Grease if necessary.) Cook Raised Flapjacks, turning when bubbles break.

BISCUIT FAN TANS

Store no longer than 24 hours. Makes enough for 6 biscuits.

2 cups buttermilk baking mix
½ cup cold water
¼ cup butter or margarine, softened

Mix baking mix and water until soft dough forms. Turn dough onto floured cloth-covered board; smooth gently into a ball. Knead 5 times. Roll dough until ¼ inch thick.

Spread half the butter on half the dough; fold in half. Spread remaining butter on half the dough; fold in half again. Roll dough until ½ inch thick. Cut with floured 2-inch cutter. Place 2 biscuits on sides in each ungreased muffin cup. (To serve immediately, bake in 450° oven about 10 minutes.) Cover and refrigerate.

■ **20 minutes before serving, heat oven to 450°.** Bake Biscuit Fan Tans 13 to 15 minutes.

CHEESE BREAD

Store no longer than 24 hours.

1 egg
1½ cups milk
3¾ cups buttermilk baking mix
1 cup shredded sharp Cheddar cheese
  (about 4 ounces)

Heat oven to 350°. Grease loaf pan, 9×5×3 inches. Beat egg in large mixer bowl. Add remaining ingredients; beat on medium speed ½ minute. Pour batter into pan. Bake 1 hour. Cool. (Can be served immediately.) Wrap and refrigerate.

■ **25 minutes before serving, heat oven to 375°.** Place wrapped Cheese Bread on oven rack; heat 15 minutes. Cut into ½-inch slices.

PUMPKIN BREAD

Store no longer than 10 days.

⅔ cup shortening
2⅔ cups sugar
4 eggs
1 can (16 ounces) pumpkin
⅔ cup water
3⅓ cups all-purpose flour*
2 teaspoons soda
1½ teaspoons salt
½ teaspoon baking powder
1 teaspoon cinnamon
1 teaspoon cloves
⅔ cup coarsely chopped nuts
⅔ cup raisins

Heat oven to 350°. Grease two 9×5×3-inch loaf pans or three 8½×4½×2½-inch loaf pans. Beat shortening and sugar in large bowl until fluffy. Stir in eggs, pumpkin and water. Mix in flour, soda, salt, baking powder, cinnamon and cloves. Stir in nuts and raisins. Pour batter into pans.

Bake until wooden pick inserted in center comes out clean, about 1 hour 10 minutes. Cool completely. (Can be served immediately.) Wrap and refrigerate.

*If using self-rising flour, omit soda, salt and baking powder.

Bread Ahead

Normally, bread is stored in its own wrapper at room temperature. But in hot weather store in wrapper in refrigerator to protect against mold.

Here's a simple do-ahead garlic bread: Cut a 1-pound loaf of French bread into 1-inch slices. Spread with mixture of ½ cup soft butter and ¼ teaspoon garlic powder. Reassemble loaf; wrap with 28x18-inch piece of heavy-duty foil. Store up to 24 hours in refrigerator. Heat in 350° oven 15 to 20 minutes.

BUTTERSCOTCH BISCUITS

Store no longer than 24 hours. Makes about 12 biscuits.

½ cup butter or margarine, melted
½ cup brown sugar (packed)
⅓ cup pecan halves
Cinnamon
Biscuit dough (enough for 10 biscuits)

Grease 12 medium muffin cups (2½ inches in diameter). Place 2 teaspoons butter, 2 teaspoons sugar and 2 or 3 pecan halves in each muffin cup; sprinkle cinnamon on top.

Prepare dough as directed on buttermilk baking mix package except—spoon dough on mixture in cups. (Can be baked immediately in 425° oven 15 minutes.) Cover and refrigerate.

■ **25 minutes before serving, heat oven to 425°.** Bake Butterscotch Biscuits uncovered 18 minutes. Immediately invert pan onto large tray. Let pan remain a minute so butterscotch drizzles down on biscuits.

CORN POCKET ROLLS

Store no longer than 8 hours. Makes 10 rolls.

1½ cups all-purpose flour
½ cup cornmeal
3 teaspoons baking powder
½ teaspoon salt
2 tablespoons sugar
1 egg, beaten
¾ cup dairy sour cream
1 tablespoon soft butter or margarine

Mix dry ingredients. Blend egg and sour cream and stir into dry ingredients. Turn dough onto lightly floured board; roll ⅜ inch thick. Cut with 3-inch biscuit cutter. Brush butter on circles. Fold circles in half, pressing folded edges, and place on ungreased baking sheet. (To serve immediately, bake in 375° oven until golden brown, 12 to 15 minutes.) Cover and refrigerate.

■ **20 minutes before serving, heat oven to 375°.** Bake Corn Pocket Rolls until golden brown, about 15 minutes.

SHOOFLY COFFEE CAKE

Store no longer than 5 days.

Batter
- ¾ cup butter or margarine, softened
- 1 cup granulated sugar
- 3 eggs
- 1½ teaspoons vanilla
- ½ cup light molasses
- 3 cups all-purpose flour*
- 1½ teaspoons baking powder
- 2 teaspoons soda
- ¼ teaspoon salt
- 1⅓ cups dairy sour cream

Filling
- ½ cup brown sugar (packed)
- ½ cup finely chopped nuts
- 1½ teaspoons cinnamon

Heat oven to 350°. Grease tube pan, 10×4 inches, or 2 loaf pans, 9×5×3 inches. Measure butter, granulated sugar, eggs, vanilla and molasses into large mixer bowl. Beat on medium speed 2 minutes or by hand 300 vigorous strokes. Mix in flour, baking powder, soda and salt alternately with sour cream.

Mix Filling ingredients.

For tube pan, spread ⅓ of batter (about 2 cups) in pan. Sprinkle ⅓ of filling (about 6 tablespoons) on batter. Repeat 2 times. For loaf pans, spread ¼ of batter (about 1½ cups) in each pan. Sprinkle ¼ of filling (about 5 tablespoons) on batter in each pan. Repeat.

Bake until wooden pick inserted in center(s) comes out clean, 55 to 60 minutes. Cool slightly before removing from pan(s). Cool thoroughly. (Can be served immediately.) Cover with plastic wrap and refrigerate.

*If using self-rising flour, decrease soda to 1 teaspoon; omit baking powder and salt.

BLUEBERRY-ORANGE BREAD

Store no longer than 1 week.

- 2 eggs
- 1 cup milk
- 1 package (14 ounces) orange muffin mix
- 1 package (13.5 ounces) wild blueberry muffin mix

Heat oven to 350°. Grease loaf pan, 9×5×3 inches. Mix eggs and milk. Stir in muffin mixes (dry). Batter will be slightly lumpy; pour into pan.

Bake until wooden pick inserted in center comes out clean, 50 to 60 minutes. Cool thoroughly. (Can be served immediately.) Wrap in plastic wrap and refrigerate.

FRUIT AND NUT BREAD

Store no longer than 4 days.

- 3 cups buttermilk baking mix
- ⅔ cup sugar
- ⅓ cup all-purpose flour*
- 1 egg
- 1 cup orange juice
- 1 cup chopped dried fruit (apricots, peaches, dates, raisins or figs)
- ¾ cup chopped nuts

Heat oven to 350°. Grease loaf pan, 9×5×3 inches. Mix baking mix, sugar, flour, egg and orange juice; beat vigorously ½ minute. Stir in fruit and nuts. Pour batter into pan.

Bake until wooden pick inserted in center comes out clean, 55 to 60 minutes. Cool slightly before removing from pan. Cool thoroughly. (Can be served immediately.) Wrap and refrigerate.

*Do not use self-rising flour in this recipe.

POTATO REFRIGERATOR DOUGH

Store in refrigerator at 45° or below no longer than 9 days.

1 package active dry yeast
1½ cups warm water (105 to 115°)
⅔ cup sugar
1½ teaspoons salt
⅔ cup shortening
2 eggs
1 cup lukewarm mashed potatoes
7 to 7½ cups all-purpose flour*

Dissolve yeast in warm water. Mix in sugar, salt, shortening, eggs, potatoes and 4 cups of the flour. Beat until smooth. Stir in enough remaining flour to make dough easy to handle.

Turn dough onto lightly floured board; knead until smooth and elastic, about 5 minutes. Place in greased bowl; turn greased side up. Cover bowl tightly; refrigerate at least 8 hours.

■ **2 to 2½ hours before serving, punch down dough; divide into 3 parts.** Use for your choice of 3 of the following recipes on pages 139 to 140: Parker House Rolls; Orange Butterhorn Rolls; Four-leaf Clover Rolls; Apricot Cream Cake; Cinnamon Braid; Rich Nut Roll.

*If using self-rising flour, omit salt.

PARKER HOUSE ROLLS

Makes 13 rolls.

Roll 1 part dough (left) into rectangle, 15×10 inches, about ¼ inch thick. Cut into 3-inch circles; fold so top half overlaps slightly. Pinch edges together. Place close together in greased pan, 9×9×2 inches. Brush with butter. Let rise until double, about 1½ hours. Heat oven to 400°. Bake until brown, about 20 minutes.

ORANGE BUTTERHORN ROLLS

Makes 24 rolls.

Divide 1 part dough (left) in half; roll each half into 10-inch circle. Spread 2 tablespoons Orange Glaze (below) on outside of circle, leaving a 2-inch circle in the center without glaze. Cut into 12 wedges. Roll up, beginning at rounded edge. Place rolls with point underneath on greased baking sheet. Let rise until double, about 1½ hours. Heat oven to 400°. Bake until light brown, 10 to 15 minutes. Spread remaining glaze on hot rolls.

Orange Glaze: Mix 2 tablespoons soft butter or margarine, 1 tablespoon grated orange peel, 1 tablespoon orange juice and 1½ cups confectioners' sugar until smooth and spreading consistency. If necessary, stir in 1 to 2 teaspoons additional orange juice.

Parker House Rolls

Orange Butterhorn Rolls

Four-leaf Clover Rolls (page 140)

Apricot Cream Cake

Cinnamon Braid

Rich Nut Roll

FOUR-LEAF CLOVER ROLLS

Makes 16 rolls.

Shape pieces of 1 part Potato Refrigerator Dough (page 139) into 2-inch balls. Place each ball in greased muffin cup. Snip each ball in half, then in half in opposite direction with scissors. Brush with butter. Let rise until double, about 1½ hours. Heat oven to 400°. Bake until brown, about 15 minutes.

APRICOT CREAM CAKE

Makes 16 servings.

Roll 1 part Potato Refrigerator Dough (page 139) into 15-inch circle; place over greased 9-inch ring mold. Fit dough into ring mold (outer edge of circle will come to rim of mold). Spoon Cream Cheese Filling (below) on dough. Lap edge of circle over filling; seal to inside ring of dough. Cut a cross in dough which covers the center of mold. Fold each triangle formed back over ring and pinch each point to the dough to seal securely. Let rise until double, about 1½ hours. Heat oven to 350°. Bake 30 minutes.

Remove Apricot Cream Cake from pan; place top side up on serving plate. Heat ½ cup apricot jam until melted; spoon on ring. Sift 1 tablespoon confectioners' sugar on top.

Cream Cheese Filling: Beat 1 package (8 ounces) cream cheese, softened, and ¼ cup sugar until light and fluffy. Stir in 3 tablespoons flour, 1 egg yolk, ½ teaspoon grated lemon peel and 1 tablespoon lemon juice.

CINNAMON BRAID

Divide 1 part Potato Refrigerator Dough (page 139) into 3 parts; roll each part into strand, 15 inches long. Mix 2 tablespoons sugar and 1 teaspoon cinnamon. Roll each strand in sugar-cinnamon mixture. Place strands close together and braid gently and loosely. Seal ends securely and tuck under. Place in greased loaf pan, 9×5×3 inches. Brush braid with milk; sprinkle remaining sugar-cinnamon mixture on top. Let rise until double, about 1½ hours. Heat oven to 375°. Bake until loaf sounds hollow when tapped, about 30 minutes.

RICH NUT ROLL

Roll 1 part Potato Refrigerator Dough (page 139) into rectangle, 12×10 inches. Spread Nut Filling (below) to within ½ inch of edge. Roll up tightly, beginning at long side. Pinch edge of dough into roll to seal securely. Stretch roll to make even. Place on greased baking sheet; seal ends securely. Let rise until double, about 1½ hours. Heat oven to 350°. Beat 1 egg white slightly; brush roll with beaten egg white. Sprinkle 2 tablespoons chopped nuts on top. Bake 40 minutes. While warm, drizzle mixture of ¼ cup confectioners' sugar and 1 tablespoon light cream on top.

Nut Filling: Beat 1 egg white until stiff. Fold in 1 tablespoon flour, ½ cup brown sugar (packed) and ½ cup finely chopped nuts.

Desserts

BAKED APPLES

Store no longer than 24 hours.

Core baking apples (e.g., Rome Beauty, Starr, Jersey Red, Winesap, Northern Spy, Golden Delicious or Greening). Pare 1-inch strip of skin around middle of each apple or upper half of each to prevent skin from splitting.

Heat oven to 375°. Place apples upright in ungreased baking dish. Fill center of each apple with 1 to 2 tablespoons granulated or brown sugar, 1 teaspoon butter or margarine and ⅛ teaspoon cinnamon. Pour water (¼ inch) into baking dish.

Spooning syrup in pan on apples several times during baking, bake 30 minutes. Cool 30 minutes. Cover and refrigerate.

■ **35 minutes before serving, heat oven to 350°.** Bake Baked Apples uncovered until hot, about 25 minutes.

STRAWBERRY CREAM

Store no longer than 24 hours. Makes enough for 6 servings.

- **½ cup confectioners' sugar**
- **1 quart strawberries, hulled**
- **1 envelope (about 2 ounces) dessert topping mix**
- **3 or 4 tablespoons orange-flavored liqueur**

Sprinkle sugar on strawberries; stir gently. Cover and refrigerate at least 2 hours.

Prepare dessert topping mix as directed on package. Gradually stir in liqueur. Fold in strawberries. (Can be served immediately.) Cover and refrigerate.

APPLE CRISP

Store no longer than 48 hours. Makes enough for 4 servings.

Butter Crunch
- **¼ cup butter or margarine**
- **2 tablespoons brown sugar (packed)**
- **½ cup all-purpose flour***
- **¼ cup chopped pecans, walnuts or coconut**

Apple Mixture
- **1 can (21 ounces) apple pie filling**
- **1 teaspoon lemon juice**
- **½ teaspoon cinnamon**
- **1 or 2 drops aromatic bitters, if desired**

Heat oven to 400°. Mix Butter Crunch ingredients with hands. Spread in ungreased baking pan, 8×8×2 inches. Bake until light brown, about 15 minutes. Stir with spoon; cool.

Mix remaining ingredients. Place apple mixture in ungreased 9-inch pie pan or baking dish, 8×8×2 inches. Sprinkle the Butter Crunch evenly on top. (To serve immediately, bake uncovered in 450° oven until golden brown and bubbly, about 10 minutes.) Cover and refrigerate.

■ **30 minutes before serving, heat oven to 450°.** Bake Apple Crisp uncovered until golden brown and bubbly, about 20 minutes. Delicious topped with ice cream.

*Do not use self-rising flour in this recipe.

CHERRY-CHERRY

Store no longer than 48 hours. Makes enough for 5 servings.

1 cup boiling water
1 package (3 ounces) cherry-flavored
gelatin
4 to 6 ice cubes
1 carton (8 ounces) cherry-flavored
yogurt
Frozen whipped topping (thawed)

Pour boiling water on gelatin in bowl; stir until gelatin is dissolved. Stir in ice cubes until gelatin thickens; remove any remaining ice cubes.

Beat in yogurt with rotary beater until smooth. Pour into individual serving dishes, glasses or molds; refrigerate at least 45 minutes. (Can be served immediately.) Serve with a dollop of whipped topping. Try toasted almonds or toasted coconut for a crunchy garnish.

Note: Please your own personal preference with other flavor combinations. Try strawberry-flavored gelatin and strawberry-flavored yogurt; raspberry-flavored gelatin and raspberry-flavored yogurt; orange-flavored gelatin and orange-flavored yogurt.

Whipping Cream

☐ Cream can be kept in the refrigerator 3 to 5 days.

☐ Remember that whipping causes cream to double in quantity.

☐ Before whipping, add 2 tablespoons granulated or confectioners' sugar for every $1/2$ cup of cream.

☐ If it is to whip well, cream must have at least 35% butterfat. To whip, chill cream, bowl and beaters thoroughly. Beat with electric mixer just until stiff. (Overbeaten cream will separate.)

APRICOT SOUFFLÉ

Store no longer than 24 hours. Makes enough for 6 to 8 servings.

1 can (29 ounces) apricot halves, drained
(reserve syrup)
2 envelopes unflavored gelatin
1 can (18 ounces) vanilla pudding
1 cup chilled whipping cream

Extend depth of 5-cup soufflé dish by securing 4-inch band of double thickness aluminum foil around top.

Pour $2/3$ of the reserved apricot syrup into blender; sprinkle gelatin on syrup. Heat remaining apricot syrup until syrup boils; pour into blender. Blend on low speed until gelatin is dissolved, about $1/2$ minute. Add apricot halves; blend on high speed until apricots are pureed, about 1 minute. Fold pudding into apricot mixture.

Beat whipping cream in chilled bowl until stiff; fold into apricot-pudding mixture. Pour into soufflé dish. Cover with plastic wrap and chill until firm, about 4 hours. (Can be served immediately.) Especially pretty with a garnish of maraschino cherries and frozen whipped topping.

MAPLE BROWNIE DESSERT

Store no longer than 48 hours. Makes enough for 9 servings.

1 package (15.5 ounces) fudge brownie mix
1 cup chilled whipping cream
$1/4$ cup confectioners' sugar
1 teaspoon maple flavoring
9 walnut halves

Prepare Cake-like Brownies as directed on package except—bake 30 minutes. Cool thoroughly.

Beat whipping cream, sugar and maple flavoring in chilled bowl until stiff. Spread whipped cream on brownies; top with walnut halves. Cover and refrigerate at least 2 hours. (Can be served immediately.)

■ **At serving time, cut Maple Brownie Dessert into squares.**

MAZARINE TORTE

Store no longer than 24 hours. Makes enough for 10 servings.

Dough
1⅓ **cups all-purpose flour***
 1 **teaspoon baking powder**
 ⅓ **cup sugar**
 ½ **cup butter or margarine, softened**
 1 **egg**

Filling
 ½ **cup raspberry jam**
 ½ **cup butter or margarine, softened**
 ⅔ **cup sugar**
 1 **cup blanched almonds, ground or finely chopped**
 ½ **teaspoon almond extract**
 2 **eggs**

Frosting
 ½ **cup confectioners' sugar**
 2 **teaspoons lemon juice**

Spread raspberry jam over the dough, then spoon the almond mixture on top of the jam.

Cover torte with plastic wrap before you refrigerate it. (Wooden picks help to keep wrap from touching the top.)

Grease layer pan, 9×1½ inches. (For ease in removing torte from pan, use a pan with removable bottom.) Mix Dough ingredients; press evenly on bottom and side of pan. Spread ¼ cup of the jam on dough; chill.

Heat oven to 350°. Beat ½ cup butter and ⅔ cup sugar; stir in the almonds and extract. Add 2 eggs, one at a time, beating well after each addition; spoon on jam. Bake 50 minutes. Cool. Remove from pan.

Mix confectioners' sugar and lemon juice until smooth. Spread remaining ¼ cup jam on top; drizzle Frosting on jam. (Can be served immediately.) Insert wooden picks at intervals around top to hold wrap away from the filling. Wrap and refrigerate.

■ **30 minutes before serving, cut Mazarine Torte into pieces and let stand at room temperature.**

*If using self-rising flour, omit baking powder.

Mazarine Torte

Melt the granulated sugar in a saucepan, then quickly coat a pie pan with the caramelized sugar. Pour the pumpkin mixture into the coated pan.

Pumpkin Flan

PUMPKIN FLAN

Store no longer than 24 hours. Makes enough for 10 to 12 servings.

> **Spice Cake (page 145)**
> ¾ **cup granulated sugar**
> 1 **can (16 ounces) pumpkin**
> 1 **cup light cream (20%)**
> 2 **eggs**
> ½ **cup brown sugar (packed)**
> 3 **to 4 tablespoons light rum**

Bake Spice Cake. Melt granulated sugar in saucepan, stirring constantly, until an even amber color. Remove from heat; pour quickly into 9-inch pie pan. Coat bottom and side of pan by tipping pan quickly in all directions.

Heat oven to 350°. Beat remaining ingredients until smooth. Pour into sugar-glazed pie pan. Place in pan of hot water (½ to ¾ inch). Bake until knife inserted halfway between center and edge comes out clean, about 70 minutes. Cool.

Run knife around edge of pumpkin custard to loosen. Invert cake on custard. Invert serving plate on cake and turn upright so custard is top layer. (To serve immediately, see below.) Refrigerate.

■ **At serving time, have ready:** frozen whipped topping (thawed).

Decorate top of Pumpkin Flan and cover space between cake and custard with whipped topping in decorators' tube.

To Serve Immediately: Have ready: frozen whipped topping (thawed).

Decorate top of flan and cover space between cake and custard with whipped topping in decorators' tube.

Using whipped topping in a decorators' tube, decorate the top of the flan and cover the space where the cake and custard meet.

SPICE CAKE

1⅓ cups all-purpose flour*
¾ cup sugar
⅓ cup shortening
⅔ cup milk
1 egg
1¼ teaspoons baking powder
½ teaspoon salt
1½ teaspoons pumpkin pie spice
¾ teaspoon vanilla

Heat oven to 350°. Grease and flour layer pan, 9 × 1½ inches. Measure all ingredients into large mixer bowl; beat on low speed ½ minute. Beat on medium speed, scraping bowl frequently, 3 minutes. Pour into pan. Bake until wooden pick inserted in center comes out clean, 35 to 40 minutes. Cool.

Note: The Spice Cake can be baked in an 8-inch round layer pan. Bake pumpkin custard in an 8-inch pie pan and 2 individual custard cups.

*If using self-rising flour, omit baking powder and salt.

To Make a Decorating Cone

Cut a 15-inch square of heavy paper or parchment into 2 triangles. Grasping edges with the thumb and forefinger, twist to form a cone (with point at center of longest side). Fold down top edges and fasten cone with transparent tape. Snip off a small opening at point or insert a metal tip into cone. (We used a star tip for this dessert.) Fill cone about half full. Fold top over. Press out whipped cream with one hand near top of cone. Use other hand to guide tip.

TRIFLE

Store no longer than 24 hours. Makes enough for 6 to 8 servings.

1 package (18.5 ounces) yellow cake mix
4 teaspoons sherry
1 package (16 ounces) frozen strawberry halves, thawed
1 can (18 ounces) vanilla pudding
1 envelope (about 2 ounces) dessert topping mix
2 tablespoons toasted slivered almonds

Bake cake in baking pan, 13×9×2 inches, as directed on package. Cool. Cut cake crosswise in half. Wrap, label and freeze one half for future use.

Cut remaining cake half into 8 pieces; split each piece horizontally. Arrange half the pieces in 2-quart glass serving bowl, cutting pieces to fit shape of bowl. Sprinkle 2 teaspoons of the sherry on cake pieces in bowl. Pour half the strawberries on cake pieces; spread half the pudding (1 cup) on strawberries. Repeat with remaining cake pieces, sherry, strawberries and pudding.

Prepare dessert topping mix as directed on package; spread on trifle. Sprinkle almonds on top. Cover and refrigerate at least 1 hour. (Can be served immediately.)

Special Tips

☐ Strawberries or other frozen fruits may be thawed quickly by putting the wrapped package in a bowl under cool running water.

☐ Toasted and/or chopped nuts may be stored in the refrigerator. The best type of container for them is a tightly covered jar.

WHIPPED CHERRY TORTE

Store no longer than 3 days. Makes enough for 8 to 10 servings.

Filling
 1 package (7.2 ounces) fluffy white frosting mix
 2 cups whipping cream

Torte Layers
 1 packet or 2 sticks pie crust mix
 1 cup confectioners' sugar
 1 cup ground or finely chopped pecans
 1 egg
 1 teaspoon vanilla
  Granulated sugar

Filling
 ¼ cup cherry-flavored liqueur
 5 to 6 drops red food color
 12 maraschino cherries, chopped and drained

Chill frosting mix (dry) and whipping cream covered in small mixer bowl at least 1 hour.

Heat oven to 450°. Mix pie crust mix, confectioners' sugar and pecans; stir in egg and vanilla. Gather dough into ball. Turn dough onto lightly floured cloth-covered board; knead until smooth. Divide into 6 parts. Roll each part into 7-inch circle; place on ungreased baking sheet. Prick circles with fork; sprinkle granulated sugar on each one. Bake until golden brown, 6 to 8 minutes. Cool on wire racks.

Stir frosting mixture and beat until stiff. Gradually beat in liqueur. Stir in food color; fold in cherries. Stack circles, filling layers with about ½ cup frosting mixture. Frost stack with remaining frosting mixture. Cover torte with plastic wrap or aluminum foil tent; refrigerate at least 8 hours. (Can be served immediately.)

CHOCOLATE SOUFFLÉ

Store no longer than 6 hours. Makes enough for 6 servings.

⅓ cup sugar
¼ cup all-purpose flour
⅓ cup cocoa
1 cup milk
3 egg yolks
2 tablespoons butter or margarine, softened
1 teaspoon vanilla
4 egg whites
¼ teaspoon cream of tartar
⅛ teaspoon salt
3 tablespoons sugar

Mix ⅓ cup sugar, the flour and cocoa in small saucepan. Gradually stir in milk. Heat, stirring constantly, until mixture boils. Remove from heat. Beat yolks in medium bowl with fork. Beat in about ⅓ of cocoa mixture. Gradually stir in remaining cocoa mixture. Stir in butter and vanilla. Cool slightly. Butter and sugar 6-cup soufflé dish.

Beat egg whites, cream of tartar and salt in large mixer bowl until foamy. Beat in 3 tablespoons sugar, 1 tablespoon at a time, just until stiff peaks form. Stir about ¼ of egg whites into chocolate mixture. Fold in remaining whites. Pour carefully into dish. (Can be baked immediately.) Cover and refrigerate.

■ **1 hour 20 minutes before serving, place oven rack in lowest position.** Heat oven to 350°. Make 4-inch band of triple thickness aluminum foil 2 inches longer than circumference of dish. Butter one side of foil band and sprinkle sugar on butter. Extend depth of dish by securing foil band buttered side in around outside edge of dish. Place dish in baking pan, 9×9×2 inches, on oven rack; pour very hot water (1 inch) into pan. Bake 1¼ hours. If desired, serve with Best Sauce (below).

BEST SAUCE

Beat ½ cup confectioners' sugar and ½ cup soft butter in small saucepan until smooth and creamy. Beat ½ cup chilled whipping cream in chilled bowl until stiff. Fold whipped cream into sugar-butter mixture. Heat, stirring occasionally, until sauce boils. Serve immediately.

RICH CHOCOLATE BAKE

Store no longer than 24 hours. Makes enough for 4 servings.

⅔ cup semisweet chocolate pieces
1 cup light cream (20%)
2 eggs
3 tablespoons sugar
  Dash salt
1½ tablespoons rum, if desired

Heat oven to 350°. Heat chocolate pieces and cream, stirring constantly, until chocolate is melted and mixture is smooth. Cool slightly. Beat remaining ingredients; stir gradually into chocolate mixture. Pour into 4 ungreased 6-ounce custard cups or 4 or 5 ovenproof pot de crème cups.

Place cups in baking pan on oven rack. Pour boiling water into pan to within ½ inch of tops of cups. Bake 20 minutes. Cool slightly. Cover and chill at least 4 hours.

CHOCOLATE REFRIGERATED DESSERT

Store no longer than 4 days. Makes 10 to 12 servings.

½ large angel food cake
1 package (6 ounces) semisweet chocolate pieces
4 eggs
1 package (about 2 ounces) dessert topping mix
1 teaspoon vanilla
¾ cup chopped nuts

Tear cake into small pieces. Place half of cake pieces in baking dish, 13½×9×2 inches. In top of double boiler over hot water, melt chocolate pieces. Cool. Beat eggs until thick and lemon colored. Stir in chocolate.

Prepare dessert topping mix as directed on package. Fold in chocolate mixture, vanilla and nuts. Pour half of chocolate mixture on cake pieces in baking dish. Cover with remaining cake pieces; pour remaining chocolate mixture on top. Cover and refrigerate at least 12 hours. (Can be served immediately.)

COMPANY CHEESECAKE

Store no longer than 10 days. Makes enough for 9 to 12 servings.

Crust
1¼ cups graham cracker crumbs (about
    15 crackers)
2 tablespoons sugar
3 tablespoons butter or margarine, melted

Filling
2 packages (8 ounces each) plus
    1 package (3 ounces) cream cheese,
    softened
1 cup sugar
2 teaspoons grated lemon peel
¼ teaspoon vanilla
3 eggs

Topping
2 cups dairy sour cream
¼ cup sugar
1 teaspoon vanilla

Heat oven to 350°. Mix graham cracker crumbs and 2 tablespoons sugar. Stir in butter. Press mixture evenly in bottom of ungreased 9-inch springform pan or in baking pan, 9×9×2 inches. Bake 10 minutes. Cool.

Reduce oven temperature to 300°. Beat cream cheese in large mixer bowl. Gradually beat in 1 cup sugar; beat until fluffy. Add lemon peel and ¼ teaspoon vanilla. Beat in eggs, one at a time; pour on crumb mixture.

Bake until center is firm, about 1 hour. Cool 10 minutes. Mix Topping ingredients; spread on hot cheesecake. Bake 10 minutes. Chill uncovered until cold, about 2 hours. (Can be served immediately.) Cover and refrigerate.

■ **At serving time, loosen edge of Company Cheesecake with knife before removing from pan.**

CANDY COOKIES

Store no longer than 5 days. Makes about 4 dozen cookies.

2 cups sugar
¼ cup cocoa
½ cup milk
½ cup butter or margarine
½ cup peanut butter
2 cups quick-cooking oats
2 teaspoons vanilla
½ cup chopped nuts

Heat sugar, cocoa, milk and butter in large saucepan, stirring occasionally, until mixture boils. Boil 1 minute. Remove from heat; immediately stir in remaining ingredients. Drop mixture by teaspoonfuls onto waxed paper. (Cookies will spread very thin.) Let stand until firm, about 40 minutes. (Can be served immediately.) Remove from waxed paper; place in covered container and refrigerate.

ALMOND DROPS

Store no longer than 8 days. Makes 7 dozen candies.

1 can (16.5 ounces) vanilla frosting
¾ teaspoon almond extract
½ teaspoon vanilla
½ cup slivered almonds, toasted

Mix all ingredients; drop by level teaspoonfuls onto waxed paper-covered baking sheet. Chill until set, about 4 hours. (Can be served immediately.) Remove from waxed paper; place in covered container and refrigerate.

Versatile Cookie Mix: Peanut Butter Cookies, Spice Cookies and Banana Cookies

VERSATILE COOKIE MIX

Store no longer than 10 weeks. Makes 9 to 10 cups cookie mix.

  4 cups all-purpose flour*
1¼ cups granulated sugar
1¼ cups brown sugar (packed)
  3 teaspoons baking powder
1½ teaspoons salt
1½ cups shortening

Mix flour, sugars, baking powder and salt in large bowl. Cut in shortening with pastry blender or with electric mixer on medium speed until mixture looks like coarse meal. Do not overmix.

Measure desired amounts of cookie mix into jars or plastic containers: 2 cups for 3 dozen Peanut Butter Cookies; 2½ cups each for 3 dozen Banana Cookies and Spice Cookies. (Can be baked immediately.) Seal tightly, label and refrigerate.

■ **30 minutes before serving, prepare one of the cookie recipes at right.**

Note: Do not use butter or margarine. If dough is dry, stir in 1 to 2 teaspoons cream.

*If using self-rising flour, omit baking powder and salt.

PEANUT BUTTER COOKIES

Heat oven to 375°. Mix 2 cups cookie mix, ½ cup chunky peanut butter, 1 egg and 1 teaspoon vanilla. Shape dough by teaspoonfuls into balls. Place about 2 inches apart on ungreased baking sheet; flatten with tines of fork dipped in flour. Bake until light brown, 12 to 15 minutes. (3 dozen cookies.)

BANANA COOKIES

Heat oven to 375°. Mix 2½ cups cookie mix, ½ cup mashed ripe banana, 1 teaspoon vanilla, 1 egg and ½ cup chopped nuts. Drop dough by rounded teaspoonfuls 2 inches apart onto ungreased baking sheet. Bake until light brown, 12 to 15 minutes. (3 dozen cookies.)

SPICE COOKIES

Heat oven to 375°. Mix 2½ cups cookie mix, 1 egg, ½ teaspoon cinnamon, ½ teaspoon lemon extract, ½ cup raisins and ½ cup chopped nuts. Drop dough by rounded teaspoonfuls 2 inches apart onto ungreased baking sheet. Bake until light brown, 12 to 15 minutes. (3 dozen cookies.)

DATE-NUT PINWHEELS

Store no longer than 6 weeks. Makes about 5 dozen cookies.

- ¾ **pound pitted dates, chopped**
- ⅓ **cup granulated sugar**
- ⅓ **cup water**
- ½ **cup chopped nuts**
- ½ **cup shortening (half butter or margarine, softened)**
- 1 **cup brown sugar (packed)**
- 1 **egg**
- ½ **teaspoon vanilla**
- 1¾ **cups all-purpose flour***
- ¼ **teaspoon salt**

Cook dates, granulated sugar and water in saucepan, stirring constantly, until thickened slightly. Remove from heat; stir in nuts. Cool.

Mix shortening, brown sugar, egg and vanilla until smooth. Stir in flour and salt; divide dough in half. Roll each half on waxed paper into rectangle about 11×7 inches; spread half the date-nut filling on each rectangle. Roll up tightly, beginning at long side. Pinch edge to dough to seal securely. Wrap and chill at least 4 hours. (Can be baked immediately.)

■ **15 minutes before serving, heat oven to 400°.** Cut rolls into ¼-inch slices; place 1 inch apart on ungreased baking sheet. Bake until light brown, about 10 minutes. Remove immediately from baking sheet.

VARIATIONS

Caramel-Nut Cookies: Omit date-nut filling. Stir in 1 cup finely chopped nuts with the flour. Shape dough into rolls, 2 inches in diameter; wrap and chill at least 4 hours.

Orange-Pecan Cookies: Omit date-nut filling. Mix in 1 tablespoon grated orange peel with the shortening; stir in ½ cup chopped pecans with the flour. Shape dough into rolls, 2 inches in diameter; wrap and chill at least 4 hours.

*If using self-rising flour, omit salt.

Pictured at left: The rolls of cookie dough make Date-Nut Pinwheels, Almond-Molasses Toppers (page 152), Brownie Refrigerator Cookies (page 152) and Candied Fruit Cookies (page 152).

NEAPOLITAN COOKIES

Store no longer than 6 weeks. Makes about 6½ dozen cookies.

- 1 **cup butter or margarine, softened**
- ½ **cup sugar**
- 1 **egg**
- 1 **teaspoon vanilla**
- 2¼ **cups all-purpose flour***
- ½ **teaspoon salt**
- 1 **ounce melted unsweetened chocolate (cool)**
- ¼ **cup chopped walnuts**
- 2 **tablespoons finely chopped maraschino cherries**

Mix butter, sugar, egg and vanilla. Stir in flour and salt. Divide dough into 3 parts. Leave 1 part plain; mix chocolate and walnuts into 1 part and cherries into remaining part. Line loaf pan, 9×5×3 inches, with aluminum foil. Spread plain dough evenly in bottom of pan. Top with a layer each of chocolate and cherry dough. Chill at least 2 hours. Remove dough with foil from pan. (Can be baked immediately.) Wrap and refrigerate.

■ **20 minutes before serving, heat oven to 375°.** Cut dough into ¼-inch slices; cut each slice crosswise in half. Place 1 inch apart on un-greased baking sheet. Bake until light brown, about 10 minutes. Remove immediately from baking sheet.

*Do not use self-rising flour in this recipe.

BROWNIE REFRIGERATOR COOKIES

Store no longer than 4 weeks. Makes about 4 dozen cookies.

1 package (15.5 ounces) fudge
  brownie mix
1 egg
½ cup finely chopped walnuts

Mix brownie mix (dry), egg and walnuts with hands. (If necessary, add about 1 teaspoon water.) Shape into roll, 2 inches in diameter. Wrap and chill at least 4 hours. (Can be baked immediately.)

■ **15 minutes before serving, heat oven to 375°.** Cut roll into ⅛-inch slices; place on ungreased baking sheet. Bake until set, about 5 minutes. Cool slightly; remove from baking sheet.

VARIATION

Cherry Refrigerator Cookies: Add ¼ cup drained chopped maraschino cherries.

CANDIED FRUIT COOKIES

Store no longer than 6 weeks. Makes about 6 dozen cookies.

1 cup butter or margarine, softened
1 cup confectioners' sugar
1 egg
2¼ cups all-purpose flour*
¼ teaspoon cream of tartar
½ cup chopped pecans
½ cup chopped mixed candied fruit
1 cup candied whole cherries

Mix butter, sugar and egg. Stir in remaining ingredients. Divide dough in half; shape each half into roll, 1½ inches in diameter. Wrap and chill at least 4 hours. (Can be baked immediately.) (Rolls of cookies can also be frozen if you prefer. Thaw before slicing.)

■ **About 15 minutes before serving, heat oven to 375°.** Cut rolls into ⅛-inch slices; place 1 inch apart on ungreased baking sheet. Bake about 8 minutes. Remove immediately from baking sheet.

*Self-rising flour can be used in this recipe.

ALMOND-MOLASSES TOPPERS

Store no longer than 6 weeks. Makes about 3½ dozen cookies.

½ cup butter or margarine, softened
2 tablespoons molasses
½ teaspoon vanilla
¼ cup confectioners' sugar
1 cup all-purpose flour*
¼ teaspoon soda
⅓ cup butter or margarine, softened
1 cup confectioners' sugar
1 cup finely chopped almonds

Mix ½ cup butter, the molasses, vanilla, ¼ cup confectioners' sugar, the flour and soda until soft dough forms. Divide dough in half; shape each half into roll, 6 inches long. Wrap and chill in refrigerator at least 4 hours. (Can be baked immediately.)

Mix ⅓ cup butter, 1 cup confectioners' sugar and the almonds. Divide mixture in half; shape each half into roll, 6 inches long. Wrap and chill at least 4 hours.

■ **20 minutes before serving, heat oven to 350°.** Cut rolls into ¼-inch slices. Place molasses slices 1 inch apart on ungreased baking sheet; top each with almond slice. Bake until delicate brown, 10 to 12 minutes. Remove immediately from baking sheet.

*If using self-rising flour, omit soda.

Easy-to-Cut Cookies

For nicely shaped refrigerator cookies:
☐ Be sure dough has been thoroughly mixed and shaped into *firm* rolls.

☐ Use a sharp, thin-bladed knife. Make slices all the same size so that they will bake in the same length of time.

QUICK REFRIGERATOR COOKIES

Store no longer than 10 weeks. Makes about 8 dozen cookies.

**1 package (15.4 ounces) creamy white
  frosting mix
2 cups all-purpose flour*
1 cup butter or margarine, softened
½ cup chopped pecans**

Measure 1½ cups of the frosting mix (dry) into large bowl; reserve remaining frosting mix. Mix in flour, butter and pecans with hands. Divide dough in half; shape each half into roll, about 1½ inches in diameter and 7½ inches long. Wrap and chill at least 4 hours. (Can be baked immediately.)

■ **20 minutes before serving, heat oven to 400°. Have ready:** reserved frosting mix; 1½ tablespoons butter or margarine, softened; 2 tablespoons hot water.

Cut rolls into ⅛-inch slices; place 1 inch apart on ungreased baking sheet. Bake 4 to 6 minutes. Cool slightly; remove from baking sheet.

Mix butter, water and reserved frosting mix. (If necessary, stir in 1 to 2 teaspoons water.) Frost cookies. (Enough frosting for about 4 dozen cookies; leave remainder unfrosted.)

*Do not use self-rising flour in this recipe.

ORANGE PECAN LOAF

Store no longer than 4 days.

Heat oven to 350°. Grease and flour 2 loaf pans, 9×5×3 inches. Prepare orange cake mix (19 ounces) as directed on package except—use 2 tablespoons less water and add ½ cup chopped pecans. Pour into pans.

Bake until wooden pick inserted in center comes out clean, 35 to 40 minutes. Cool thoroughly. (Can be served immediately.) Wrap and refrigerate.

PUMPKIN CAKE

Store no longer than 1 week.

**1 package (18.5 ounces) yellow cake mix
2 eggs
¼ cup water
2 teaspoons soda
1 can (16 ounces) pumpkin*
2 teaspoons pumpkin pie spice**

Heat oven to 350°. Grease and flour 12-cup cast aluminum bundt pan or baking pan, 13×9×2 inches. Stir all ingredients in large mixer bowl. Beat on medium speed 4 minutes. Pour batter into pan. Bake until wooden pick inserted in center comes out clean, 40 to 45 minutes. Cool 10 minutes; remove from pan. Cool; wrap and refrigerate.

*1 can (18 ounces) pumpkin pie mix can be substituted for the pumpkin and pumpkin pie spice.

ALMOND TORTE

Store no longer than 24 hours.

Bake a chocolate layer cake mix (18.5 ounces) in 2 layer pans, 8 or 9×1½ inches, as directed on package. Cool. Split to make 4 layers.

Prepare Almond Whipped Cream Filling (below). Fill layers and frost top of torte, using ¼ of the filling (about 1 cup) for each layer. Sprinkle chocolate shot around top edge of torte. Decorate with blanched almonds. Chill at least 4 hours. (Can be served immediately.) Insert wooden picks at intervals on top and side of torte to prevent wrap from touching filling. Wrap and refrigerate.

■ **35 minutes before serving, remove torte from refrigerator and unwrap.** Cut Almond Torte and let stand at room temperature.

ALMOND WHIPPED CREAM FILLING
**2 envelopes (about 2 ounces each)
  dessert topping mix
1 cup milk
1½ teaspoons almond extract
½ cup confectioners' sugar**

Mix dessert topping mix, milk and extract in bowl. Gradually beat in sugar; beat until stiff.

FRUIT SALAD PIE

Store no longer than 24 hours.

Pastry for 9-inch Two-crust Pie (page 77)
2 tablespoons soft butter or margarine
1 medium banana
2 cans (17 ounces each) fruits for salad, drained
1 can (16 ounces) mandarin orange segments, drained
⅓ cup honey
2 tablespoons granulated ascorbic acid mixture
3 tablespoons quick-cooking tapioca
¼ teaspoon salt
¼ teaspoon allspice

Prepare pastry. Spread butter on pastry in pie pan. Slice banana into bowl; add fruits for salad and orange segments. Pour honey on fruits; toss until fruits are coated. Mix ascorbic acid mixture, tapioca, salt and allspice; stir into fruit mixture. Turn fruit mixture into pie pan; cover with top crust. Do not cut slits in top crust. Seal edge; flute. (To serve immediately, see below.) Refrigerate.

■ **1 hour before serving, heat oven to 425°.** Cut slits in top crust. Cover edge with 2- to 3-inch strip of aluminum foil to prevent excessive browning; remove foil 15 minutes before pie is done. Bake until crust is brown, 45 to 55 minutes. Cool slightly.

To Serve Immediately: Heat oven to 425°. Cut slits in top crust. Cover edge with 2- to 3-inch strip of aluminum foil; remove after pie has baked 25 minutes. Bake until crust is brown, 40 to 50 minutes. Cool slightly.

STRAWBERRY MINUTE PIE

Store no longer than 48 hours.

8- inch Baked Pie Shell (page 77)
1 cup boiling water
1 package (3 ounces) strawberry-flavored gelatin
1 package (16 ounces) frozen sliced strawberries

Bake pie shell. Pour boiling water on gelatin in bowl; stir until gelatin is dissolved. Add frozen strawberries; stir to break berries apart. When mixture is partially set, pour into baked pie shell. Chill until set, about 2 hours. (Can be served immediately.) If desired, serve with frozen whipped topping.

VANILLA CREAM PIE

Store no longer than 48 hours.

9- inch Baked Pie Shell (page 77)
⅔ cup sugar
¼ cup cornstarch
½ teaspoon salt
3 cups milk
4 egg yolks, slightly beaten
2 tablespoons butter or margarine, softened
1 tablespoon plus 1 teaspoon vanilla

Bake pie shell. Mix sugar, cornstarch and salt in saucepan. Beat milk and egg yolks; stir gradually into sugar mixture. Cook over medium heat, stirring constantly, until mixture thickens and boils. Boil and stir 1 minute. Remove from heat; stir in butter and vanilla. Pour immediately into baked pie shell. Immediately press plastic wrap onto filling. Chill at least 2 hours. (Can be served immediately.) If desired, serve with sweetened whipped cream.

VARIATIONS

Chocolate Cream Pie: Increase sugar to 1½ cups and cornstarch to ⅓ cup. Omit butter and stir in 2 ounces melted unsweetened chocolate with the vanilla.

Coconut Cream Pie: Decrease vanilla to 2 teaspoons and stir in ¾ cup flaked coconut. Sprinkle ¼ cup flaked coconut on whipped cream if desired.

EGGNOG PIE

Store no longer than 48 hours.

9- inch Baked Pie Shell (page 77)
1 envelope (about 2 ounces) dessert
   topping mix
1 teaspoon rum flavoring
½ teaspoon nutmeg
¼ teaspoon ginger
1 can (18 ounces) vanilla pudding

Bake pie shell. Prepare topping mix as directed on package except—omit vanilla; stir in rum flavoring, nutmeg and ginger. Fold pudding into whipped topping; pour into pie shell. Chill until set, at least 4 hours. (Can be served immediately.)

STRAWBERRY CHIFFON PIE

Store no longer than 48 hours.

9- inch Baked Pie Shell (page 77)
¼ cup sugar
1 envelope unflavored gelatin
1 package (10 ounces) frozen strawberry
   halves, thawed
3 egg whites
¼ teaspoon cream of tartar
⅓ cup sugar
½ cup chilled whipping cream

Bake pie shell. Mix ¼ cup sugar and the gelatin in saucepan; stir in strawberries. Cook over medium heat, stirring constantly, just until mixture boils. Place pan in bowl of ice and water or chill in refrigerator, stirring occasionally, until mixture mounds slightly when dropped from spoon.

Beat egg whites and cream of tartar until foamy. Beat in ⅓ cup sugar, 1 tablespoon at a time; beat until stiff and glossy. Do not underbeat. Fold strawberry mixture into meringue. Beat cream in chilled bowl until stiff; fold into strawberry meringue. Pile into baked pie shell. Chill until set, at least 3 hours. (Can be served immediately.)

Note: For ease in cutting pie, dip knife into hot water.

LEMON CHIFFON PIE

Store no longer than 48 hours.

9- inch Baked Pie Shell (page 77)
½ cup sugar
1 envelope unflavored gelatin
4 eggs, separated
⅔ cup water
⅓ cup lemon juice
1 tablespoon grated lemon peel
½ teaspoon cream of tartar
½ cup sugar

Bake pie shell. Mix ½ cup sugar and the gelatin in small saucepan. Beat egg yolks, water and lemon juice; stir into sugar mixture. Cook over medium heat, stirring constantly, just until mixture boils. Stir in peel. Place pan in bowl of ice and water or chill in refrigerator, stirring occasionally, until mixture mounds slightly when dropped from spoon.

Beat egg whites and cream of tartar until foamy. Beat in ½ cup sugar, 1 tablespoon at a time; beat until stiff and glossy. Do not underbeat. Fold lemon mixture into meringue. Pile into baked pie shell. Chill until set, at least 3 hours. (Can be served immediately.)

Note: For ease in cutting pie, dip knife into hot water.

For Great Chiffon Pies

☐ Look at the photo on page 80 to determine when gelatin "mounds slightly."

☐ Separate eggs while they are cold; then let whites come to room temperature (they'll beat up faster and to a larger volume). Be sure there is no yolk in the white.

☐ Fold thickened gelatin mixture into meringue carefully but thoroughly. Use a rubber scraper, cutting down through the mixture. Slide scraper across the bottom of the bowl and up the side.

Index